I'd like to thank my amazing fiancé, Michelle, for unwavering support and unconditional love! I would also like to thank our kids, grandkids, parents, brothers, sisters, nieces, nephews and friends

Whom all provided assistance or motivation to complete this project.

Thank You and Love You All!

Disclaimer

All information in this title or at MyRepairKit.com is published in good faith and for general informational purposes only. My Repair Kit LLC has made every effort to ensure that the information, recommendations and techniques are accurate to the best of the author's knowledge and ability.

My Repair Kit LLC does not make any warranties about this information and will not be held liable for any losses and/or damages in connection with the use of this book/title, videos, supplies or website, MyRepairKit.com.

Do-it-yourself activities, specifically furniture repair/restoration and refinishing involve a degree of risk. A person's skill, knowledge of product formulations, application techniques and site conditions may cause products in some instances to perform suboptimally.

Always use gloves, protective mask and other personal protective gear while performing any repair, otherwise known as PPE. My Repair Kit LLC will not be held responsible for injuries, losses, methods, materials, tools, supplies or related products.

Always refer to the downloadable SDS (Safety Data Sheets) sheets available at MyRepairKit.com for product descriptions and warnings prior to use.

Do not use any products that you may have an allergic reaction to. Do not consume, inhale, breathe vapor, fume or spray of any restoration product. If you're feeling unwell, move to fresh air. If on skin or in eyes, rinse thoroughly with water for several minutes. Call poison control, emergency services or a doctor.

Some restoration products may be extremely flammable. Keep restoration supplies away from open flames and sparks and store in a cool ventilated space.

Table of Contents

About the Author: Pages 5-6

Introduction: Pages 7-9

Chapter 1: ***Let's Talk About Wood***
Characteristics of Furniture - Pages 10-47

Chapter 2: ***Crash Course on Color and Light***
Light Sources and Their Effect on Color - Pages 48-65

Chapter 3: ***Hand Applied Finishes***
Finishes and Product Descriptions - Pages 66-80

Chapter 4: ***French Polishing***
Application Techniques - Pages 81-117

Chapter 5: ***Toners***
Spray Finishes - Pages 118-124

Chapter 6: ***Pigments and Their Application Techniques***
Pigment Descriptions and Techniques for Application - Pages 125-162

Chapter 7: ***Broken Wood***
Repair Techniques for Broken Wood - Pages 163-186

Chapter 8: ***Surface Damages***
Repair Techniques for Gouges and Scratches - Pages 187-203

Chapter 9: ***Veneer Damage***
Repair Techniques for Veneer Damage - Pages 204-207

Chapter 10: ***Problems***
Inevitable Problems and Solutions - Pages 208-241

Chapter 11: ***Other Cool Stuff***
Repair Techniques for Unique Items Other than Wood - Pages 242-255

Chapter 12: ***Fabrication of Molded Parts***
Fabrication Techniques for Missing Parts - Pages 256-271

Chapter 13: ***Odds & Ends***
Other Pertinent Information With Regard to Furniture Repair - Pages 272-281

Chapter 14: ***Be A Boss***
Information on Career and Money Making Opportunities - Pages 282-289

In Closing: Page 290

Photo Credits and Sources: Pages 291-294

About the Author

Often I look back on my life and wonder where I would be if it wasn't for my uncle, Tom Schoenbauer. I'd like to give a special THANK YOU to Uncle Tommy for being instrumental in my growth personally and professionally!

My journey unknowingly began around 6 years old, while staying at my uncle's house. At this point Tom was already a seasoned furniture restorer, but he was not a furniture refinisher. He carved out his own niche, strictly performing repairs, in clients homes, primarily for moving and insurance companies.

As a child I would sit back and watch my uncle perform repairs. I would be amazed that something that once was shattered, broken or horribly damaged, looked virtually perfect once he performed his magic.

I only lived with my uncle briefly, but that didn't stop him from paving the way for the rest of my career. It really started when I was around twelve or thirteen years of age, uncle Tommy owned an art gallery in Annapolis, MD, off of State Circle.

Several weekends for months, Tom would have me come help prepare the gallery for its grand opening, which included creating some stucco walls, painting, carpentry and the occasional lesson in restorations.

Once the gallery opened, there was a back room dedicated to art and ceramic restoration along with furniture or anything else he was working on that could fit around the workbench.

Through the years I continued going to the gallery, but instead of working on the building, Tom would give me several small projects like a broken plate or ceramic statue to work on. He would give me direction on what he wanted done and the technique required to do the task.

Through Tom's guidance I grew a love for performing restorations, primarily because I started to be the one that took something shattered or broken and had the ability to restore it, which was really satisfying once I understood all the repair products and processes.

Even though Tom had his art gallery, he still regularly performed repairs in clients' homes, for moving damages or insurance claims. Often on weekends I would assist him on jobs that required two people, being the muscle, helping by performing my own repairs, or just sitting back watching the master at his craft.

In 1996 I graduated high school and shortly thereafter Tom set up a meeting with my cousin, Bill Schoenbauer, who owned a larger restoration company named Schoenbauer Furniture Service, in Charlotte Hall, MD.

Schoenbauer Furniture Service is where I further developed and honed my skills. I started primarily refinishing furniture in the shop. This gave me immense insight into the construction of furniture, along with a lot of experience sanding, gluing, filling, replacing parts and so much more.

After about a year, I started riding with some of the other techs, out on the road, doing repairs and being a helper. Shortly thereafter I received my own van and started performing my own inspections and repairs.

In 2004, after working at Schoenbauer Furniture Service for around eight years, I felt I had realized my full potential there, and decided it was best to branch out. I had a few small accounts I was working for, but it wasn't enough to cover everything so I briefly worked for a distant cousin in the industry, Gene Shontere, of Shontere Restorations.

I really appreciated working at Shontere's because it gave me the opportunity to work with another one of my uncles, Uncle Ron, who also greatly helped my growth in restorations.

I left Shontere's in 2006, after obtaining enough consistent work to officially start my own business, Jacobson Restoration LLC. Things were going great for a while, at least till the 2008 housing crisis hit, which really affected the moving industry, and me!

I found myself still having some work but not enough to sustain. A guy who assisted me in my time of need was Phil Termini with Termini Brothers Furniture Repair. Phil hired me part time to help out around his shop in Gaithersburg MD, performing repairs and refinishing.

Phil always took additional time to show me new techniques or explain to me why he did certain unique things when performing restorations and repairs. Phil is a phenomenal mentor and I still go to his shop regularly, as we still trade some jobs back and forth. He still takes time to teach me new things whenever I walk in on one of his projects.

Eventually sometime around 2009-2010 things got back to normal and I've been self sustained ever since. I couldn't have done it without all my mentors, along with many others that were not mentioned.

It's with great hope that I've streamlined and condensed all the knowledge and techniques I've learned into this book for your reading satisfaction!

Introduction

There is a big difference between furniture refinishing and furniture repair. Refinishing entails completely removing an existing finish to bare wood, usually by means of chemicals.

Followed by an extensive amount of sanding to smooth out the surface and remove damages like scratches or gouges. Application of a stain and adding several layers of finish while also sanding in between those coats to completion.

This isn't a book about refinishing, but most of the techniques you will learn throughout these chapters will be applicable, as there are almost always defects or imperfections that need to be addressed during the refinishing process.

There's an extensive amount of information, books, videos or in person courses available to teach you how to refinish furniture, but rarely will you find resources with a large amount of instruction with regard to furniture repair.

Most often you will only find a chapter dedicated to the topic in a book about furniture refinishing. A chapter here and there is nowhere near enough information to give you the full scope of the complexity involved with most repairs.

Furniture repair is taking some type of furniture which sustained damage (gouges, scratches etc.), and using products like glue, fillers, pigments, padding finishes and skill to disguise the damage, while also manipulating the existing finish back to a condition that has limited diminishment of beauty and utility.

Before delving straight into the nitty gritty details of performing repairs, it's important to go over a few things and give you a quick synopsis of what you're getting yourself into, with regard to this book.

The first chapter, "Let's Talk About Wood", will expand on some of the most common wood species, along with some of their unique characteristics, so you can identify what type of wood furniture you'll be working with most often.

Understanding some species attributes, like strength, will also be critical while performing structural restorations (something's broken).

Secondly, each species of wood will project a specific "color". You can't always see this "color" in fresh cut wood, but when wood has been dried, and a clear finish is applied to a raw wood surface, the color and natural beauty of the wood becomes visible and greatly enhanced.

From here on out the term "color" will be referenced, the majority of time, with two different terms, "hue" or "tone".

Tone can be considered the "base color" exhibited naturally by the wood, which has not been altered by the use of stains or paint. As we just spoke about, every unique species of tree will have their own inherent tone.

For instance, tones can vary even within the species but in general, pine may have a naturally whitish to yellowish tone, mahogany may have an orangish to reddish tone, rosewood may have a purplish tone, poplar may have a greenish tone, among countless other unique wood types.

Hue is a description of a precise, concentrated color, i.e. hot pink, cobalt blue, chartreuse, olive, etc. Hue will be mentioned more often with pigments or wood that has been stained/colored, or has a dyed protective clear coat/finish already, possibly even painted.

Any species of wood can have any hue by the application of particularly colored stains or paint. The chapter titled "Crash Course on Color and Light" will greatly expand on the topic of color, which will assist with color blending during the repair process.

Ultimately you're going to be "painting" an area, in an attempt to disguise the damage you were tasked with repairing. I refer to this part of the process as performing "cosmetic repairs". These techniques are covered extensively in the chapter, "Pigments & Their Application ", accompanied by several other restoration samples throughout this book.

From here on out the term "painting" will be replaced, the majority of the time, with "touch up". When performing various touch ups, your job will be to figure out what mixture of pigments are required to create the targeted hues needed to conceal an area of damage. Notice the term "hues" is plural, as almost no piece of wood will consist of just one "color".

With regard to both types of restorations, structural and cosmetic, more often than not, you'll have to incorporate the use of a synthetic filler to "fill" those damages, more on that topic in the chapter titled, "Surface Damages".

Some of the purest craftsmen may not agree with the way I perform some repairs. They may say that performing a repair in a certain manner is not ideal, or for an antique piece of furniture, a repair will depreciate the value.

My response is usually to say, it's completely up to the client to decide whether they want to have their damaged piece of furniture repaired, we are going to make a structural or cosmetic repair virtually undetectable to 99% of the people who will see that piece of furniture.

If you're not a collector or never plan on selling your furniture, you should, in my opinion, at least have your furniture functional. What's the point in having a broken or unappealing piece of furniture because of a few irrelevant dollars?

Over the 25+ years that I have been in the restoration business I've come to two conclusions. First, just about everyone, private or commercial, owns a piece of furniture, and secondly, nearly every piece of furniture owned likely has some type of damage, unless you have one of those "off limit" rooms.

Additionally, on countless occasions while performing repairs for various clients, they would request I look at or assess damages to other pieces of furniture they own, and ask me to explain to them some easy process that they could perform to repair the damage themselves.

Unfortunately, there was no easily accessible information or products/systems available for repairs that I could tell them about. For the most part, I could only point them in the direction of obtaining touch up markers, stain pens or something similar from their local hardware store.

Those solutions are usually just temporary, or the limited selection of hues don't really match the furniture they have, making any potential repair or touch up remaining completely noticeable.

Due to these factors I saw the need to create a system, which includes all the information and products a professional would use. By following the instructions and recommendations in this book, anyone can learn to perform repairs just like a professional, to a multitude of items, not just wood.

There are a few other chapters with cool projects or additional information about other unique restorations. If you find yourself successfully performing repairs, I've also included a blueprint for you to start your own business, which with hard work and dedication, could gross you well into six figures, titled "Be A Boss"

Let me also forewarn you, I get sidetracked easily. There are several facts or information throughout these chapters that you may think has nothing to do with furniture repair. Occasionally it's hard to capture the full scope of a discipline without expanding on some background information to support the topic at hand.

Everything written in this book, in my opinion, is pertinent information to assist with comprehending the restoration process, whether realized immediately or not.

Thank you for your interest in restorations! I wish you good luck on your new found journey of repairs!

Let's begin with some of the basics with regard to wood. Looking at the picture of this freshly cut tree to the right, you can see there are three distinct areas.

The outer ring is the bark of the tree, but inside the bark, there is a light area called *"Sapwood"*, and the darker center of the tree is called *"Heartwood"*. Both areas play a significant role in the tones that every wood species produce.

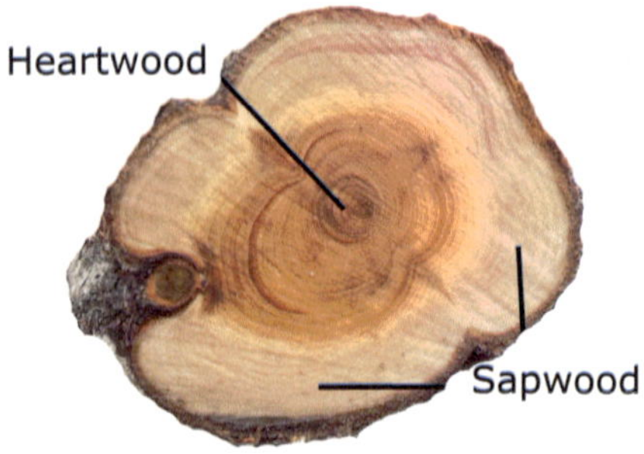

Sapwood is the living, outermost portion of a stem or branch, all wood begins as sapwood. It's formed just under the bark by a thin layer of living cells known as cambium.

Cambium produces bark cells to the outside of the tree, and wood cells to the inside of the tree. A tree increases in girth during each year of growth because every year a new layer of wood cells are added inside the cambium, these are the "rings" that you see in a freshly cut tree.

A tree ring equalling one year isn't always an accurate measurement. On occasion, trees can create more than one ring per year, which could be the result of drought or stress during that singular growing season; those are called false rings.

On the other hand, some trees may not produce rings, like the palm tree (right), as they do not produce cambium, palms use a vascular system to grow.

For most other trees, as they mature, in conjunction with the increased need for structural support due to their surging weight, their trunks increase in diameter and significant changes are occuring at the cellular level.

As the older sapwood cells nearest the center of the tree die, remaining mostly intact, they transform themselves into heartwood. Heartwood is very dense, and you can usually distinguish sapwood from heartwood by their contrasting tones.

Although some tones in various wood species can be deceiving, as not all sapwood is light and not all heartwood is dark. Additionally, the relative amounts of sapwood and heartwood in any tree can vary greatly among species, individual trees, and on growing climate or soil conditions.

All species of trees generally fall into two categories, *"Hardwood"* and *"Softwood"*. A common misconception about hardwood vs. softwood, is that it somehow indicates how hearty the wood is, or its resistance to damage.

In fact, the term "hardwood" simply means the wood came from a dicot tree. Dicot (dicotyledon) trees, also known as "*Angiosperms*", have broad leaves and produce either seeds, nuts or flowers. Examples of hardwoods include walnut, cherry, maple, oak, mahogany, among many others.

"Softwood", on the other hand, refers to wood which comes from *"Gymnosperm"* trees, like conifers. Examples of softwoods are pine, fir, cedar, and others, all which produce cones.

Even though I just stated that the hardwood/softwood moniker doesn't define a wood's heartiness, the terminology usually does translate in the grand scheme of things. Hardwoods do tend to be more dense than softwoods, which in turn make them harder and more durable.

The *Janka Scale* (right) is what determines the hardness or softness of a wood. To perform the test, a steel ball is placed onto the surface of a piece of wood, force is applied to the steel ball until it is embedded halfway into the wood surface.

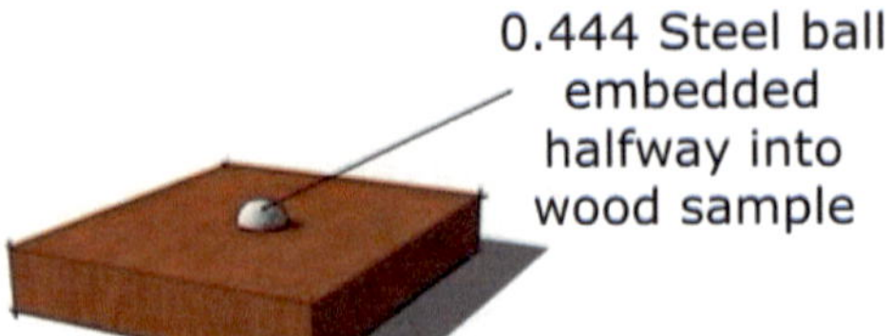

The force is measured in Pounds Force (lbf). The lower the number, the softer the wood, and as I'm sure you can imagine, the higher the number, the more dense/harder the wood will be. Additionally, differing hardwoods/softwoods mostly all have their own unique measurement on the Janka scale.

For example, Lignum Vitae can be found in abundance in Central and South America, it's the national tree of the Bahamas, and is often acknowledged as the "hardest" known wood.

Lingum Vitae, latin for "wood of life", has the finest grain of any wood, creating an iron-like density, so dense that a one foot cube weighs in at 83 lbs., and will not float.

In fact, the first nuclear powered submarine, the USS Nautilus, has its aft, main shaft strut bearings made out of this almost impervious product.

Even to this day, due to the wood's natural self lubrication and virtual indestructibility, ball bearings made of Lignum Vitae are still used in certain ships and hydroelectric power plant turbines.

Lignum Vitae measures in at 4,500 lbf on the Janka scale, compared to red oak, which is 1290 lbf, that's almost four times harder!

On the other hand, Balsa (Ochroma Pyramidale) is also a hardwood, but it's one of the "softest" hardwoods, only registering around 100 lbf on the Janka scale.

Aromatic cedar, which is an example of a softwood, is often used to line the inside of closet walls and the inside of this antique pine dresser, that was converted into a blanket chest, is one of the "hardest" softwoods, measuring in around 900 lbf on the Janka scale.

These were just a few examples of why I stated that the hardwood/softwood moniker doesn't always translate into a wood's physical ability.

Softwoods are used to create furniture, flooring, doors, among many other things, but mostly you'll see it used in the construction of roof trusses or house stud partitions, in the form of 2x4's.

Softwoods do tend to be softer than most hardwoods, which make them far more susceptible to damage like gouges and scratches, but a super power of softwood is that it usually won't crack or split when nailed or screwed, unlike hardwoods.

Since I told you about the hardest wood, it's only right to expand on the softest wood known. The Cuipo tree (left) is considered to have the softest known wood, which on the Janka scale only registers at 22 lbf. This means you can probably create damage simply by squeezing a piece of its wood between two fingers.

When first looking at furniture, you may initially find it difficult to identify all the different wood types, as there are literally thousands of unique tree species.

However, even though any piece of furniture technically could be made from any type of wood, the vast majority of furniture is manufactured from a select few species.

In this chapter, I will expand further on the different characteristics to look for in the composition of various types of wood, which hopefully will assist you with differentiating and identifying the various species simply just by sight.

I usually make two observations at first glance when looking at a piece of furniture. First, I recognize which various common species of wood that a piece of furniture is made of.

The second observation I will make is specifically to the damage in question. The extent of the damage to a surface will determine initially whether a repair is even possible, or if the damage is too severe and the piece of furniture in question is in need of refinishing. You can't always put lipstick on a pig!

In this picture of a nightstand top, the finish is severely chipping and flaking off due to neglect and water damage. Damage similar to this is far too advanced for a "spot repair". I would consider this top, not repairable, without refinishing.

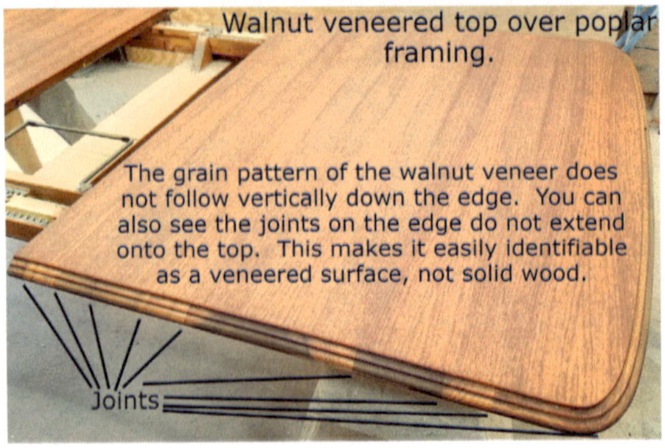

My third observation is whether the piece of furniture in question is solid wood or veneered. This observation alone usually doesn't make much of a difference in the grand scheme of things, unless the piece in question requires refinishing.

There are a few ways to determine if the piece of furniture is solid wood or not, as solid wood furniture will usually consist of more than one plank of wood glued together.

Depending on the width and construction of any particular piece of furniture, you should expect to see none, one or several "joints".

Observing "joints" of a wood surface alone will not always be an identifier of solid wood vs. a veneered surface, as a veneered surface can easily duplicate the appearance of "joints".

Most often you'll have to rely on the "side edge" (left or right edge) or "rear edge" to determine the construction.

You may possibly even look at the underside of the wood panel in question, if you can access it, to see if the same grain pattern that is on the top continues through to the underside, which if so, would likely make it a solid wood surface.

Look at the top surface and follow the grain pattern of the top down the left or right edge. If it's a solid wood surface, you should see what is referred to as, "end-grain", like in the picture to the right.

You can easily see that the grain pattern continues from the top surface, vertically down the item's edge.

Be cautious when looking at the front edge of a top surface, such as a dresser or buffet, as that edge may not always be a true detector of solid wood vs. veneer.

On a front edge (and possibly rear), the grain pattern most likely will run parallel with the grain pattern of the top surface, therefore appearing to be one consistent piece of wood, which could make it easier to mistake for a solid surface.

Conversely, some solid wood constructed items may have edges that are veneered (right) to cover some unsightly end grain, or there may be a thicker, solid wood edge attached to a veneered or plywood surface (second picture right).

Some edges may not be either, on a finished piece of furniture it's not uncommon to see the edges painted by the manufacturer, in an attempt to mimic a grain pattern.

Look closely at the picture to the left, that's the top edge of a nightstand.

It appears that there is a grain pattern, but in reality, the edge is completely "painted" by the manufacturer to blend with the top surface.

This piece of furniture is being refinished, and after the finish has been removed you can see from the picture, the top is actually made of MDF (medium density fiberboard), with only the center of the top surface being a veneer.

That is the reason the edge was painted, now I'll have to "repaint" that edge during the finishing process to make it look like wood again.

In our case, this was part of a bedroom set which included an additional nightstand, dresser with a tri-fold mirror, and a two piece tall chest.

Re-painting the edges of everything probably added two hours to the total restoration. If you were observant and pointed that out to the client, you may be able to increase your refinish cost slightly to reflect the additional time needed.

As you may have noticed, the client also wanted to completely change the appearance of the set to a darker walnut tone.

Along the same lines as painting the edges, some faux painters are amazingly talented! Take this cabinet below, which is actually a built-in unit, owned by my absolute favorite clients, Mr. and Mrs. F.

It was painted by Mr. F.'s brother and that's not real wood that you see, it's entirely painted to simulate wood, most people would have no clue.

The picture to the left is a close-up of the top edge, it's still hard to tell that it isn't even "real wood".

In this case, I can tell the unit is completely painted because the grain pattern doesn't appear "true" to me, but additionally, the miniscule bumps in the finished surface appear like the "bumpy" pattern of house paint on a wall, it's not as smooth as a sprayed finish.

A sprayed finish shouldn't have any texture, but finishes applied by hand often will.

See the picture to the right for the texture. Now look at your painted wall, the texture is virtually the same.

If you were to start sanding this painted surface, you would immediately begin to remove the color/paint and the simulated grain pattern from the surface completely.

The further you sand, the larger the area will become, and the more simulated grain pattern you lose, the more difficult it may be to replicate, possibly getting you in trouble if you cannot recreate that area with your touch up products.

Other identifying characteristics of a veneered surface, may be, if the grain pattern on the edge is running perpendicular, compared to the grain pattern of the top surface.

If the grain pattern runs in two completely opposite directions, that is a sure sign the edge, either consists of veneer, or it's painted.

Just understand that solid wood surfaces most likely will not have any veneer on the edges, unless we're talking about inlay.

Inlay, is a type of veneer, which is often a secondary (or more) wood type, that is usually a different species of wood than what is used in the overall construction of a particular piece of furniture

Inlays can be seen on solid wood or veneered surfaces. Various woods are cut into very thin pieces, made into a pattern and installed into a pre-cut void or pocket, often to add an artistic aspect to any piece of furniture, like the picture to the right.

It may take more of a trained eye to decipher if a wood panel is actually solid, veneered or painted, but once you begin to recognize the varying characteristics, identifying solid wood vs. veneer will become second nature with most furniture you'll come across, and it should be something that only takes a couple seconds to notice.

Try going to a furniture retailer and see how many characteristics you now notice that you wouldn't have in the past. You should now be able to observe how "low quality" most newer furniture is constructed and finished, but go to an estate sale, antique dealer or hi-end retailer/consignment shop and you'll be better prepared and understand the quality of what you are viewing/purchasing.

Determining whether something is solid wood or veneered still doesn't tell me what type of wood it is. When it comes to actually attempting to identify a wood species, there's one characteristic that is unique to every piece of wood, its grain pattern!

"Wood-grain" refers to the alignment, appearance and texture of the wood fibers.

All species of wood fall into three basic "wood-grain" categories, which also could be thought of, as to how deep, or visually apparent the grain cavity is.

Coarse-grained has the deepest of cavities, examples are Oak (right), Butternut and Ash, among others.

Medium-grained, the grain cavity is apparent, but minimally shallow, examples are mahogany and walnut (right), among others.

Lastly, there is fine-grained, the surface has extremely miniscule, to non-existent grain cavities, as found in birch, maple, pine (below) and others.

All the factors that we just went over should greatly assist you in identifying unique characteristics of any particular piece of furniture.

Further, I will attempt to expand on some of the most common wood species that you may come across with regard to furniture.

I will do my best to provide an example of the wood in its natural, unstained, unfinished state, along with accompanying pictures of what that stated wood may look like if finished in various traditional hues.

PINE

Pine, is part of the Gymnosperm family, and consists of four major groups, Conifers, Cycads, Ginkgo and Gnetophytes.

Conifers are by far the most diverse, ecological and economically important gymnosperm group on the planet, with approximately 588 species, grown on every continent in the world except Antarctica.

There are more than 100 species of pine in the northern hemisphere, making them the most abundant species of tree in North America.

Being a soft, fine grained wood, It's relatively easy to recognize pine furniture by the frequent presence of dark knots throughout, along with its traditional light beige to yellowish tone.

Even though there are plenty of examples of pine furniture used in people's homes as of today, due to the wood's relative softness, and its ability to easily attract gouges and scratches, pine is not generally used by craftsmen that produce high end furniture, cabinetry or flooring.

On the Janka scale, pine only registers around 380 lbf, in comparison, walnut is 1010 lbf.

Even though pine may be gouged and scratched easily, it is actually an extremely versatile, very strong, wood species with numerous uses. A few beneficial characteristics are that it doesn't shrink or swell very much and is extremely shock resistant.

Pine was an extremely important resource in the colonial years of the United States, which included the building of virtually all structures, including their interior millwork and furniture.

American and British shipbuilding during this period also depended on the resource to build their fleets, which eventually led to the Pine Tree Riot of 1772.

This was considered a major precursor to the Revolutionary War, and partly fueled America's rebellion for independence.

Pine sapwood usually appears pale and creamy, sometimes with yellow tones. The heartwood may vary from a straw-like color to a deep yellowish-tan.

The resin ducts are also seen as the darker portions of the grain pattern, often appearing as fine, light to medium brown lines. The knots of pine could appear as light to dark, various shaped and sized brown circles.

WALNUT

Walnut, specifically black walnut (Juglans Nigra), is by far the most common species of walnut used by furniture manufacturers, looking to create high quality furniture.

English Walnut

Walnut is also the most valuable commercial timber species in North America, and the only domestic, dark brown wood species.

All walnut trees produce walnuts, but the walnuts we commonly consume are from the English Walnut tree, not the black walnut tree.

Black walnuts are very flavorful but their hard shell and laborious hulling characteristics make them not commercially viable.

Black Walnut

What you may not realize, walnuts are not even in the nut family, even though we consume them in grandma's famous holiday spread of finger foods, they are actually an edible seed.

Another interesting fact, their shells are commonly ground and used as a soft grit abrasive to debur, descale, polish, and are commonly used to clean fiberglass, plastics, wood, stone and soft metals. I personally use it during the process of cleaning and polishing metal furniture hardware.

This recyclable, environmentally friendly, soft grit abrasive has a few other uses I couldn't resist at least mentioning, the shells are also used as a paint thickener, in oil drilling and as a filler in dynamite!

"Figure", refers to the appearance of wood, as seen on a longitudinal surface. We'll delve more into the different types of figuring in various other sections of this chapter, but one type that is highly coveted by woodworkers, with regard to walnut and mahogany, is called "crotch".

Crotches are an extreme compression of the wood, caused by the forces exerted within the trunk of a growing tree, where two main branches meet the trunk.

In other words, at the first "V" section of a tree, where the large branches grow from the trunk and begin to separate. The bigger, heavier the branches, the more compression there may be in the grain pattern.

Walnut and mahogany trees dominate the crotch market because they are some of the only trees to grow big enough to consistently produce a large crotch area.

A popular way to apply crotch veneer is called "bookmatched". Bookmatching is when two or more extremely thin sheets of veneer, one after another, are sliced off of a log.

The sheets of veneer are laid down and attached to a surface in a manner so that one sheet is a mirror image of the opposing sheet, like pages in a book. This walnut door, to the left, has been bookmatched four times.

Walnut grain may be irregular, but is typically straight, with a medium texture. Walnut sapwood can be creamy white, while the heartwood can vary from a light to dark chocolate brown, occasionally having a purplish cast or dark streaks.

Kiln-dried walnut tends toward a dull brown tone, but when air-dried, the wood can tend to have a rich purplish-brown tone. It's only the heartwood of the tree which produces the dark wood, but some manufacturers will steam the entirety of a walnut plank which darkens the sapwood and creates a more even color distribution across the wood surface.

Most craftsmen like to avoid the steamed planks and will look for only the heartwood, as steaming may bring out more of a grayish tone.

Walnuts' tone will actually lighten with age, unlike oak, maple or cherry which darken with age.

POPLAR

Poplar wood is most commonly derived from the Tulip Poplar (Liriodendron Tulipifera), and is one of the softest (540 lbf on the Janka scale), and least expensive hardwoods available.

Poplar is also not prized for appearance like cherry, oak or walnut, but it still may be one of the most popular woods used in furniture manufacturing that you are unaware of.

Poplar is known as utility wood, and may be most commonly incorporated as pallets, crates, framing of furniture, drawer guides, inner framing of a sofa, cabinetry and countless other uses.

A way furniture manufacturers may mislead you, is they may try to sell you "solid wood" furniture. You may think that because the top is made of walnut as in the previous example eleven pages ago (and below), the entire table is made of walnut.

In actuality, only the top veneer consists of walnut, often you will find poplar used as "filler wood".

It's true that this table is made of "solid wood" but it's misleading because it's not made entirely of the type of wood you are expecting, and often a salesman will not necessarily expose that fact.

Often due to the higher prices of solid hardwoods like walnut, a craftsman may build a piece of furniture out of poplar, only to have the more prized veneer applied to all the flat surfaces, like the top, sides, drawer and door fronts.

After this piece of furniture is fabricated, it's very likely that the edges of the entire piece of furniture are not veneered, which may also include the legs and other exposed parts, leaving this "walnut" piece of furniture needing additional work to color match all the exposed edges and any other un-veneered parts.

A positive is that poplar generally accepts stain well and a competent craftsman should always be able to properly color match the different woods together to create a near uniform hue.

Even the chairs included in this set were entirely made of poplar, with only the center plywood carved backs being veneered with walnut, therefore dye stains were used/required during the finishing process to create the proper match.

You may, though, at some point come across a solid wood, stained and finished piece of poplar furniture, but because of the unpopularity of poplar's appearance, it will be the least common.

You may also see poplar in kitchen cabinetry and not even realize that it's poplar because the cabinetry will often be completely painted.

One unique type of poplar occasionally used in furniture construction is called rainbow poplar (right). Rainbow poplar is not a different species of tree, in fact it's from the standard Yellow Poplar, but it's been mineral stained, and can exhibit a plethora of streaking colors ranging from green, purple, black, red and more.

The precise cause of these colored streaks are not fully understood, but as with most trees, soil and growing conditions usually are the determining factor in every aspect of growth.

To the untrained eye, solid poplar furniture may be confused with maple or cherry furniture as the grain pattern may appear similar, if they both are traditionally stained and finished in similar light hues, though poplar usually will exhibit more of a green tone.

Poplar usually has a fairly straight, uniform, medium texture grain. Its sapwood is pale yellow to a creamy white, and may be streaked. The heartwood is usually tan but can vary from pale yellowish brown to olive green. The green hue of the heartwood will tend to darken over time, due to exposure to light, and will become more brown.

Sorry, no other great photos of poplar furniture exist.

Walnut Veneered Radio Cabinet

CHERRY

Cherry is the fourth most harvested wood in the US, behind Oak, Poplar and Ash.

Cherry wood is harvested from the American Black Cherry (Prunus Serotina) tree, and may be considered the most prized hardwood used in America, for furniture manufacturing.

Black cherry does have several aliases; rum cherry, whiskey cherry, mountain cherry, wild cherry, along with others, depending on your whereabouts.

Black cherry grows abundantly throughout the midwest to the eastern US, but grows particularly well in the Appalachians. Cherry trees can grow as tall as 80 feet and live upwards of 200 years.

Black cherry trees produce wild black cherries, which are edible, but have to be pitted, because they contain amygdalin, a naturally occurring chemical, when metabolized produces cyanide.

A single black cherry seed yields roughly 0.17 grams cyanide per gram, so depending on the size of the kernel, ingesting just one or two freshly crushed pits could lead to serious illness or death.

It's not only cherry pits that you need to watch out for, the same compound can be found in the seeds of apricots, apples, plums, peaches and more. So the PSA of the day is to definitely stay away from eating most fruit seeds, even pets can be susceptible!

Cherry wood has a smooth closed grain, similar to that of maple. Unlike maple though, cherry has what appears to be black specks, in various areas throughout the surface.

These black specks are naturally developed mineral deposits, where sap was once stored, often referred to as "pitch pockets", or "gum patch/pockets", and may look similar, but shouldn't be confused with spalting.

Pro tip: occasionally instead of filling a small gouge on the surface of the cherry, depending on the size and shape of the damage, you may be able to disguise a gouge by just adding a small amount of black or dark brown, to make the damage appear similar to a pitch pocket.

It's not only with cherry, but all wood repairs, I recommend trying to incorporate the unique characteristics of the wood, not everything has to be filled and touched up perfectly to become invisible.

The main goal of a repair, in the end, is to not see the damage, which often requires getting creative by tricking the eye into not recognizing that there was ever damage. I even occasionally paint large, fake knots on a piece of pine furniture.

Cherry wood, when cut, usually starts out with a golden/pink tone, but as the wood oxidizes or is exposed to UV light, the color of the heartwood darkens to a rich, reddish brown. The sapwood of cherry is usually a creamy, satiny white.

MAHOGANY

Mahogany belongs to the family Swietenia, which really only consists of three species, Honduran, West Indian and Swietenia Humilis. These three species are the only types of mahogany to be considered "Genuine Mahogany".

There are numerous other species of trees which have extremely similar characteristics to the three Swietenia species from countries in Africa, Asia as well as several other parts of the world, including the United States.

Because these other species are only close in visual appearance, and not of the same genus, they are considered to be "True Mahogany" (or in my opinion, false mahogany, haha).

True mahoganies are usually far lighter or browner in hue, have a more coarse grain, are less dense and may be more prone to warpage, than genuine mahoganies.

In the US, mahogany trees only grow in Florida, and are listed as a threatened species by the state. Even though low in numbers, mahogany is one of the most dense and hardest woods grown in the United States, in fact, mahogany is so dense and heavy that it sinks in water.

What's ironic, is that several manufacturers create high end boats made from solid, genuine mahogany. That is in part due to the wood's fantastic ability to resist rot, warpage and cracking.

The United States is the biggest importer of mahogany in the world, and Peru is the world's biggest exporter of genuine mahogany. It's estimated that up to 90% of the trees felled in Peru are illegally harvested and traded by gun toting loggers.

There is one mahogany tree that is considered to have the most notorious "figure" in history. The term figure, refers to the appearance of wood, as seen on a longitudinal surface. In other words, unique patterns of the grain, on the flat surface of a piece of wood, not the edge.

The figure of any particular piece of wood is in part due to the cut, combined with the unique, innate properties of the tree.

It's basically just referred to as "The Tree". So what happened to The Tree, what makes it so remarkable, and is there any of The Tree left in the world?

In 1965, deep in the Honduran rainforest of Chiquibul, a party of loggers happened upon this massive mahogany tree with a trunk greater than 20 feet across.

The legend begins when loggers, outfitted only with axes, began to chip at the base for weeks in preparation to fell it. Finally, when The Tree was ready to topple, it took an unexpected turn, falling backwards, deep into a ravine.

An unfortunate turn of events for the loggers, as they could not extract it, giving up, leaving the forest floor to be The Tree's home for the next ten years

Around 1975, Alan Mauney, a sawmill owner, discovered The Tree during an expedition in search of timber. Immediately Alan recognized the significance of his finding and enlisted the help of Robert Novak (an American specializing in importing wood to the US) and set forth a plan for extraction.

The decision was made to cut the tree into sections. With the help of large tractors and trucks, Alan and his crew were able to drag the timber out and transport the sections 100 miles, through the heart of the jungle to the Chiquibul river, where the logs then had to be floated 70 miles downstream to Alan's steam powered sawmill.

Milling of The Tree took several weeks and produced somewhere around 12,000 board feet of timber. It was immediately apparent that this was no ordinary wood, the figure was like nothing that's ever been seen before.

Through the 70's and 80's much of the wood was sold to high end furniture craftsmen, in fact, it's rumored that George Lucas (creator of Star Wars) used wood from The Tree to panel the walls of his entire office in San Francisco. I can neither confirm nor deny.

It wasn't until the late 80's when The Tree found serious use in guitars thanks to Tom Ribbecke and Richard Hoover, founders of Santa Cruz Guitars. The guitars made with wood from The Tree routinely sell for $20,000-$40,000 each.

The Tree's figure is classified into three categories, quilted, blistered and tortoise (pictured), with the latter being the most coveted.

To this date, there have been no other mahogany trees found that even come close in comparison to The Tree and it's estimated that there may be less than 100 boards from The Tree remaining in the world.

Genuine mahogany has an even, straight, medium textured grain which is relatively free of voids, pitch pockets and knots.

Mahoganies sapwood is yellowish-white to pale brown, while the heartwood may vary from medium to deep brown or red-brown, and in some instances, a deep, rich, red or purplish tone.

TEAK

Teak is considered to have two "types", old growth and plantation teak. Old growth teak, considered the best teak, mostly from Myanmar, can also be referred to as Burmese teak.

The Indonesian government has strict guidelines for the production of their teak supply. Since the best teak wood comes from mature trees, it can take up to 80 years to harvest a tree that's planted today.

Each year the Myanmar government decides a predetermined amount of trees which can be felled, ensuring each tree felled is replaced by a new sapling.

Burmese teak is considered the best because of its high silica content, which is attributed to the soil they grow in. The silica content is what makes the wood resistant to decay or insects and also makes it naturally slip resistant in wet conditions, (i.e. a boat deck or boat interior).

Plantation teak, which is now produced throughout the world, are teak trees produced and felled as rapidly as possible, usually within 25 years, to try and keep up with the demand for the natural product.

Growing these trees so rapidly lowers the silica content, the wood is not as dense, could warp easier, and can be less rot and insect resistant.

Teak is ideal for the outdoors and is frequently used for patio furniture and shipbuilding. Even without a protective coating, due to the natural resins and oils produced in the wood, teak is virtually water resistant!

As teak ages outside, the hue will transform from a beautiful golden brown to an elegant gray patina, if the wood is not properly sealed, but maybe you like that appearance.

If you want to keep teak from turning gray as long as possible, if storing outside, it is recommended to seal the wood with an exterior, UV protected varnish.

But last I checked, mother nature is undefeated. There is no type of finish that I'm aware of, that will last indefinitely, outside in the elements.

Most interior teak furniture, on the other hand, is simply finished with Teak oil, or has minimal finish. Teak oil is usually a combination of Tung oil and Linseed oil, along with a few extra additives mixed in, which seep under the surface and may provide only minimal additional strength and durability, while the oil on the surface will eventually evaporate.

As evaporation occurs, so does oxidation, slowly starting the graying cycle. So, teak furniture without a "finish" will be high maintenance if you want to keep that beautiful golden brown hue, but if the wood has a protective clear coat, like lacquer or urethane, kept inside with proper care, the original wood hue could potentially last indefinitely.

Despite teak's widespread cultivation, it's still perhaps one of the most expensive lumbers on the market.

Teak grain pattern is usually straight, though occasionally it can be wavy and interlocked.

Additionally, the grain usually has a coarse uneven texture. Raw, unfinished teak may also have an oily or greasy feel due to the natural oils secreted from the wood.

ROSEWOOD

Rosewood has 300 different species around the world, but due to overexploitation, rosewood is an endangered species of flora, now protected worldwide.

Due to the endangered species tag, there are several different species of trees which are sold as "rosewood", only because they have similar characteristics, but they are not genuine rosewood species. Examples of imitation rosewood include Blackwood, Pau Ferro and others.

The most popular species of rosewood used for furniture is either Brazilian (Dalbergia Nigra) or East Indian (Dalbergia Latifolia) rosewood. One of the main ways to differentiate the two species is to pay attention to the endgrain and the pore density. East Indian rosewood will have twice as many pores per square inch than Brazilian rosewood.

Genuine rosewood is referred to as the "ivory of the forest". It's illegally traded far more than rhino horn, elephant tusk and pangolin scales combined.

It's even more expensive by weight than cocaine and it's the world's most trafficked wild product, a trade worth north of $2 billion per year

A single small rosewood log in China can sell for over several thousands of dollars. In fact, rosewood furniture made in the "hongmu" style (Chinese high end reproduction furniture), routinely sells for over one million dollars.

Another fact, in 2011, the world famous Gibson Guitar company was raided by federal marshals for trafficking what the government thought was illegally obtained rosewood, and that wasn't even the first time, they were also raided for the same issue in 2009.

You should be cautious when working with rosewood as dust from sanding is considered a sensitizing irritant, and can trigger asthma and other respiratory ailments, so I suggest wearing a dust mask when sanding.

In fact, I always recommend wearing a mask when sanding any type of wood, it can't be good to consistently inhale tiny wood particles.

Rosewood has a narrowly interlocked medium textured grain. Its yellow sapwood has an appearance distinctly different from the heartwood which can appear in alternating dark and light streaks with black markings.

OAK

Oak (Genus Quercus), in my opinion, may be one of the most distinguishable species of wood. There are more than 90 species of oak in the United States alone, and over 600 species across the world.

Even though there are many different species of oak, all will usually fall into one of three classifications, White Oak (above), Red Oak (right), and you guessed it, Intermediate Oak.

Often oak is described for the way it is milled, either plain (flat) sawn, quarter sawn, rift sawn or live sawn with each type of milling creating its own unique grain pattern, and various cuts can incorporate other attributes like added strength and warpage resistance.

All wood could be milled in one of the following ways described, but most of the time you won't hear "quarter sawn walnut" like you would hear "quarter sawn oak". Oak is synonymous with this type of milling.

Plain/Flat sawn lumber is cut parallel to the growth rings so that the growth rings are cut from 0°-30° to the wide face of the board. Plain sawn lumber is also the most vulnerable to warping and distortion.

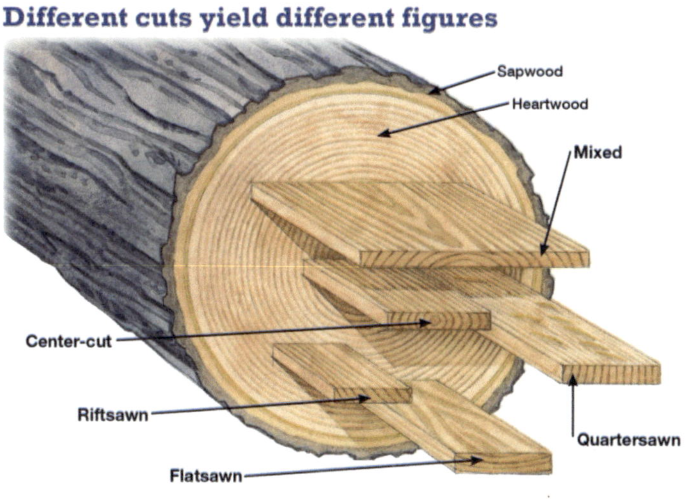

Quarter sawn, by definition, is the angle that the annular growth rings intersect with the face of the board. However, there is no standard agreement about what exactly that milling angle is, most define it as between 60°- 90° degrees, although some experts define it as between 75°- 90° degrees.

A lot of non-experts may suggest it's between 45°- 90° degrees. One downside to quarter-sawing, is that up to 30% of the wood on a log could be wasted.

Quarter sawn lumber is also more stable and less prone to expanding and contracting, it also provides a straighter face grain.

Even though any type of wood can be quarter sawn, Oak is most known for this cutting process which creates unique, beautiful, subtle, wavy, ribbon-like patterns in the grain called "Medullary Rays", or may also be referred to as "ray and fleck".

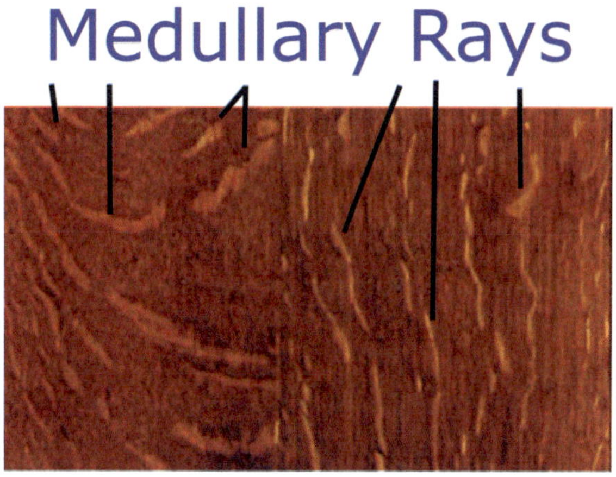

White oak has larger medullary rays than red oak. Some other tree species most commonly cut in this fashion are Sycamore, Lacewood, Beech, Ash and a few others, because they too have beautiful medullary rays.

Rift sawn wood is milled strictly along a log's radials, perpendicular to the annular growth ring orientation. This is a technique of cutting planks from logs so the grain is between 30°– 60° to the face of the board, with 45° being optimum. Rift sawn lumber typically has a narrow, very straight grain pattern, which also is void of medullary rays.

Live sawn milling is the most efficient way to cut a log into planks. Each plank is cut straight off of the log in one direction without changing the orientation of the log.

This cutting method produces boards with a full range of angles of the log's rings. The angles range from 0 to 90 degrees, so each plank could include all of the log's unique visual characteristics.

Interestingly, white oak has a cell structure so tight that water can't even pass through. In white oak, this is due to the grain being sealed off by tyloses (a simple description would be a waterproof foam material) in the pores (left).

This "waterproofing" feature is why most spirit (alcohol) barrels (below) are made of this type of wood.

Weirdly enough, red oak does not have these same tyloses. In fact, the cellular structure of red oak is so open that on a flat sawn piece of wood, you can blow smoke through it from end-grain to end-grain.

The differing cell structures between the two also make white oak slightly harder than red oak on the Janka Scale.

MAPLE

Maple comes in two different forms, hard maple and soft maple. "Hard Maple" really refers to only one species of maple, *Acer Saccharum*, otherwise known as Sugar Maple. The sugar maple tree also produces maple syrup.

"Soft maple" is a broad term which actually includes several different species of maple tree, and the term is used merely to differentiate those species from the singular, hard maple tree (sugar maple).

Soft maple, comparatively on the Janka scale, is about half as hard as the sugar maple. Soft maple clocks in somewhere between 700-950 lbf., while hard maple registers at 1450 lbf.

Another term you may run into often when speaking about maple, or any other wood for that matter, is "figure", which you've already read several times throughout this chapter.

The often heard term, "curly maple", is not a new species of maple tree, in fact, it's a catch all term which basically refers to a tight, undulating, rippling effect in the grain of a piece of wood, sawn in a particular fashion. You can see this effect throughout the unfinished piece of maple to the right.

There are possibly dozens of different terms that are used to describe the visually different characteristics which fall under this "curly" or "figured" moniker.

"Fiddleback", is a very specific type of figure (right). Typically, the spaces in between a curl have to be a quarter of an inch or less for it to be classified as a "fiddleback".

Tight and uniform, fiddleback curls are prized for use in guitars, mandolins, and violins. Fiddleback figure may also be found in some maple furniture.

"Quilted" (below) is a pattern that almost looks like bubbling, or tubes, on a surface. Most often found in big leaf maple, quilted figures are another highly sought after quality by furniture and guitar makers.

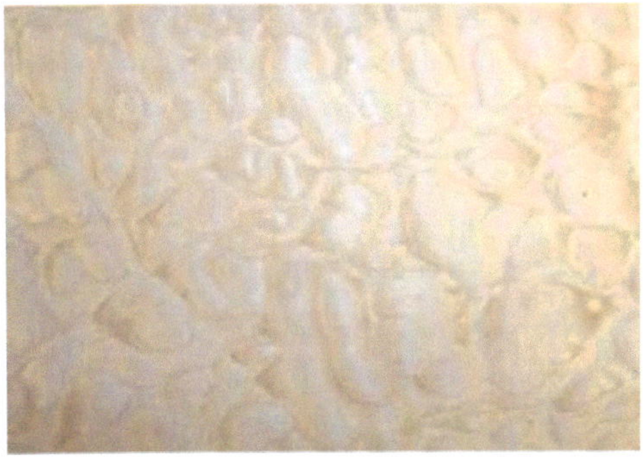

"Tiger Stripe" (below), as you can see, has a pattern similar to fiddleback, but what sets it apart is that the "stripes" are not all separated within a quarter inch of each other.

"Spalting" (below) is different from the other types of figure we've talked about so far. Spalting can happen in almost any wood species, but it's quite often found in maple.

When the ends of a freshly-cut log are exposed to moisture, a fungus finds its way inside the log and begins to eat.

If left too long, fungi could rot the log from the inside out, but if the fungus is caught in time, it will leave what looks like a black ink line of varying thicknesses, drawn by a Sharpie® with spectacular irregularity.

It may not seem possible, but the black lines/spalting is actually the front line of an epic fungi battle, with different groups of fungi attacking each other. The black line is actually a line of dead fungi!

Some fungi cannot colonize the wood by themselves, they require other fungi to have preceded them, to create favorable conditions. Fungi arrive in waves of primary and secondary colonizers. Primary colonizers initially capture and control the resource, and by doing so, they change the pH (power of hydrogen) of the wood, and its structure.

The primary, original fungi, must defend against secondary colonizers that then have the ability to fully colonize due to the ideal conditions created by the original colonizers.

Not sure who was victorious! But in my opinion, we're the winners because we ultimately have the opportunity to admire these beautiful characteristics.

"Birdseye" figuring is as synonymous with maple, as quarter-sawn is for oak, but birdseye is rare, only found in approximately 1% of all felled maple trees.

The figure appears to resemble a "bird's eye", and these "eyes" can have several different shapes, consider it, figuring within the figure.

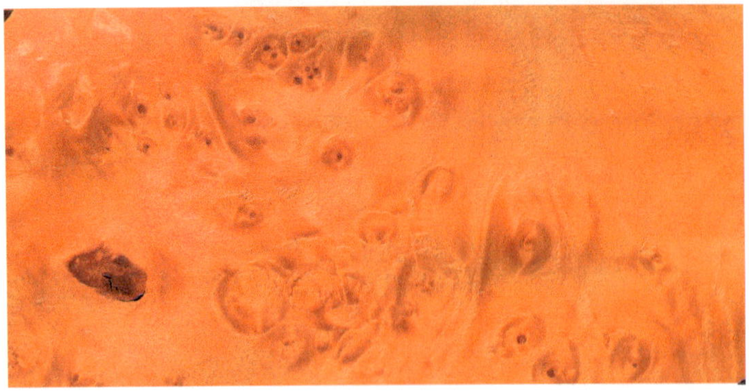

There are "C" shaped eyes, oval eyes, eyes that look like raindrops streaking down a window pane, and others. The eyes can also vary in spacing from dense to sparse.

It's thought that the figure is a result of unfavorable growing conditions for the tree, but scientists have yet to be able to replicate the phenomenon.

This definitely was not a complete, comprehensive list of the different "figure" types, just some of the more common grain patterns you may run into when dealing with maple furniture.

Also remember, “curl” or “figure” isn’t only found in maple, and it isn’t always found in maple, but may be more apparent in maple than other wood types, even though any wood can have figure.

More descriptive names of figuring that you may come across, but aren’t limited to include; angel step, bear scratches, blister, burl, ribbon curl, dimple, flame, wide flame, ghost, pinstripe, and a host of other terms.

Remember these are not differing types of wood, these are just adjectives that someone invented to describe the visual effects produced by the grain pattern from a particular cut on a finished piece of wood.

FAKE WOOD?

One major caveat that I just want to mention about furniture, is that on occasion, you may come across what appears to be a standard piece of furniture, but what you may not realize is it could consist of a laminate veneer, which is made of synthetic materials, usually either a paper type material, or plastic.

On this conference table, the top is essentially a sheet of plastic glued to a particle board (MDF) or plywood framing. If you sand the surface, you will only remove the imitation grain to expose the true color of the plastic underneath the "printed grain".

Again, these desks are not made of cherry, they are completely covered in plastic that imitates wood.

Think of it as a photograph, furniture manufacturers, computers and printers have become so advanced that they can produce wood grain patterns virtually indistinguishable to the untrained eye.

There are not many exceptional repairs that can be produced on a paper or plastic laminate, think big box stores (Walmart, Target, some IKEA) furniture.

Be cautious and temper your expectations if attempting to repair furniture with these types of veneers, as repairs will rarely turn out invisible, but that in no way means that repairs are impossible, in most situations, with enough experience, you will most likely still be able to perform sufficient cosmetic repairs.

Most laminates will have a low luster, though some plastic laminates could potentially have a gloss. If you look extremely close, possibly using a magnifying glass you can usually see a pattern from the printing machine on the laminate.

Laminates are also void of grain cavities, so the surface will most always be perfectly smooth. Some higher end laminate office furniture may have solid wood edging, with only the top and sides consisting of laminate.

Even though this chapter didn't have much information pertaining to the actual aspect of repairing furniture, my goal is that you now have a better general understanding of wood so you can distinguish between various types of furniture far more easily than before. Having this basic knowledge will help expedite your repairs in the future. Good luck!

Other than knowing what type of wood you are working with, in my opinion, light and its effect on color is one of the most important aspects to comprehend with regard to furniture, repairs and finishing.

Color plays a significant role in our daily lives, as soon as you open your eyes in the morning we are inundated by color. Whether it be on our walls, carpets, coffee mugs, computer screens, pictures, cars, commute to the office, kids football practice.

Basically everything in this entire world is one big collage of never ending colors. So where are these colors derived from? More about the scientific answer later, for now we'll discuss how colors throughout history have been primarily created from natural organic materials like plants, rocks, soils, and animals.

In other words, almost anything that exists in this world that is not man made can and likely has been manipulated in some way to create some type of colored pigment. Yes, even humans, search for "mummy brown" pigment.

Natural pigments have been used since the beginning of the Middle Paleolithic era. Humans throughout the world, have collected and utilized all different types of organic materials, local to them, while discovering unique ways to process those materials by either grinding, sifting, washing, mixing or in some rare cases, heating (causing oxidation), to create a pigment which has a particular, specific hue (color).

In fact, Ochre is the oldest known pigment to be used by humans, thought to have been used some 300,000 years ago, close to the emergence of Homosapiens.

Some archaeologists believe that ochre (a natural clay) helped evolve early humans' cognitive abilities and could have been beneficial in birthing communication between strangers.

Painting one's body or environment would have been done as a way to convey a message or something else in particular to another individual, who hopefully would in turn have the ability to understand that signal.

For instance, civilizations were able to portray themselves or something unique from their culture, like depicted in this parietal art, located at Serra da Capivara National Park, in Brazil, which is estimated to be over 20,000 years old.

I'm not an archeologist, but I'm positive that we've (today's humans) learned something historically significant about that civilization based solely on this hand painted representation.

These types of renderings, along with painted hieroglyphics from the Egyptians, Mayans, Chinese and other cultures eventually lead to scripts (writing), and also in turn gave us unparalleled insight into what the world was like through their eyes, at a particular given time throughout history.

In my opinion, that should make pigments one of the most important discoveries in the history of mankind, probably up there with fire or the wheel.

In 1706, German chemist Johann Jacob Diesbach created Prussian Blue (ferric hexacyanoferrate(II)) by accident, inventing the first known chemically synthesized color.

This new blue pigment was less expensive to manufacture, more readily available and was far easier to produce as compared to ultramarine blue or other blue pigments which were in use at the time.

This first written account of prussian blue was published anonymously. This early report revealed almost nothing pertaining to the discovery of Prussian Blue nor the method for preparation of the pigment.

The written account was really no more than an advertisement for the new material and stated that the prussian blue pigment could be purchased directly from the book dealers, thus creating the first market for a synthetically fabricated color.

The first known painting to contain prussian blue was painted in 1709 by Pieter Van Der Werff, titled, "Entombment of Christ" (right). It was used in Mary's viel and in the sky.

Today there are synthetic versions of virtually all colors we use, but nearly all of them refer back to hues originally developed from organic sources.

For instance, actual burnt wood produces charcoal (below left), used to make black pigment.

Different clay soils (below right) or minerals could be used to create browns such as umber, ocher and sienna pigments.

One of the more exotic coloring agents may have been the dye that creates Tyrian Purple. The use of tyrian purple dates back over 3000 years to the ancient Phoenicians.

The dye is harvested from a species of a medium sized predatory sea snail named Bolinus Brandaris (right), from the eastern Mediterranean Sea.

The dye substance is a mucus secretion from their hypobranchial gland. The snails secrete this substance when they are attacked by predators, or physically antagonized, like poked by annoying humans.

Therefore, the dye can be collected either by "milking" the snails, which is extremely labor intensive, but a renewable resource, or by collecting and destructively crushing the snails.

In ancient times, extracting this dye involved tens or even hundreds of thousands of snails. It's estimated that it required approximately 250,000 snails to create no more than one ounce of pure purple dye.

The color purple also has ties to the kings and queens that date back to the ancient world, where, because the color purple was so rare and difficult to make, it was often reserved only for royalty or for the elite upper class.

The Persian King Cyrus wore a purple tunic as his royal uniform, and some Roman emperors even forbid their citizens from wearing purple clothing under penalty of death.

Purple was especially revered in the Byzantine Empire, where its rulers wore flowing purple robes and even signed their decrees in purple ink. It's thought by some, that even Jesus was donned in a purple cloak or robe at his crucifixion.

You've probably heard the saying "born with a silver spoon", meaning a child was born into wealth, well similarly, thousands of years ago, children of wealth were described as being "born in the purple".

You may be more familiar with the color Royal Blue. This too was discovered by the Phoenicians using the same process, except it was a different species of snail needed to create the royal blue color that we now know today.

For an example of a pigment that was initially developed by pure coincidence, we can delve into Lead-Tin Yellow (right), which is considered a historically important yellow pigment used in oil paintings.

Lead-tin yellow is often referred to as the "yellow of the old masters", because of the frequency in which it was used by some of the most prominent artists in history during the Renaissance era, including Rembrandt and others.

Lead-tin yellow is an oxide of lead and tin that was produced by heating 3 parts lead oxide with 1 part tin oxide somewhere between 800-900℃. Slightly lowering or raising the temperature produced different hues of yellow, varying from an orangey-yellow to a lemon-yellow.

This pigment was initially discovered as a byproduct of crystal glass production, but ironically after the year 1750, no known paintings have been found that used lead-tin yellow, and it is unknown why the pigment was lost from collective memory, but Naples Yellow is widely thought to have taken its place during that time period.

It wasn't until 1941, by a scientist named Richard Jakobi, that the compound was rediscovered. Of course, the fact that it was lead based also meant that the pigment was highly poisonous if ingested, inhaled or contacted, so maybe it could be considered a positive that it was lost for a couple hundred years, and may have saved the lives of countless artists for generations.

In Rembrandt's famous masterpiece, *Portrait of a Couple as Isaac and Rebecca*, also known as "The Jewish Bride", as seen under a macro x-ray fluorescence scan, shows the highlights of the tin in the pigment where the lead-tin yellow was applied.

Most dry pigments used today are referred to as dry colorants, and can be either organic or inorganic. Organic means that the dry colorant is made of natural resources.

Inorganic also may be known as synthetic organic. Inorganic pigments are derived from petrochemicals and coal tars, which are formulated to create colored polymers, otherwise known as (colored) plastic.

When in use, you really can't tell the difference between the two. These dry colorants, natural or synthetic, are processed into fine granules similar to the consistency of baby powder.

The fine powder pigment needs to be mixed with a "binder/medium". The finish used is referred to as a binder because it adheres the pigment to a surface during the touch up process.

If pigments are needed during the refinishing process, your binder will be the finish that you are using during that process, whether it be lacquer, urethane, shellac or any other type of finish.

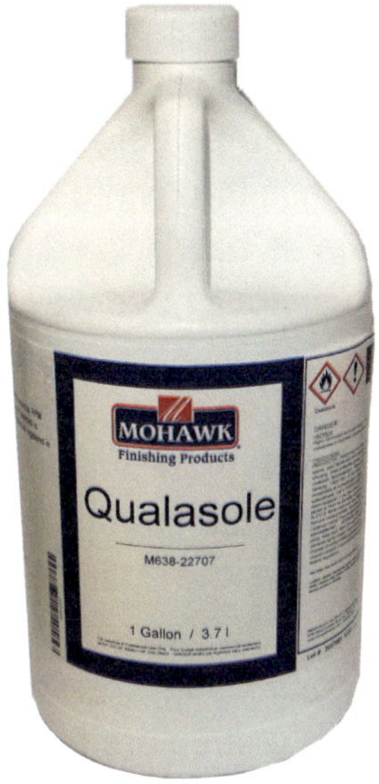

For repairs, we primarily use a padding finish (right) as our binder. A padding finish is usually a neutral or nearly colorless type of finish formulated so it can be applied to a surface by hand (with a rag). Padding finishes and sprayed finishes in most cases are not compatible to be intermixed.

The padding finish that I've used for the majority of my career performing restorations and touch ups, is either Qualasole® or Lacover®, both manufactured by Mohawk®. There are several other similar products, manufactured by various companies, which are covered extensively in the "Hand Applied Finishes" chapter.

Pigments differ from dyes in that they are generally insoluble. Some organic pigments may be able to dissolve in a medium, but the vast majority of synthetic pigments will not dissolve in water, oil, varnish or other mediums. Ultimately, pigments are simply suspended in whatever medium is used.

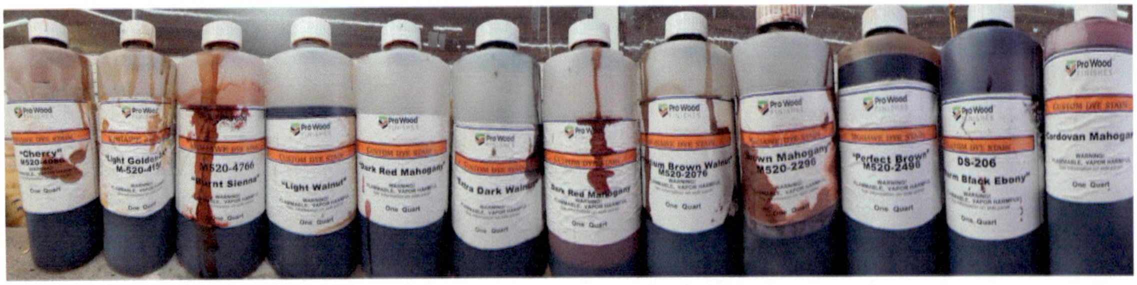

Dyes (above) on the other hand are very concentrated colors, usually in liquid form already, which when combined and agitated into another medium, creates a homogenous mixture.

A colorant may be able to act as either a pigment or a dye depending on the formulation and the liquid medium involved with the application.

Now we can begin to explore the science of color that I mentioned earlier. With reference to humans, color is often mistaken as a property of light, but in my opinion, I feel color is a property of each individual's brain. One could say, "color is a pigment of your imagination".

To perceive a color, our experience depends not only on the wavelength of light that hits the retina, but also the way in which our brain processes that information. Things such as background colors, lighting, surroundings and familiarity all play an active role in the various hues we perceive.

Within the retina there are millions of receptor cells called rods and cones (right). When light energy strikes them, neural signals are created as a result of chemical changes, then routed through neighboring bipolar and ganglion cells that form the optic nerve.

The optic nerve transmits information to the brain's primary visual cortex. The primary visual cortex, often called V1, is a structure that is essential to the conscious processing of visual stimuli.

The human eye consists of 120 million rods that are responsible for our perception of black, white, and gray. Rods are most sensitive in dim light. Each eye also has 6 million cones, which enable us to see color and fine detail. Cones function best in well-lit conditions and become more ineffective with diminished illumination.

Each eye contains three color receptors, green, red and blue. These receptors generate the experience of color when stimulated in various combinations, this is known as the Young-Helmholtz Trichromatic Theory.

Perceived colors also vary with their light source, which could be from either natural/white or artificial light. White light is what we refer to as the "light" that is emitted from the sun, also commonly known as "natural light".

White light carries roughly an equal mixture of the entire spectrum of visible light and all the wavelengths of color. The hue of everything in this world is intimately connected to the "color" of the light source. Without light, there is no such thing as color.

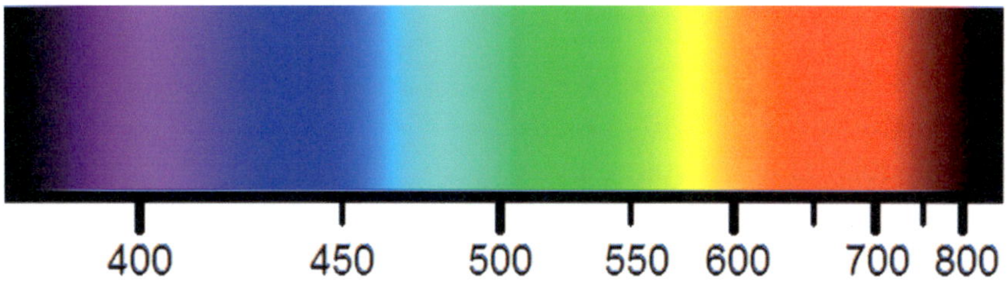

Visible light is an electromagnetic wave that has a wavelength range of approx 380 to 740 nanometers.

The colors of a rainbow, red, orange, yellow, green, blue, indigo and violet, all have their characteristic wavelengths within this range.

When a surface absorbs all wavelengths equally, we perceive it as black, and when a surface reflects all wavelengths equally, we perceive it as white.

Unlike white light, not all wavelengths of color may be present in artificial light. This is the reason an object may appear to be a different color when moved from white light to artificial light.

In other words, an object taken from the outside on a sunny day, to the inside of a house, with only light generated from artificial sources like lamps or ceiling lights, no windows.

Color Rendering Index, also known as CRI, is a way to measure a light source's distinctive attributes. It's an assessment of how the light source shows object colors "naturally" when compared using either LED, incandescent or white light.

The color rendering index is measured as a number between 0 and 100. At zero, all colors look the same, but a CRI of 100 will show the true hue of an object.

Usually, a light source with a CRI of under 80 is considered poor, 80 to 90 is considered good and those with a CRI of 90+ are considered excellent. In general, the higher the CRI, the more accurate the color rendering capacity of the light source.

Incandescent lights have a notoriously good ability to render color. The color rendering index for an incandescent bulb with a color temperature of 2700K is 100, a perfect score!

Unfortunately, incandescent lights have the worst energy efficiency and lifespan of any light source. About 90% of the energy used in incandescent lights goes toward producing heat, while a measly 10% of energy is what produces "light".

LED lights on the other hand can be designed to generate the entire spectrum of visible light without having to use the color filters required by other traditional lighting solutions.

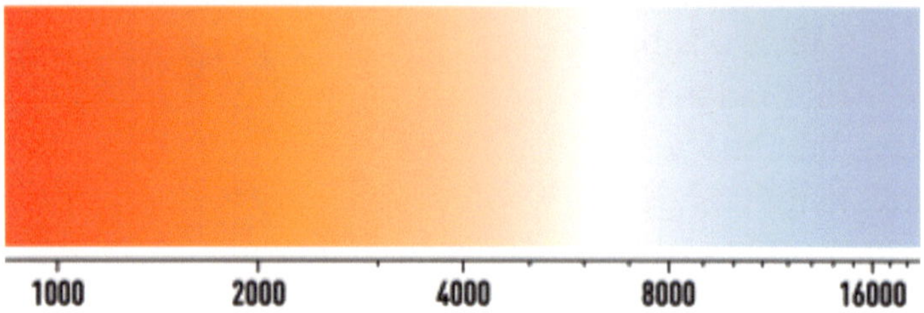

The color rendering index is also independent of color temperature. Color temperature is a way to describe the light appearance provided by a light source, which is measured in degrees of Kelvin (K) on a scale from 1,000 to 16,000

Lightbulbs are available in a wide range of color temperatures that generally span from 2200K, a warm yellow, to over 6000K which produces a cool blue spectrum, the latter is more closely related to the spectrum emitted by the sun..

The first color wheel was created by Sir Isaac Newton around 1704 after he discovered the visible spectrum of white light as it passed through a prism.

Newton saw the sequence red, orange, yellow, green, blue, indigo, and violet, commonly known by the acronym ROY-G-BIV.

From those experiments Newton determined that red, yellow, and blue are the colors from which all the other colors were derived.

For the lack of a better analogy, consider the three primary colors red, yellow, and blue the "grandparents" of all future generations of colors. This analogy could get weird so we'll stop at grandparents, but also imagine these three colors mysteriously appeared, because as we were taught in kindergarten, primary colors cannot be recreated by intermixing any other colors together.

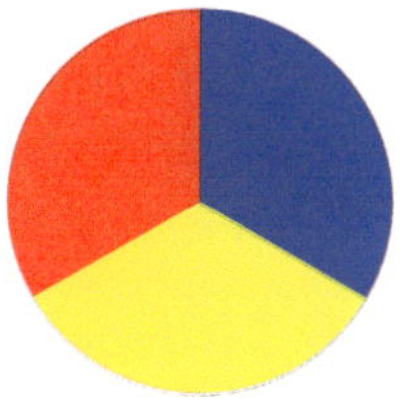

Through the prism experiment Newton also discovered secondary colors. The three secondary colors are, in no particular order, orange, green and violet (purple).

Secondary colors are obtained when you mix equal amounts of two adjoining primaries. For instance mixing red and yellow will make orange, mixing yellow and blue will make green and mixing blue and red will make violet.

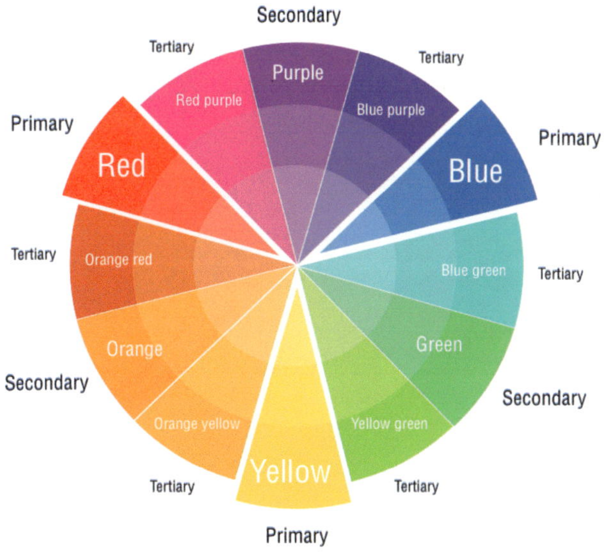

Tertiary colors are the result of mixing a primary and a secondary color together. Traditionally when naming a tertiary color the primary color is named first followed by the name of the secondary color, divided with a hyphen.

There are six tertiary colors; red-orange, yellow-orange, yellow-green, blue-green, blue-violet, and red-violet.

What comes after tertiary colors you may ask? The sequence may seemingly go on forever, but by mixing equal proportions of any two tertiary colors together, the end result is called quaternary colors.

Mixing equal proportions of any two quaternary colors together create quinary colors, mixing equal proportions of any two quinary colors together create senary colors. Next in the sequence would be septenary, octonary, nonary, and denary, although most of these terms beyond tertiary are rarely used.

Are you ready to have your mind blown? Everything that was just described is considered the "artist's color wheel". The artist's color wheel is based on red, yellow, blue, and everything I just told you, which we all learned in elementary school, could be at the least, considered misleading according to more science.

What if I said that you truly cannot make every color by mixing only those three primaries? The artist color wheel predates modern science and doesn't properly address the true range of spectral color.

It is common to still use the blue-red-yellow model for mixing paints, and it is the most ordinary color wheel typically found in art or specialty stores but the truth is, the more pure a primary color is, the less colors that can be created. The best primary colors are not pure.

Ask Xerox® or HP®, companies that manufacture printers. Upon discovering more scientific information about spectral color, how wavelengths of light work in conjunction with the absorption or reflection of surfaces, and interaction with a human's visual system, the blue-red-yellow model has shifted to the cyan-magenta-yellow model becoming the standard, which are called "pigment color primaries", or also known as subtractive primaries.

There are two different types of color mixing, "subtractive" and "additive". Subtractive color mixing is creating a new color by the absorption of wavelengths on a surface, from a light source with a complete spectrum.

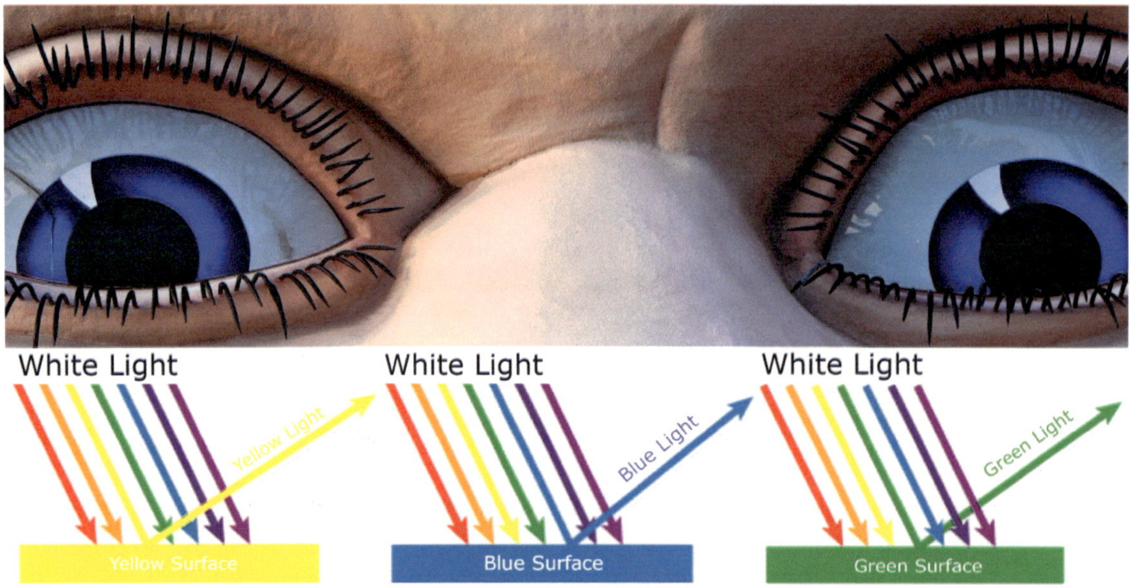

Subtractive color mixing occurs when we mix paints, dyes, or pigments. It is called subtractive, because when paints mix, certain wavelengths are deleted because each paint will absorb some wavelengths that each individual paint reflects, thus leaving us with a lesser number of wavelengths remaining afterward.

The paints still absorb all of the wavelengths that they did previously, but what we are left with is only the wavelengths that the paints reflect.

If we combine all the pigment color primaries, cyan, magenta, yellow, we would create black, but if you notice, the secondary colors in this model are, in no particular order, red, green and blue.

Which leads us to our third version, the red-green-blue color model, otherwise known as, "light color primaries" (colors created by light), this is considered an "additive" color model.

James Clerk Maxwell has been credited as being the father of additive color. In 1861 Maxwell had a photographer, Thomas Sutton, photograph a tartan ribbon on black-and-white film three times, first with a red, then green, then blue color filter over the camera lens.

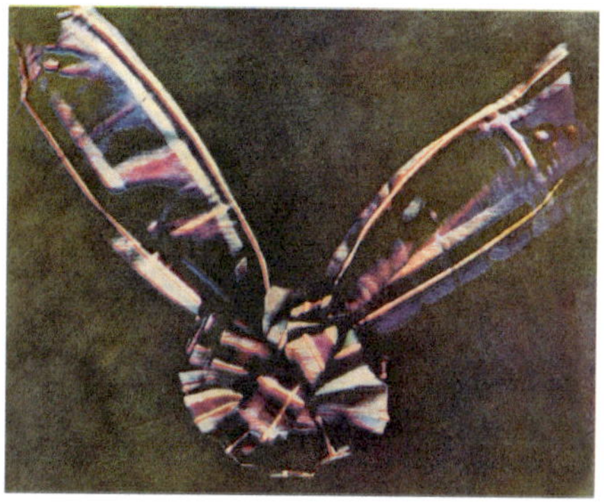

The three images were developed and then projected onto a screen with three different projectors. Each projector was equipped with the corresponding red, green, or blue color filter used to take the initial images.

When the photographs were brought into alignment, the three images formed the first full color image, thus demonstrating the principles of additive color.

When all of the different wavelengths of sunlight are combined, we see white rather than the individual colors. Did you notice the secondary colors in this model are cyan, magenta and yellow? Confused yet?

It is called additive because wavelengths of light still reach our eyes. It is the combination of different light wavelengths reflecting off of a surface that creates the diversity of colors.

In summary, color systems that remove colors through absorption are called "subtractive" and color systems that create colors through reflection of light wavelengths are called "additive".

You may now ponder "is there an infinite amount of colors?", or not, but I'm going to attempt to tell you.

Earlier in the chapter I mentioned cones in the human eye, well in the retina there are millions of these tiny color receptors. The cones found in the human eye are red, green and blue. Because humans have three color receptors, we are referred to as "trichromats".

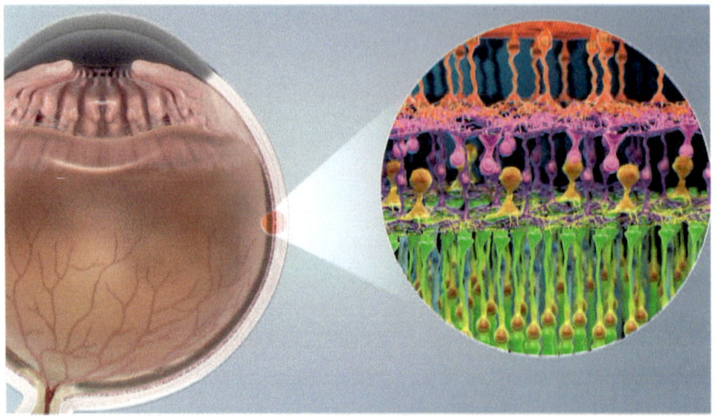

Therefore, all of the colors we observe are just approximations of red, green and blue.

It's been thought that humans can only see about one million different colors, but Psychophysicists, scientists who study human responses, like seeing color, in reference to things in the world, including surfaces and light, have taken meticulous measurements of the human's visual systems (our eyes) best performances.

Psychophysicists have shown that the average human can see about 1000 levels of light-dark, 100 levels of red-green, and 100 levels of yellow-blue, for any single viewing condition in a laboratory. This means that the approximated total number of colors that humans can see is about 1000 x 100 x 100 = 10,000,000 (10 million).

An experiment you'd be able to perform in order to prove this, is to take a magnifying glass and put it close to your computer screen. Whatever you are observing on your computer screen, I'm sure appears to have the entire gamut of colors, but when you zoom in and focus the magnifying glass what you will see are a lot of little lights, and all these lights will be either red, green or blue.

That means every single pixel on a computer screen uses a juxtaposition of these three colors to create every other color. 16,777,216 is the magic number, regarding all the different colors that a computer screen projects to create a full color picture, which seems like overkill since science just told us that's about 6.8 million more colors than the human eye can perceive.

The picture below has all sixteen million, seven hundred seventy seven thousand, two hundred and sixteen colors! Since this is just a picture in a book, you'll have to take my word for it, but if you are interested in zooming in to find your favorite, this is the source: https://commons.wikimedia.org/wiki/File:16777216colors.png authored by Marc Mongenet.

Just remember, everything you look at is greatly affected by the viewing conditions, like the type of lighting, volume of lighting, and other colors of surrounding objects in any viewable scene.

There is also a difference in the way some people view and interpret color.

For instance, some people only have two cones or color receptors in their eyes, therefore they can only see variations of two colors. These people may be considered "dichromats".

This means a person may be partially colorblind and not even recognize the existence of a certain object's true hue.

Protanopia is a state in which the red cones are absent, leaving only cones that absorb blue and green light.

Having the green cones absent is known as Deuteranopia, this creates the inability by a person to decipher between the colors red and green.

Tritanopia is when a person cannot distinguish between blue and yellow, and lastly there is total color blindness, known as monochromacy or achromatopsia, which is due to non-functioning or absent retinal cones.

What is even rarer, are people called "tetrachromats". People with this condition (if you consider it a condition) have a fourth color receptor in their eye and are thought to be able to see up to one hundred million colors. That's ten times more colors than the average person can see.

Hopefully you're not color-blind, it may make performing furniture touch up and color blending more difficult, but that doesn't mean it is impossible.

I actually have a slight form of deuteranopia, though not extreme, I have been in the furniture restoration industry, mixing colors and creating flawless or what I think is nearly flawless repairs for over 25 years.

I've never tried and can't necessarily endorse, but there are glasses available which can "correct" various forms of colorblindness, from different manufacturers. Try them if you have a form of color blindness, the result could be life altering.

I keep rambling, blah, blah, everyone sees light, reflected or absorbed, from surfaces, sources and in volumes. Did you already forget what the question was? Is there an infinite amount of colors?

Since the average person can see at least 10-million colors in any single viewing condition and the variety of viewing conditions for the observer is endless, scientists far smarter than I have determined that there are about 18 decillion colors. That's an 18 followed by 33 zeros, 18,000,000,000,000,000,000,000,000,000,000,000.

That might not quite be infinite, but we can consider that it may be close enough, since those estimated numbers are likely to be on the low side and there is no way to exactly measure each of them or account for each color individually. This would be a great project for some type of supercomputer, to determine every color that exists.

Even though we now know humans can see about ten million colors, compared to some animals, we could all be considered color blind.

Unlike humans with only three color receptors, a blue bottle butterfly has 15 color receptors, and a mantis shrimp has 12 color receptors.

Some birds and other animals can even see polarized or ultraviolet light, which means they too can pick up highlights not visible to the human eye. It's not yet completely understood in certain animals, what all the different receptors in their unique eyes perceive.

Now off that tangent and back to the topic of colors. When primary or secondary colors are not mixed equally you get what are called "intermediate colors". For instance if you mix in more yellow than green you would get a chartreuse hue, but if you mix more green than yellow you would create an apple green hue.

Another seldom known fact is that white and black are not actually considered "colors". White is considered a tint and black is considered a shade. White has the highest level of light reflectance to which black has the lowest degree of light reflectance, so if you are adding white, you are effectively making your color mixture more reflective and adding black effectively makes your color mixture less reflective.

Gray is considered a tone. Neutral gray is an equal amount of white and black mixed. A tone is any pure hue (name any color) with neutral gray added. The original hue remains the same, but now only less vibrant.

Understanding color and its terminology is important in any application involving the use of colors. I often use the HSB model to classify colors. Hue, Saturation and Brightness (value).

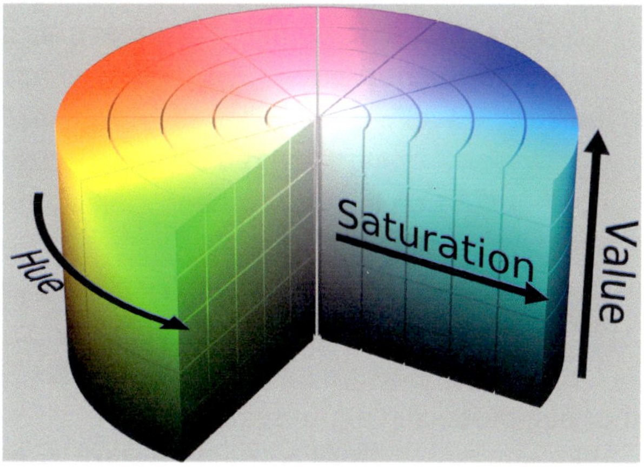

Hue (a term you've read numerous times at this point) is a term which describes a dimension of color we readily experience when we look at an object.

Hue is the term for the pure spectrum colors which are referred to by their "unique color names", like amber, baby blue, turquoise or parakeet green. Hue is any particular color, in its purest form.

Did you know that the language you speak may also play a determining factor in your interpretation of color? In the majority of industrialized cultures, most people get by with only 11 different words for all the various colors. In English they are, black, white, red, green, yellow, blue, brown, orange, pink, purple and gray.

Greeks rely on 12 distinctive words, because they separate light and dark blue. It's been scientifically tested and verified that because of this distinction, Greeks are more sensitive to colors in that region of the spectrum.

The Pirahã language, spoken by indigenous people of the Amazon in Brazil, only has two distinctive terms for color, "light" and "dark". They use descriptive phrases to explain a color, they'll say "such as" or "like" a plant, to describe green, or point to the sun for yellow. They do not have a specific term for green, yellow, or any other color for that matter.

Even a person that you would think may have a vast knowledge of colors, like an interior designer, may only be able to "name" or identify less than 100 different colors. How many unique colors do you think you can name out of 18,000,000,000,000,000,000,000,000,000,000,000,000?

Saturation, often referred to as Color Value, is defined as a relative lightness or darkness of a color. When a color is lightened by adding white, a new color is created called a tint. When a color is darkened by adding black that becomes a shade. Value distinguishes a light color from a dark one.

Brightness, also known as chroma or value, is the third dimension of color. Chroma distinguishes a strong, saturated, vibrant color from a weak one. For instance, the three primary colors, red, yellow and blue are at their greatest chroma before intermixing with other colors or any addition of white or black. Basically chroma is the intensity or brightness of a color.

There are are few other terms that may be important as it pertains to color mixing;

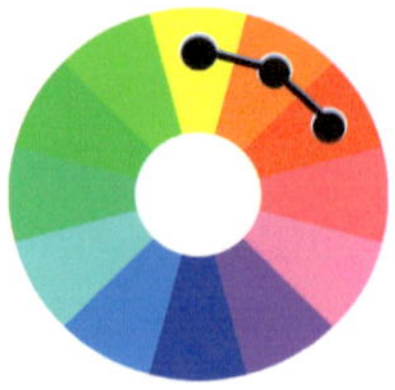

Analogous colors (right) are colors that are next to each other on the color wheel with no spaces in between. For example, yellow, orange and red are categorized as analogous colors on this color wheel, making them generally the same family of colors.

Complementary colors (left) are any two hues positioned exactly opposite each other on a color wheel, for instance, red and green or yellow and blue. Complementary hues will cancel each other out, producing a grayscale hue.

Split complementary colors (left) is a color scheme using one base color and two secondary colors. Instead of using a complementary color, two colors placed symmetrically around it on the color wheel are used. The base color is main, while the secondary colors should be used only for highlights and accents.

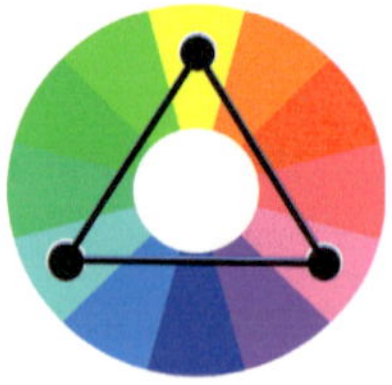

Triadic colors (right) is a color scheme that consists of three colors evenly spaced on the color wheel. The two most basic triadic palettes are the primary colors red, blue, and yellow and the secondary hues orange, purple, and green.

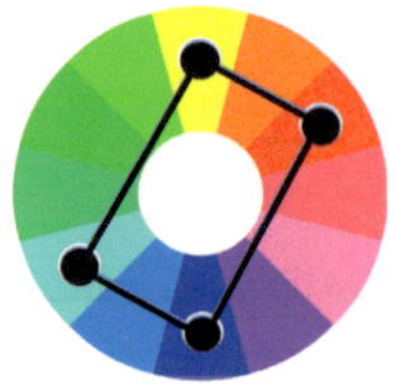

Tetradic colors (left) is a scheme that uses four colors, that are two sets of complements, for example, yellow-blue and green-red. The tetrad colors do not need to be equally spaced in the color wheel, as long as they are couples of complementary colors.

In the furniture restoration industry, the most common color matching system developed, and the most widely accepted is the Prang System (right).

Developed by Lewis Prang in 1876, the system lends itself well to wood tones and color mixing for furniture finishing.

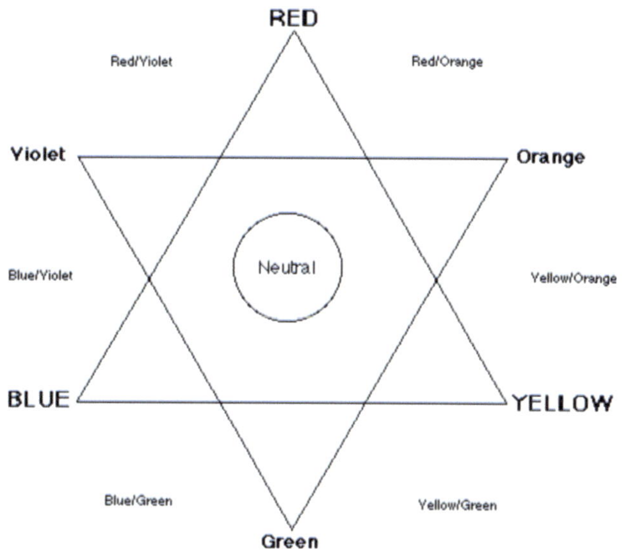

In my opinion, for furniture restoration, the "Finishers Color Wheel" (below) may lend itself better towards ease of use for novice woodworkers and finishers, unfamiliar with how colors may interact with each other.

This unique revolving disc was developed to help woodworkers and finishers better understand how typical woodworking tints can be intermixed to create specific hues.

To use the finishers color wheel, you simply rotate the inside wheel and watch for the desired color to appear through one of the windows. When you have found the closest color match, mix the appropriate colors as shown.

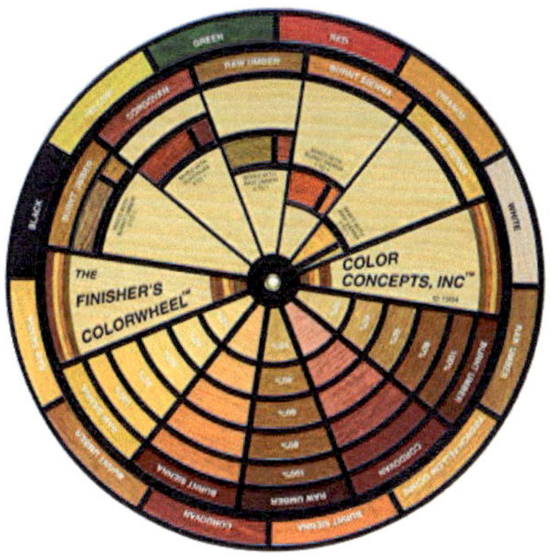

This color wheel can be used in conjunction with liquid dyes, pigments and also standard premixed liquid stains.

This lesson in colors is important to comprehend because as you progress through your journey in restorations, and your skills increase, you will likely be expanding your restoration capabilities to far more than just wood, you may eventually work yourself towards learning how to restore artwork, ceramics, marble, or weird, unique items and much more!

Just remember, everything in this world consists of a "color", and understanding how to achieve your target color is imperative in every repair, no matter what you are restoring. It's generally the color work that will separate a poor repair from a good one and make a good repair undetectable!

Shellac can be considered the "godfather" of finishes, discovered somewhere between Thailand and India, with written evidence of its creation dating back some 3000 years.

The period where shellac went into widespread introduction seems to be sometime between 1550-1650, when it began to be imported in high volume to Europe and other areas around the world.

In America, prior to and during the early 1800's, traditionally furniture was finished by applying beeswax in several thin layers, then polished with a cloth to a desired gloss.

The problem with wax finishes is that they do not wear well, and could easily be damaged by water or abrasions. Wax finish offers very little in the form of protection, and was predominately replaced by shellac sometime during the early 19th Century.

Shellac is a resin secreted by a tiny female insect named Laccifer Lacca, a.k.a the Lac Bug, which resides on particular trees in India and Thailand. The lac bug may also be referred to by its binomial name “Kerria Lacca”.

The only reason for the existence of the male lac bug is to fertilize the female. The life cycle begins at the larvae stage, with the first instar (#3), which are known suitably, as “crawlers”.

At this stage the lac bugs crawl along, piercing the branches and feeding on the phloem of their host trees.

As they traverse the tree, their secretions cover all the piercings they make on the branches.

Depending on the crop and differing environmental conditions, the female lac bug's life cycle is only estimated to be approximately 62-148 days, while the male lifespan is only 2-3 days, though the longest female lifespan observed has been 8 months and 5 days.

During the lac bugs time, they grow, propagate, continuously secrete resin, lay up to 1000 eggs and eat until they literally feed themselves to death. The indigenous people call this process “the feast of death”.

While alive though, the consumed sap is chemically altered inside of the female lac bug's body then excreted onto the tree branch.

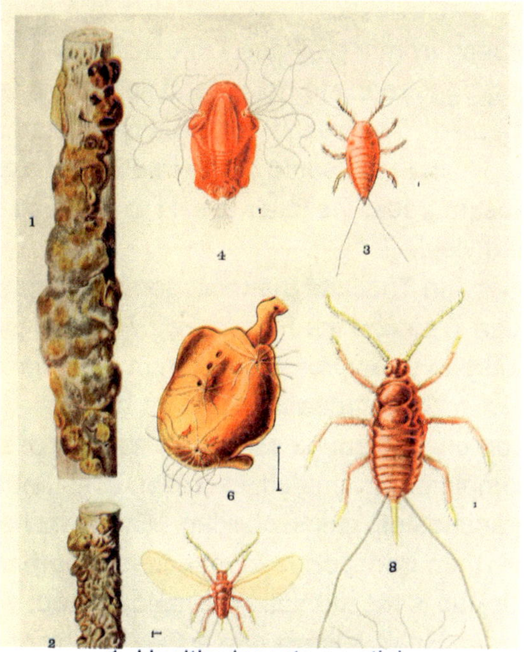

1. Healthy insects on stick
2. Unhealthy insects on stick
3. First instar, active stage. 40x
4. Female, 4 weeks after inoculation. 35x.
5. Female, 13 weeks after inoculation. 15x.
6. Dead female cell, with young emerging. 4x.
7. Male cell, 13 weeks after inoculation. 15x.
8. Wingless male. 12x.
9. Winged male. 40x.

Upon contact with the air, the excretion forms a hard shell-like covering referred to as the "cell", which not only consumes the eggs, but often traps and kills the adult lac bugs. This process continues until eventually most of the twigs and branches on a particular tree are covered.

The term "Lac" itself, is an abbreviation of the Sanskrit word "Lakh", which is a unit of measurement in the Indian Numeral System which means one hundred thousand. It has been estimated that it requires between one hundred thousand and two hundred thousand lac bugs to create one pound of dried shellac.

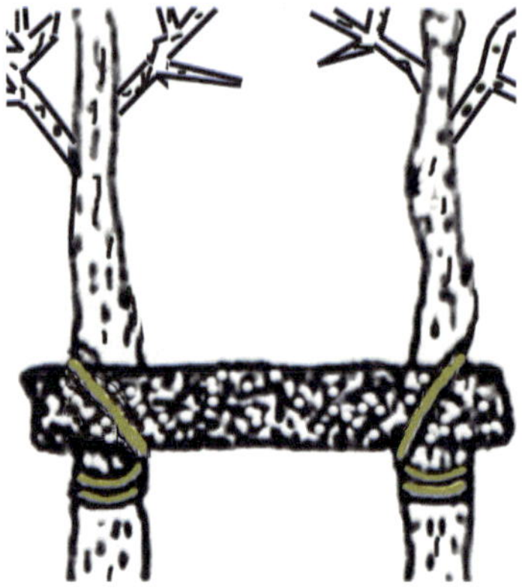

Cultivation begins when a farmer cuts off a stick or branch from a previously infested tree, which contains lac bug eggs ready to hatch, and ties it to a new tree to be infested. The freshly cut branch is called brood lac.

In India, some of the trees used are Dhak, Ber and Kasum trees, the latter is said to produce the best quality and yield.

In Thailand the most common trees used are the Rain Tree and the Pigeon Pea Tree. In all there has been noted to be approx 400 different host plants.

When trees are ready to harvest, workers can cut off seemingly millions of small, completely encrusted, secretion consumed branches off, called sticklac. The branches are then transported to refineries, where the sticklac is mechanically or hand refined.

Hand refiners use knives to scrape and mallets to hit the branches, to break the secretions from the bark of the trees, like breaking ice off of a branch after a sleet storm.

Workers place the scrapings into canvas tubes, similar to long socks, and heat over a fire.

Heat makes the "Lac" liquify and seep through the canvas tubes, filtering out contaminants like tree bark or bug substance, leaving only the thick, sticky molten shellac, which are formed into "pucks",referred to as "buttonlac" (right).

In mechanically advanced refineries, the secretions are ground with rotating millstones. The resulting milled material contains far more impurities compared to that of the hand refiners at the same stage.

The mixture is then forced through a screen to remove the largest impurities. The sifted mixture is then placed into large containers and stomped by workers who crush the granules which force the dye and remaining insect parts from the lac.

There are several rinsings to wash away scum, dye, bugs and tree impurities. The mixture is then spread onto a concrete floor to dry.

At this point it would be referred to as "seedlac" (left), due to the material's resemblance to seeds. Seedlac is the raw material in which all shellac is produced.

Further refining with heat melts seedlac onto steam heated grids. The molten lac is then, by hydraulic pressure, forced through an additional fine screen to remove any remaining impurities, collected and transferred to a steam kettle.

Through the kettle, the molten liquid lac is dropped onto rollers and forced to form large, thin sheets of shellac. When dry, the sheets are transported into another area where they are broken into flakes (right) and packaged dry, or combined with alcohol to produce a liquid shellac, ready for the consumer.

The end user, after purchasing shellac flakes, would crush the flakes into a powder, a mortar and pestle works well, then mix with denatured alcohol, creating their own fresh liquid shellac, ready for use.

Liquid shellac is available for purchase pre-mixed at most hardware stores, but it has a shelf life, that is why primarily it's suggested to buy dried flakes or pucks, which if stored properly, have no expiration.

Shellac has some amazing uses that most people may be unaware of, it's edible, used as a glazing agent on candy and chocolate covered nuts, usually referred to as "confectioners glaze" in the ingredients.

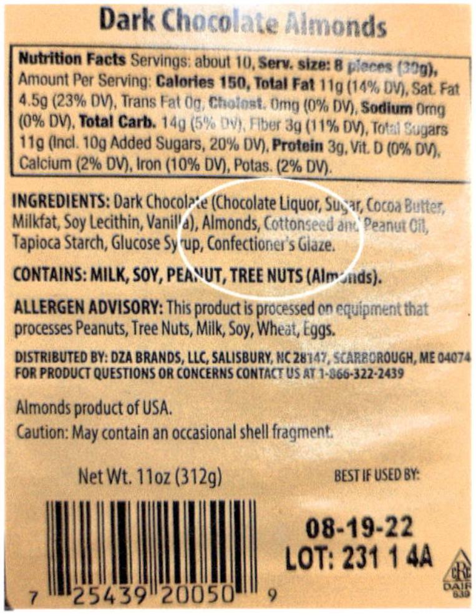

Shellac is also used as a coating on citrus or dried fruit to prolong its shelf/storage life, and has GRAS (generally recognized as safe) status by the Food and Drug Administration (FDA).

It's also approved for use in products certified as organic by The United States Department of Agriculture (USDA).

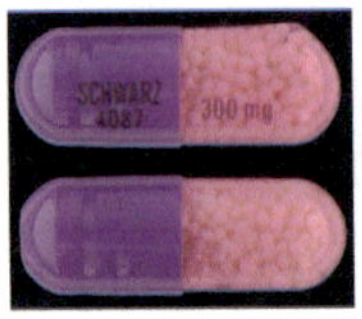

Other uses include, pill coatings which may have timed enteric or colonic release, a dye for cotton, in makeup, or finger nail polish, and much more.

Shellac has also been known to protect electronic parts because of its exquisite dielectric properties, low thermal conductivity and minimal expansion.

Even gramophone records were pressed from shellac compounds prior to using vinyl, and amazingly, until the 1960's shellac was used to glue dinosaur bones together!

As you can see shellac is extremely versatile and still has many uses in today's world. In the furniture industry though, stronger more durable finishes were invented and shellac was primarily replaced by nitrocellulose lacquer in the 1920's.

Today there are even harder, more durable finishes, like urethane and varnishes, which can be applied to floors, furniture, architecture. There are even epoxy finishes which are used on bar tops, restaurant tables and countless other products which are virtually impermeable.

Some of these specialty finishes may require adding catalysts, thinners or other products, which require mixing precise ratios for the finish to properly cure.

So far we've covered a lot about how shellac is created and manufactured from the bug to the market, but we haven't expanded much about its path to popularity in America.

Unfortunately for shellac, I personally rarely use the product during our restorations, unless it is specifically requested, but to this day the finish is still used by countless woodworkers and do-it-yourselfers, so I will show shellac the respect it deserves.

In 1848, William Zinsser, a foreman at a shellac factory in Mainz, Germany, decided to move to Manhattan, New York. I would have put a picture here but I didn't get authorization, so here's the link if you're compelled. https://www.zinsseruk.com/about-us/

Upon moving to America, Zinsser realized that shellac was a fairly unknown type of finish. Within a few years, working from his factory in Manhattan, Zinsser developed and opened the first bleached shellac manufacturing plant in the United States.

The Zinsser family owned the company, producing shellac and other coatings until 1987, when they sold it to RPM International Inc., which continues to produce shellac under the Zinsser® name, continuing as one of the only shellac manufacturers in America.

Shellac sold in liquid form, is referred to as "cuts". There are 1, 2, 3 and 4 pound cuts. Cut, is the measurement term for the weight of dry shellac flakes, dissolved per one gallon of alcohol.

The higher the "cut" number, the more solids (shellac flakes) that are in the solution, the more solids, the thicker the solution will be. Most pre-mixed, commercially available shellac is sold in a 3lb. cut.

When shellac is sold in liquid form, there are generally three types that may be available at your local hardware store, amber, clear, and dewaxed (sealer/sealcoat).

Both amber and clear shellac have wax included in the mixture which is extruded by the lac bug, and is usually 3%-5% by volume. Dewaxed shellac has the wax removed during the manufacturing process.

The natural wax in shellac will settle in the bottom of the can or container. When you open a can of shellac and mix it, you will notice the lighter colored wax rise and mix in with the finish creating a slightly cloudy appearance. The wax does slightly reduce the transparency of the finish and also may make the finish slightly less water resistant.

Dewaxed shellac in its premade liquid form, from the manufacturer, is generally produced in a 2lb. cut. Dewaxed shellac is used more commonly as a sealer rather than a top coat finish.

In the grand scheme of things, not all types of finishes are compatible, but dewaxed shellac is considered a universal binder.

This means, if you use dewaxed shellac as a sealer in between two different types of finishes, i.e., lacquer and polyurethane, shellac in theory allows the new finish to bond without causing much, if any, negative reaction.

Dewaxed shellac also acts as a barrier to silicone contamination (referred to as fish eye, right), blocks odors, for instance, if the furniture received smoke damage from a fire, and it also blocks resin secretion from knots in various woods like pine.

If you can't obtain dewaxed shellac, you can create it at home. Leave the can of shellac alone for a day or two to ensure all the wax has settled at the bottom of the can, undisturbed, then you can siphon, pour or strain the top portion of undisturbed shellac into another container.

As long as you were careful not to siphon or pour any wax out, you have just successfully created dewaxed shellac, or it's also possible to obtain dewaxed shellac in dried flake form.

In my opinion, unless these are some of the specific issues you are having during the finishing process, there really is no need to always use the dewaxed shellac as a sealer, you can usually just begin with the application of standard shellac, if that's what you plan on using as a finish on your project.

Amber shellac is slightly orange in hue. The orange tint is created by the sap that the lac bugs ingest during the infestation of a tree.

Amber and clear shellac created by Zinsser® will be a consistent, but unrefined shellac can greatly vary in hue.

Amber shellac will create a beautiful hue on naturally darker toned woods, like mahogany or walnut. This mahogany bookcase we finished has 5 coats of amber shellac, as specifically requested by the client. We did not use any stain in the finishing process! That's Mike on the left.

"Clear" shellac also may be referred to as blonde and has been refined to have the amber tint removed.

Clear shellac is great for finishing light or bleached woods when you want minimal color change.

Unlike shellac in liquid form, flaked shellac can be sold in a variety of colors from blonde, super blonde, lemon-yellow, orange, garnet, ruby, extra dark and more.

These names all refer to their hue, ranging from pale yellow to very dark orange, reddish or greenish.

To the right are a few samples of the stark contrast in color the different types of shellac flakes produce.

Each color is a byproduct of the different sap the lac bugs ingest from varying trees in various regions, and also dependent on the harvest season.

There are primarily three types of alcohol that can be used to dissolve the shellac flakes.

All three types of alcohol when mixed properly should dissolve the flakes, but one characteristic that sets each type apart, aside from price, is their evaporation rate.

Methanol, also referred to as methyl, is extremely toxic and can be very expensive due to state liquor taxes. Methanol also has the fastest evaporation rate of all the alcohols, which means that the time needed to work with the shellac prior to curing on a surface will be the shortest.

Isopropanol, also referred to as rubbing alcohol, can range from 99% to about 70% ethyl, the latter (70%) contains too much water to be a good solvent, therefore the least recommended alcohol to be used.

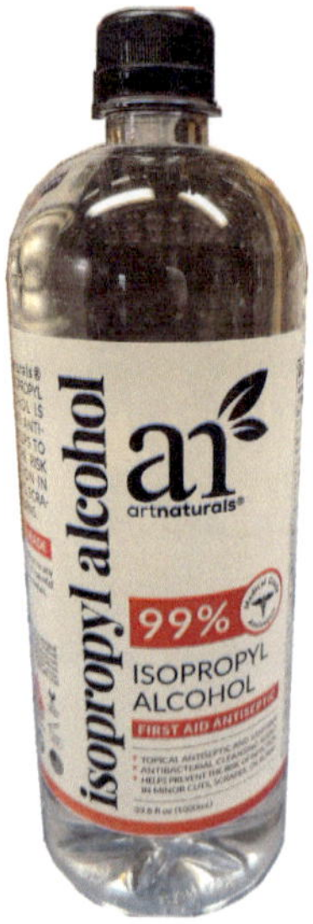

Ethanol, also referred to as denatured alcohol, is in my opinion the best option. It's fairly inexpensive, not very harmful unless it is ingested or you inhale excessive amounts of the fumes, and it evaporates slowly which gives you extended work time with the shellac mixture.

Of the three, denatured alcohol has the slowest evaporation rate, but you can also make the dry time even slower by adding 10% or less of Propyl or Butyl alcohol.

An additional note on denatured alcohol, they are not all created equal. It's best to find 190+ proof which is 95% pure Ethyl. The other 5% (denaturents) are additives which make it non-drinkable, to bypass state liquor taxes.

Most hardware stores carry high grade denatured alcohol but just be wary, some denatured alcohol is used as fuel and may consist of only approximately 50% pure ethyl, making it not the ideal solvent to use when creating a shellac mixture.

Previously, I suggested making your own shellac mixture rather than purchasing it pre-mixed. The main reason for that is premixed shellac will have a shelf life.

The manufacturer states the shelf life is usually 1-3 years, but that is also dependent on how it is stored. You have no idea what that can of shellac has been exposed to on its trip from the manufacturing plant to the store.

The manufacturer in the past would put a date on the can to tell you when it was made. They've halted stamping on the "date", and have started stamping on a "lot number".

We will decode the lot number on the two cans pictured below to figure out when the shellac was manufactured. The can on the left is lot number S95064, the can on the right is lot number S8O233.

The first letter in the lot code states where the shellac was manufactured. The "S", in our example, stands for Somerset, NJ.

The first number after the letter will be the last digit of the year of manufacture. The can on the left was produced in 2019 and the can on the right was produced in 2018.

Keep in mind that at the time of this writing, it is March 2020, and both of these cans were available for purchase at my local hardware store.

That was easy enough, and usually the only information you need since soon you'll understand how long the shelf life of premixed shellac is, but I'll explain what the rest of the lot number represents.

The second number, after the year indicator, stands for the month of mixture. In our case, the can on the left was manufactured in the fifth month, May. For the can on the right, what you may think is a zero, is actually the letter "O".

The manufacturer will use "O" for October, "N" for November and "D" for December, instead of using a two digit month format. So the can on the right was manufactured in October.

The third and fourth numbers in the lot code refer to the exact day it was manufactured. The can on the left was made on the 6th day of the month and the can on the right was made on the 23rd day of the month.

This makes the manufacture date for the can on the left, May 6, 2019. The can on the right was manufactured on October 23, 2018. Remember I told you it was March 2020 at the time of this writing, so that means that one of the cans of shellac is already almost one year old and the second can is almost a year and half old, and both were available for sale, just waiting for some unwitting customer to buy some deteriorating product.

It is for this specific reason I recommended you create your own fresh shellac mixture. Old shellac mixtures will thicken with time and eventually will never harden if too old, more on that later.

The last number in the lot code refers to the batch. The manufacturer will usually run more than one batch per day, the codes on the cans we were referring to would say that they are batch four and batch three respectively on their day of manufacture. The batch numbers are irrelevant for our knowledge as long as we are aware of the date of manufacture.

Now that I've primarily suggested that you create your own shellac and recommended using denatured alcohol to dissolve it, you now need to know the mixture ratios.

As previously mentioned, there are "cuts" of liquid shellac. You will be "cutting" or using the raw materials to create this mixture yourself. The formulation you will create will depend ultimately on how "thick" you want your shellac mixture.

For instance, one gallon of denatured alcohol (128 fluid ounces) combined with one pound of shellac flakes (16 ounces) will create what is referred to as a "1 pound cut." This manifestation will be a very thin finish, possibly near the consistency of water.

But if we combine one gallon of denatured alcohol (128 fluid ounces) with three pounds of shellac flakes (48 ounces), we have essentially created a "3 pound cut" which will be a thicker finish and more in line with what is available for purchase in stores.

If you don't need quite as much finish, just cut your ratios. For instance, if you want to create one quart of 3 pound cut shellac, you would mix 32 fluid ounces of denatured alcohol with 12 ounces of shellac flake.

Below is a convenient chart I have created for your ratio mixing pleasure.

Denatured Alcohol	***1 Pound Cut***	***1.5 Pound Cut***	***2 Pound Cut***	***2.5 Pound Cut***	***3 Pound Cut***
One Gallon (128 fl. oz.)	One pound (16 oz. flake)	1.5 Pound (24 oz. flake)	2 Pound (32 oz. flake)	2.5 Pound (40 oz. flake)	3 Pound (48 oz. flake)
Half Gallon (64 fl. oz.)	Half Pound (8 oz flake)	12 oz. flake	One Pound (16 oz. flake)	20 oz. flake	1.5 Pounds (24 oz. flake)
One Quart (32 fl. oz.)	¼ Pound (4 oz. flake)	6 oz. flake	Half Pound (8 oz. flake)	10 oz. flake	¾ Pound (12 oz. flake)
One Pint (16 fl. oz.)	2 oz. flake	3 oz. flake	¼ Pound (4 oz. flake)	5 oz. flake	6 oz. flake
One Cup (8 fl. oz)	1 oz. flake	1.5 oz. flake	2 oz. flake	2.5 oz flake	3 oz. flake

These formulations are recommended standards, the mixture itself doesn't always need to be exact. You can't really mess up the mixture unless the ratios are extremely off, like one pound of flakes to seven gallons of alcohol or three pounds of flakes to one ounce of alcohol.

The finish you create in general will either be thicker or thinner depending on the ratio of flakes to denatured alcohol. Just keep in mind that a thinner consistency is better for hand application (french polishing), and thicker is better for brush application.

Through the drying process, the alcohol evaporation is what allows the shellac to cure to a hard durable finish. It's also, in my opinion, better to build up several thin coats, rather than a few thicker coats. Be sure to always allow each coat to thoroughly dry before sanding or applying additional coats.

I would recommend initially starting with a two pound cut, which is a little thinner than store bought shellac. Before you dissolve your flakes in the alcohol, I suggest using a mortar and pestle (right) or something similar to crush the flakes into smaller particles.

This will assist the shellac to more efficiently dissolve into the alcohol. Using a plastic or glass container, combine the dry flakes and the alcohol.

Stir the mixture several times throughout the next few hours to ensure that any undissolved flakes keep from solidifying into a lump, and make sure to keep the jar closed when not stirring the mixture.

When the shellac flakes appear to be totally dissolved, it's recommended that you strain the mixture through a paint strainer or cheesecloth to remove any leftover impurities.

Immediately, once the dry flakes are properly dissolved in the alcohol, a chemical process known as "esterification" begins.

Esterification happens when the alcohol reacts to the organic acids of the shellac flakes. This reaction produces esters, which is a gummy substance that inhibits the shellac from drying to a hard durable finish.

Don't worry too much though, it takes a long time to negatively affect the curing process, but that is the reason there is a shelf life with shellac, and eventually there will be too many esters present and the finish will no longer properly harden.

This process will not happen overnight, but in general, you should store your mixture in a cool dark place and use it within four to six months.

If your mixture has been around for a while, to check for freshness, pour a small amount of the shellac onto a non porous surface and create a nice level uniform thickness, let it dry for twenty minutes to an hour.

You should not be able to leave an imprint with your finger on the surface if the shellac has dried properly, it should still be fresh enough to use.

To use shellac as a padding finish, I recommend a 1.5 or 2 pound cut mixture, poured into a plastic bottle or container with a squirt top or a lid, for easy application onto your padding rag/cloth during restorations.

If applying shellac by hand with a padding rag/cloth, whether you are applying to a new wood surface or a pre-existing finished surface, you can find recommended application techniques in the "French Polishing" chapter, next.

French polishing is when a finish, in liquid form, is applied to a padding rag/cloth, then by hand, the finish impregnated rag is briskly wiped across a surface in a particular pattern, like side to side or circular.

I highly recommend you initially learn how to apply a padding finish on spare pieces of wood or non important pieces of furniture, as the first attempts that you make will likely seem awkward and may not turn out as well as they may with additional experience and practice.

Today, with regard to the products that are used daily in our repairs, most of the products are manufactured by Mohawk® Finishing Products, a subsidiary of RPM International Inc.

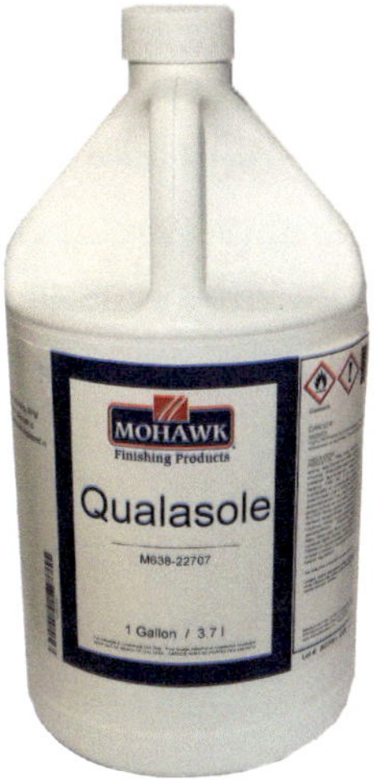

RPM International Inc, manufactures some of the most well known brands of paints and coatings sold at your local hardware store, like Rustoleum®, Varathane®, Dap®, Gator® and so many more.

There are a few different brands of padding finishes that I've used, but primarily Qualasole® has been the padding finish of choice, which I have personally used virtually every day of work since I began in the furniture restoration industry, in 1996.

Qualasole® is a finish formulated to be applied by hand (with a rag), to raw, unfinished wood as a primary finish, or applied over pre-existing finishes to restore faded or damaged areas on furniture, instruments or any other finished wood product.

A second type of padding finish I use is Lacover®, which functions in virtually the same exact way as Qualasole®, but there is one apparent difference, Lacover® is available in different "weights".

The lighter the weight, the thinner the liquid. A thick liquid will build up the finish faster to completion of a repair, but thicker finishes may become finicky and take slightly longer to cure than their thinner counterparts.

A light to medium weight formulation may be better to use during the pigment touch up process, a thinner finish may lay more flat on a surface during a repair.

It may make sense, in some instances, to use a medium to heavy weight padding finish when building up the finish over a surface, as a thicker finish will fill in sanding scratches or other defects more efficiently than its lighter weight counterpart.

But don't get it twisted, you can use either weight from start to finish during a repair, and ultimately the end result should be very similar, it just may take time to get acquainted with the various products.

Names of other padding finishes that I can throw at you are, Rapid Pad®, Wood Turners Padding Finish®, Will Pro Padding Finish®, Lac French Padding Finish®, Lubricite Padding Lacquer®, and I'm sure there are others I'm probably not even aware exist.

All these products that were just listed, in my opinion, work in a similar fashion. Some professional restorers may prefer to use certain finishes in certain applications over others, but the end result of a completed french polish or repair with any of the different padding finishes should end with a similar, satisfactory restoration.

I definitely have not used the majority of padding finishes available, but I can guarantee that It would take extensive time and practice with each product to notice any slight variations of the different formulations.

By using one product regularly you will learn the characteristics and understand any quirks or particular application techniques required for whichever finish you choose.

Now comes the fun part, as we are finally able to delve into the nitty gritty of the repair process!

FRENCH POLISHING? OUI S'IL TE PLAÎT!

Now that you've chosen which type of padding finish you'll be using, it's time to talk about application and the infamous technique, ***"French Polishing"***.

French polishing is not a product, but in fact it is a wood finishing technique that if done properly, results in a very beautiful high gloss finish on a surface.

Ironically, the roots of French polishing have nothing to do with France, and french polishing was likely not the term used when the process originated near India in approximately 250 AD.

The term french polishing was derived from the introduction of the process to France around 1810-1820. France quickly favored the finishes that resulted and began to french polish all of their finest furniture.

The first known documentation of the process ran in the *Mechanic's Magazine* on November 22, 1823. It states: "The Parisians have now introduced an entirely new mode of polishing, which is called *plaque,* and is to wood precisely what plating is to metal. The wood by some process is made to resemble marble, and has all the beauty of that article with much of its solidarity. It is even asserted by persons who have made trial of the new mode that water may be spilled upon it without staining it."

Many are too frightened to attempt the process citing, they'll likely ruin their piece of furniture. Others even say, "I'm great at woodworking, except for finishing".

In my opinion, those are all just easy excuses by the inexperienced and unknowledgeable. It undoubtedly can be difficult to leave one's comfort zone and try something new. Like most things, it may or most certainly will seem difficult at first, but just like most other tasks you are now proficient at, you had to start somewhere.

As the late great Bob Ross would say, "Talent is a pursued interest. Anything you're willing to practice, you can do!" The biggest hurdles, in my opinion, usually begin with that voice in your own head, don't listen to it!

You will not get better at any task until you have the desire to learn and improve yourself. There's no such thing as failure, but there is such a thing as not trying, or giving up too soon!

Those words can be applied to anything and everything you do. Being self-motivated is a major key to having success in life.

After all, look at me, at some point in my life I had absolutely zero experience in furniture repair, possibly like you, and now I'm writing a book on it. There's no limit to what you can accomplish if you put your mind to it!

And let me be the first to congratulate you! By taking the first step and reading this book, you're already ahead of 99% of the population in this world, on this subject, numbers approximate.

To a seasoned furniture restoration technician, french polishing may actually be one of the easier tasks, often easier than other aspects of a particular repair. You will likely find a cornucopia of techniques from varying craftspeople on the internet, or in books and videos describing this complex, mysterious, mythical process.

As with most things, there is more than one way to achieve great results. It may take some time, and trial with error, but once you master the simplistic factors listed forth in this chapter, you will be able to consistently create beautiful finishes on any type of wood, piece of furniture, cabinetry or wooden instrument (and several other non-wooden items like leather, ceramics and so much more).

It's inevitable that you are going to make mistakes while learning this process. Just consider mistakes, learning the proper ways not to do something. I couldn't begin to count all the ways I've learned not to do something, but as with life, mistakes are often correctable, especially in wood/furniture finishing, which I consider an inexact science anyway. So maybe it's a good idea not to start learning on your best piece of furniture!

On the topic of french polishing, in theory, you are simply applying a liquid (padding finish) with a rag, to a surface. This sounds like it should be extremely easy. Let's go over the steps one more time, pour liquid on a rag, check. Wipe liquid filled rag across a surface, double check.

How hard can that really be? Initially though, it often can be trickier in practice than it sounds. Additionally, remember that no amount of french polishing can hide poor surface preparation.

Total success depends on your attention to detail throughout a repair. Each step, if done properly, cleaning, gluing, filling, sanding, or other repairs along the way, including pigment touch up, all play an equally significant role in the outcome of any restoration.

If you try to cut corners in some cases, the final result of your restoration may not reach its full potential, or at the least, be quite as perfect as it could have been. You could say that poor planning and preparation is a precursor to poor performance.

As an example, if you fill and sand a large gouge, and you don't use a block when sanding, the filled area may not be perfectly flat. If the "area" is not perfectly flat after you've begun to apply a finish, you will easily see a "dip", "high area" or general unevenness/waviness when you look in the reflection of the surface, which means your completed repair may be easily detectable, at least to the trained eye.

Don't get deterred easily if things don't work out perfectly right away. Aside from the aspect of performing a repair, I would say that patience may be one of the greatest determining factors in a successful french polish.

In fact, in my opinion, french polishing may be 5% skill, 90% patience and 5% arm durability. I'd even go as far to say that, "a trained monkey could do it". Key word, trained!

When working on your own furniture, you have the luxury of working at your own pace, where I, as a hired repair technician, will usually charge hourly. If a professional repair technician comes to your home to perform a repair, that repair has to be completed, as perfectly as possible, with the client being completely satisfied, in the shortest amount of time feasible.

The client does not want to pay me to take a break for a few hours in between the application of additional coats of finish, and frankly, I have other things that I need to take care of also!

The biggest, most difficult french polishing jobs, in my opinion, usually involve dining room tables. Dining room tables, in most cases, are going to have the largest, flattest surface area of most furniture you'll come across.

Even for the largest of dining room tables, with a few leaves, depending on the extent of the damage, I can usually complete a repair, similar to this table, from start to finish in three to five hours.

That usually entails cleaning, filling gouges or scratches, sanding the entire surface, touching up any repaired areas and applying the padding finish with the french polishing technique to completion.

With some companies charging $150 an hour or more, you can see how that can add up to be a pretty costly repair ($450-$750).

I have been able to perform this type of repair in a short time frame because I've learned, and am now keenly aware of the characteristics and dry times of the french polishing products I am using, and with practice you will also!

That example wasn't a humble brag, it was primarily to make you aware that the vast majority of projects, once proficient, can be completed in a matter of hours, not days. I would say that I have never begun a repair, in a client's home, that could not be completed the same day, and I've fixed some pretty messed up stuff!

Since you have the ability to work at your own pace, on your own piece of furniture, you don't need to rush anything, you have the ability to step away and allow extended drying times in between the application of coats which can almost never be a bad thing.

This is where patience tends to come into play. Initially, if you try to build up the finish too fast, there may be issues when applying the different "coats". You may start off with your padding rag overly wet, or the existing applied finish may be too "soft" because of insufficient drying time and you may actually damage the finish/coats you've already applied.

Conversely, if keeping your padding rag on the drier end of the spectrum, it may seem like the finish isn't building up sufficiently, expeditiously enough. A drier padding rag will have an exponentially less chance of creating additional damage, but it will take more time to build a substantial finish.

You'll have to find a happy medium at various stages through a french polish. Just a word of advice, if you ever think that the finish you are applying is not laying down on a surface properly, possibly appearing as if it's creating more damage, simply stop what you are doing, let the area in question dry.

Once dry, sand the area with a fine grit sandpaper, usually 600+ grit wet/dry, and start the process over again. I'll expand further on this topic as these chapters proceed. Also check out the chapter "Problems" for other varying issues that may arise during a restoration.

There may be many other aspects that go into performing a repair before you get to the french polishing step, like filling the touching up of scratches or gouges, but the further steps that will be detailed in this chapter will strictly refer to applying a new padding finish to a raw wood surface, or a surface of a piece of furniture, cabinetry or wooden instrument, which may already have a pre-existing finish.

Let's say you bought or fabricated a new piece of furniture yourself. The piece is still in its raw wood state (below), and you want to put a "finish" on it.

Even though it's definitely possible to apply a finish by french polishing to completion of the project, in my opinion, ultimately though you would be successful, the amount of time and effort that it would take to build up a nice uniform finish over an entire piece of initially raw wood furniture, would be substantial, and your arms will fall off your body.

Just joking, but at the very least, your arms would be extremely fatigued after numerous hours or days of applying the finish simply because each coat of finish applied by the french polishing technique is extremely thin.

If you're starting from a raw, unfinished piece of wood or furniture, I would recommend beginning the process by initially applying some type of high build finish, like shellac, lacquer or varnish.

Unless you own a spray system like a HVLP (high volume low pressure) or similar, you should choose a finish that could be initially brushed on.

After building up a solid base of finish, which ultimately may only consist of two or three coats of a high build finish, once dried thoroughly, you may need to sand out any brush marks created from the initial application with a fine 400 or 600 grit wet/dry sandpaper.

After cleaning the dust from the surface, you can then move onto applying the remainder of finish with your french polishing technique, padding finish and padding rag to achieve the desired appearance and sheen to complete the project.

If you plan on repairing or applying additional finish to a piece of furniture that already has an existing finish on it (which will be most repairs), then half the battle is already completed for you, someone else has already built a substantial finish.

If a surface is dirty, visibly soiled, has an excess amount of polish or cleaning product residue, you may want to clean it prior to repair, otherwise you'll just be applying a new finish over soilage, which won't end well.

Cleaning may entail wiping the surface with a rag impregnated with Naptha or denatured alcohol. If using a solvent, the original finish may soften slightly and become sticky. You may need to wait a few extra minutes for the solvent to evaporate and the surface to resolidify before proceeding.

I don't always use a solvent to clean a surface prior to a restoration. If there doesn't appear to be any soilage, I just may begin by sanding, cleaning off the sanding dust, performing any repairs, or begin building a finish by french polishing right away.

To perform the french polishing technique correctly there will be a few key factors that you will have to learn before you are able to achieve great success.

The first determining factor begins with choosing the proper material/fabric, and folding technique to create (what I consider) the perfect padding rag.

The second factor will be determining the padding finish that you decide to use for the french polishing. Several craftspeople use shellac primarily. I have a formula listed to create your own padding shellac which can be used for french polishing a few pages ago, along with touching on several other padding finishes.

Don't fret too much though, no matter the finish you choose or the formulation, the application techniques do not vary. From this point on, I will be referring to the finish/liquid (finish of your choice) used, as "padding finish" or simply, "finish".

Privately, semi-jokingly-seriously, among family, or friends like you, I may refer to it as liquid gold, because using this liquid to perform repairs is essentially how you make the majority of your money in the furniture restoration world, in addition, it conveniently has a golden hue.

The third factor includes the amount of padding finish that is applied to the padding rag throughout the duration of a repair. You'll likely read this often, but in general you will likely use a "wetter" padding rag in the earlier stages of the process, and a "dryer" padding rag towards the end.

Wet doesn't mean dripping, and dry doesn't mean bone dry, this is where trial and error may begin to factor in. I guarantee there will be times in which issues arise, until you get the hang of using different proportions, but this will ultimately lead to experience!

The fourth factor, which goes hand in hand, as far as importance with the amount of padding finish used in the padding rag, is the amount of downward pressure that you are exerting when applying the padding rag to a surface.

Think of it as the "lightness of hand". As similar to the amount of finish that is used throughout the french polishing process, the "weight" (downward pressure) of your hand should be heavier in the beginning stages and lighter towards the end.

As I just mentioned in the beginning of your building coats, you can apply the finish from the padding rag with more downward pressure. I'm not talking about "scrubbing", if you use too much pressure, you may actually begin to remove or damage the existing surface.

Don't be too timid though, try using different pressures at varying stages on your practice pieces, see what happens. You'll also need to mess up sometimes so you know how to get yourself out of a sticky situation, just like in real life.

I can't think of a great analogy but imagine you are cleaning crumbs off your kitchen counter with a sponge, forget about the scrubbing aspect, for the most part, you are, with medium pressure, wiping across the surface to remove any crumbs or the like.

That is similar to the amount of downward force you will be exerting in the early to mid stages of the process. Mid to latter stages of the process you are applying less pressure and often, virtually trying to "glide" over the surface.

The only time this rule isn't 100% accurate is at the extreme end of the french polishing process. With your rag being on the far dryer end of the spectrum, you may be able to apply slightly more pressure than just "gliding" over the surface.

This may be implemented if needing to remove any final surface defects, but remember if using more pressure at the end of a french polish, your rag has to be virtually dry (or barely moist, depending on whether you're a glass half empty or a glass half full kind of person).

The first and most important rule (that you will also read more than once) is:
Never stop your motion with your padding rag anywhere, when it is in contact with the surface you are working on. You should be making contact and releasing contact with a surface with momentum and motion!

If you do stop your motion, the padding rag will immediately begin to stick, or at the minimum, leave visual defects on the surface which you may have to further sand out to remove. This would create additional work, but it happens to the best of us. Just be patient with the process.

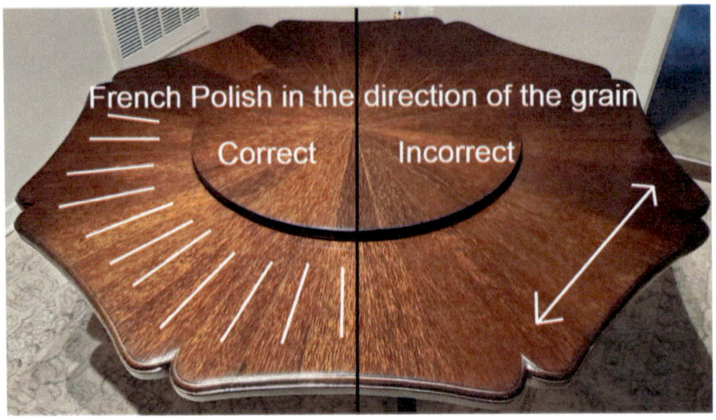

The fifth and last element will be the pattern in which you are applying the finish, side-to-side, left to right, right to left (those three are the same), which I may refer to as "east to west", along with circular and other patterns.

Certain patterns may also be more effective than others in certain situations, which will be expanded on further, shortly.

Also if I say east to west, really what I am referring to is padding in the direction parallel with the wood grain. So if the wood grain is north to south on a surface, just consider that I am referring to the direction of the wood grain.

Applying finish/padding in a direction against the grain may be noticeable in a final finished product.

You may find furniture that could have a perpendicular inlay a couple inches around the edge of a surface or an inlay with no particular direction, like the example to the right.

In these circumstances, you usually don't need to try to french polish in the direction of the grain of the inlay. I would just pick one direction and continue to french polish in that direction over the entire surface until complete.

In general, I suggest you french polish in the direction of the grain that covers the majority of the surface. If you perform a good french polish, you won't even notice any variation of the finish over any limited perpendicular inlay.

There's one more thing to consider with technique, because your arm is attached to your body, your shoulder will act as a pivot point, which will make the east to west motion of your arm more of a semicircle rather than straight lines.

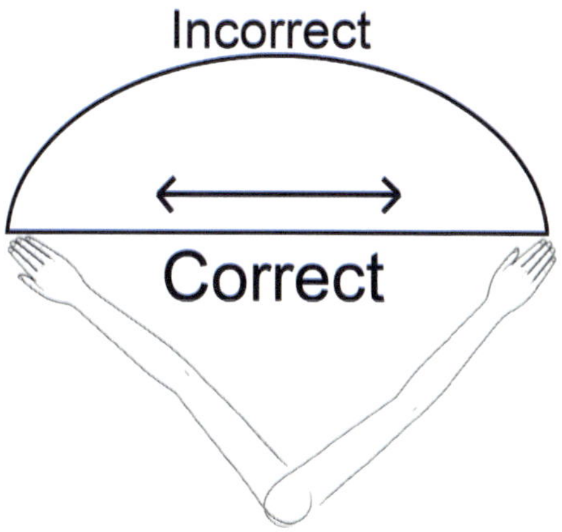

You have to be consciously aware of the motion that you are creating and understand that you have to keep that motion as straight as possible. The pattern in which you lay down the padding finish will be apparent if it's curved.

During various stages of french polishing, I don't always look at, or focus on my hand and padding rag actually gliding across the surface, I usually try to find a focal point of wood grain or a joint line in the construction of the furniture or surface.

This assists in keeping my strokes as straight as possible as I begin my french polish from one end of a surface, and continuing that stroke through that focal point, and off the opposite side of the surface, then back again, and again, and again and a...

Joint lines are my favorite things to focus on because they are always going to be straight, which helps to keep my arm moving in a straight line, and they often repeat every 6" - 8" across a surface.

My focal point will continue to change, as I work my way north to south, front to back, up/down (those three are also the same thing) on a surface.

You may repeat this motion seemingly hundreds of times on a single surface. This is the repeated motion that you will have to perfect to be able to perform a great french polish, to not leave streaks or have any unevenness in the sheen over the entire surface.

All those factors combined, determine how quickly or slowly you will be building up the finish on a surface. In some instances, you will want to build up the finish at different rates, in different areas, on the same surface.

For instance, often it is necessary to focus more on individual areas of a repair, like areas with sanding scratches where you may have filled a gouge, to build the finish up to a comparable level of the surrounding finish prior to feathering out or expanding to the entire surface.

I'd like to now expand a little more on some of these individual factors we just went over, so rounding back to the first factor, I referred to, which is creating a padding rag.

I recommend using a cotton material, most synthetic materials are not absorbent enough to use as the application rag. You should look for a 100% cotton material with a fairly tight weave.

The tighter the weave, the smoother the surface of the padding rag, in general but if the surface of your rag is too smooth, it may not transfer the padding finish to a surface properly.

Secondly, use a white rag (or natural unbleached cotton). Do not use colored materials, as once the padding finish is introduced to the padding rag, it may cause any dye in the material to transfer to the surface you are working on.

Third, stretchy t-shirt material, even though cotton, does not work well as a padding rag. You ultimately need your padding rag to be firm, there cannot be any loose fabric moving back and forth uncontrollably as you're crossing a surface.

T-shirt material has too much elasticity and also does not evenly disperse the padding finish well when you are french polishing a surface.

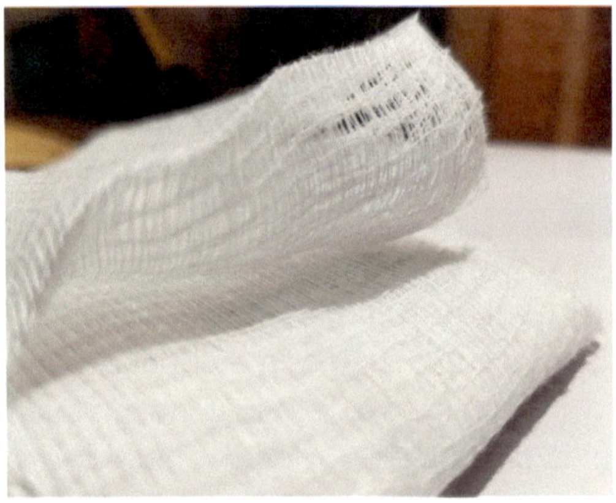

I cannot tell a lie though, in emergency situations, running out of standard padding rags during a large job, I have ripped up my undershirt to use as a rag, so it is possible, just not ideal.

The different types of materials used can vary, but common padding cloth/materials are cheesecloth (right), trace cloth, "lint free" cloth, recycled diapers, muslin and others.

Cheesecloth may be last on the list as far as usage because in general it has a very open weave, similar to medical gauze, though cheesecloth comes in different grades, grade 10 through grade 90.

The higher the number, the tighter the weave. If using cheesecloth, I wouldn't recommend using anything lower than grade 90, and in some cases, fabric may need to be washed and dried to "soften".

Trace or muslin cloth (right) are virtually indistinguishable. They have a higher thread count which gives them a tighter weave than most cheesecloth.

These types of clothes, trace and muslin, are likely the most commonly referred to french polishing material/rags, used by craftspeople.

Recycled diapers (below), are probably the best rags you've never been exposed to!

There are local diaper services (likely in your area) that have to sell their cloth diapers that have met the end of their lifespan for use with babies.

These services then recycle their diapers, which are virtually perfectly white, possibly with a stain here or there, may be a little frayed, but could be up to 10 times thicker than a single piece of trace/muslin cloth due to their inherent layers.

You may even be able to buy recycled diapers at a cheaper rate per pound, than some hardware stores' bags of inferior rags, and far cheaper than most other alternatives, per pound, like muslin/trace cloth.

To create a padding rag, there are a couple different ways you can go about it. I'll give you two options. The first configuration is a more triangular/rectangular shape (right).

The second option, which will be expanded on later, creates a padding rag in the shape and size as small as a golf ball, or as big as a baseball, which you grip primarily in your palm.

Either way you choose to make your rag, ultimately the size padding rag you create will be dependent on the size of the rags you have on hand, or configured based on the need for the project.

The main goal is to create a padding rag of substance, it has to be created in a way that you can easily, confidently, ergonomically, securely hold in your hand.

The second most important aspect is that the underside of a padding rag, the area which will be in contact with a surface, has to be firm and wrinkle/crease free.

There is no predetermined size of rag you need to perform a job, but in general, if I have to french polish a large surface like a dining room table top or dresser top, I will create a larger padding rag than if I had to perform a repair on a small edge of a nightstand. Feel free to cut your rags into smaller pieces.

The first option to create a padding rag, which is my preferable method, as I mentioned, will appear more rectangular/triangular, slimmer and longer, compared to the "ball" technique. I find that this configuration sits comfortably in my hand and is easier for me to hold onto.

Depending on the thickness of your padding material and size of rag needed, this folding method usually will only consist of only one rag, if you're using a diaper or large enough piece of cloth to begin with.

I find beginning with an approximate 20"-24" squared piece of single layer cloth makes the perfect size "large" padding rag, fit for my hands. If you're using cloth cut into smaller rags, say 12" squared, it's possible you may need two or more rags combined to give your rag substantial substance.

Recycled diapers on the other hand, since they're already several layers thick, you would only need one rag. Additionally, you will most likely have to cut the diameter of the diaper down in size. I probably use ⅓ - ½ of a diaper per large rag required.

In my opinion the most ideal size for most projects, the resulting folded padding rag, with the rectangular/triangular folding method will create an approximate 5" - 7" long, and approximate 1 ½" - 2 ½" wide surface area on the underside of the pad that when in use, will be the portion of the rag which would be in constant contact with a surface (third picture).

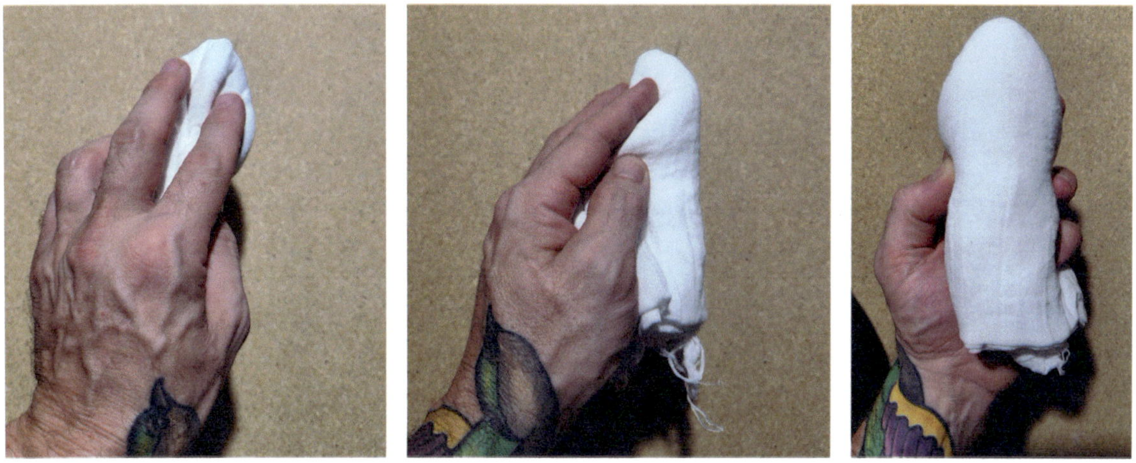

Also in my opinion, by creating a large padding rag, in theory, it should create a more expeditious repair because you are able to cover the entire surface more efficiently. Don't get me wrong though, I use smaller padding rags all the time too, just find what works for you.

If you are watching videos I've created at MyRepairKit.com, you may notice I only create and use padding rags folded in this manner. It's true, I do not often create/use rags with the "ball" method. I'm not saying one is necessarily better than the other, it's just what I happen to be most comfortable with.

The technique I use to hold the rag is similar to flashing a peace sign. My thumb, pinky and ring finger are essentially gripping the mass of the rag (this is how I am primarily securing the rag in my hand), while my middle finger and index finger are extended out, securing the "front" of the rag.

By holding the rag firmly in your palm with your extended fingers, it gives the ability to apply even pressure throughout the length of the entire padding rag.

Another way you may also grip this type of folded padding rag, is mainly between your thumb on one side and the rest of your fingers on the other side, whichever way may feel more comfortable.

The same grip technique works for both left and right hands because either method you use to create your padding rag, it should be symmetrical.

In fact, you'll likely learn to use both hands during a french polish because if one arm gets exhausted, you can always switch to the opposite arm, and in theory do the same amount of work as the previous, therefore doubling your output ability. It's also a good way to work on being ambidextrous.

The first step to creating a padding rag would be to begin folding a full rag in half multiple times, basically step 1-6.

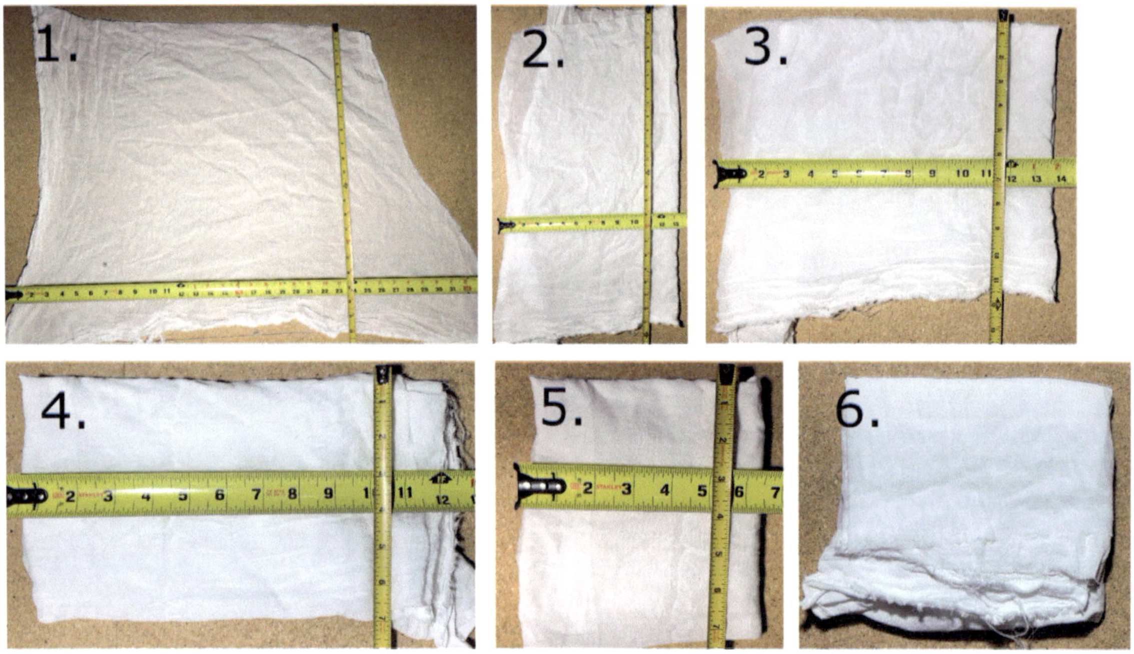

If you are using a recycled diaper that may mean just folding it in half. If you are using trace/muslin cloth, start with a flat rag approximately 24" x 24". As you can see we don't need perfectly square material!

In step five, after folding four times, our folded rag is about 7" x 7", remember, there are no perfect numbers, just go for it. I would consider this the beginning of a "large" padding rag. Additionally, by folding the rag four times, we have now created essentially an eight layer thick rag.

Once you've folded sufficiently to step five, your rag should be anywhere from five to eight inches squared. Over ten inches squared is probably too big of a padding rag, unless you have humongous hands of course.

A rag five inches squared or smaller at this point, I would consider to be a medium to small rag respectively. Step six is the same rag as #5, just flipped over and without the tape measure.

In steps seven and eight, take the "top" left and right corners, and fold each in on themselves, tightly at an approximate 45° angle, so that all the fabric from both sides has met in the middle, or slightly overlapping is fine also.

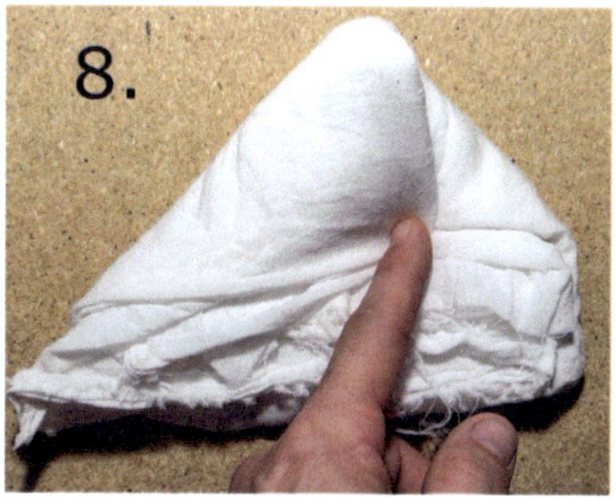

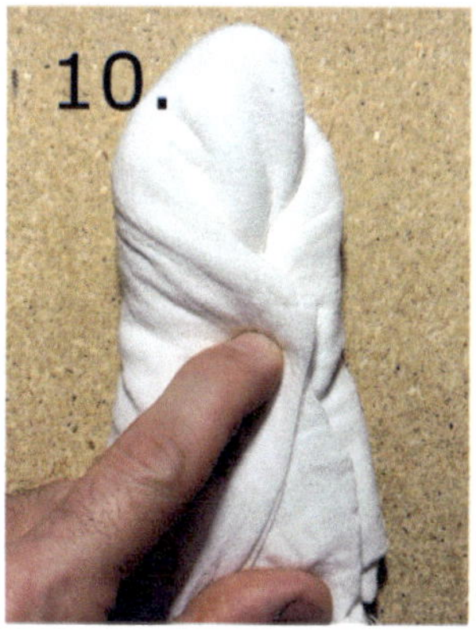

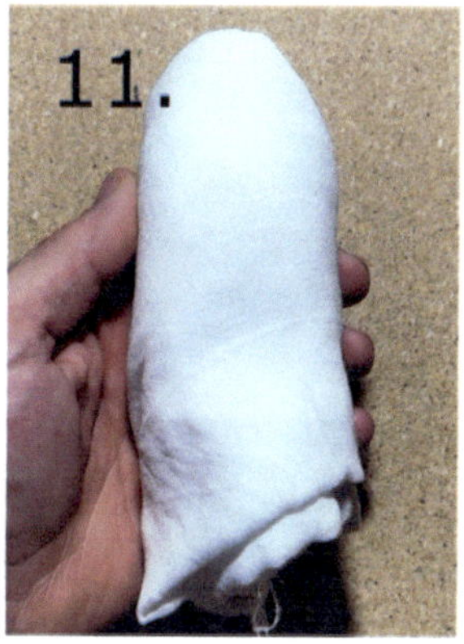

In steps nine and ten, fold/roll the remaining outer left and right sides inward. Folding/rolling the rag in on itself tightly multiple times creates firmness. Step eleven is the completely folded padding rag, which looks similar to the shape of a blunt nose paper airplane, without wings of course.

The "top" of the rag may be slightly more slender than the "rear". This is why I say that the shape may be more triangular than rectangular, but the contact surface of the pad should resemble something in-between the two, while being firm and taut. Tuck in any loose ends or frays at the rear and this rag is ready for a restoration!

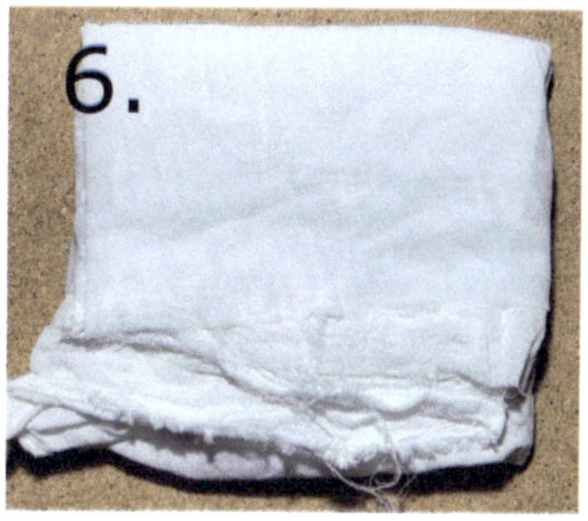

The second method I'll recommend for creating a padding rag, is referred to as the "ball" method. To create the ball, you will need two rags, an outer and an inner.

Let's revisit step six for this example.

If we fold that rag three more times, the result is an extremely dense small rectangle approximately 2 ½" by 1 ½" or so, this will be the *inner* rag, (right).

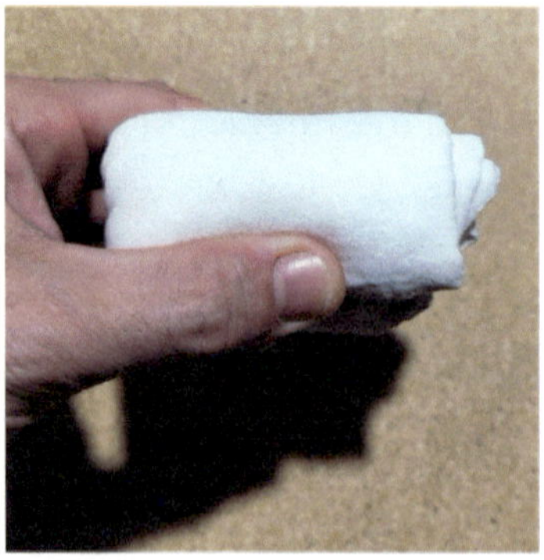

Taking a second full rag, we'll call the *outer* rag, fold that a few times, keeping it much larger than the initial rag of course (below), and place the small dense rag in the center of the outer rag.

It's not recommended to "wad" the inner rag, as that may create unwanted creases or uneven areas in the surface of the outer rag.

Combining the two rags is what creates the additional "thickness" needed to create a good, firm "ball" padding rag.

Once you place the inner rag in the center, lift all the corners and edges of the outer rag upward over the folded cloth to create a "ball" (right).

Secure all the loose material at the top, and holding the rag in between your thumb and index finger, slightly twist the top edges of the loose material, similar to closing a bread bag.

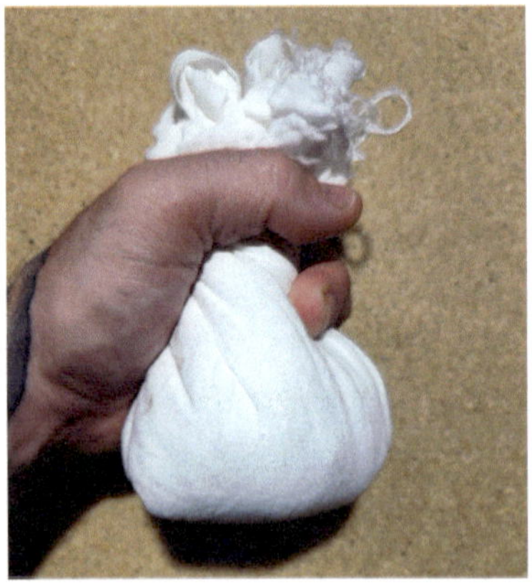

The slight twist pulls the fabric taut to create a smooth wrinkle free surface at the bottom of the pad allowing for an effortless glide over a surface.

Even though you have now created a padding rag similar in shape to an actual ball, when in use, the downward pressure you apply by the weight of your hand, will further flatten out the underside of the rag creating more overall contact with the surface you will be working on.

Again, for a padding rag that may need to be smaller, lower your rag measurements, it's possible to create a little cute padding rag (right) if that's what the task requires.

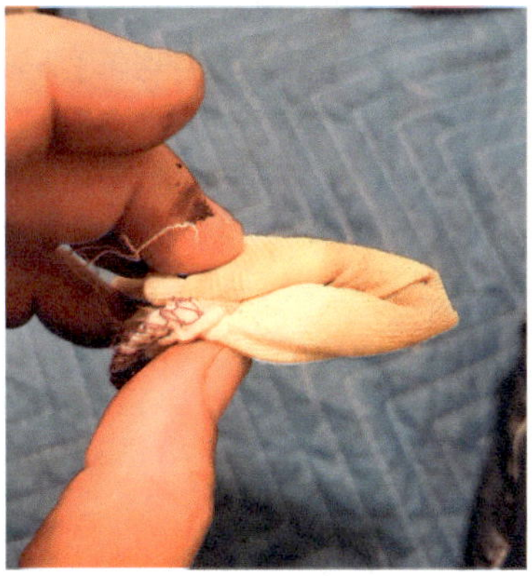

Now that we have spent an incredibly inordinate amount of time talking about folding rags, it's time to begin explaining the actual process of french polishing.

There are really only three ingredients you need (possibly four), a padding rag, which thankfully you've already created, your chosen padding finish, which we also went over, and of course, yourself.

The fourth item, as we touched on earlier, may be an initial cleaner like Naptha or denatured alcohol. Just remember, I don't "clean" every surface I work on but if you feel there may be significant silicone, polish or dirt built up on a surface you may want to wipe it down first.

Proceeding further will be a synopsis of applying the finish to the rag, while expanding more on techniques for application.

First, for your health, and for legal reasons, I suggest you wear gloves. You'll notice for the most part, I don't. Solvents and padding finishes may remove the oily fats and will dry out your skin, possibly causing irritation, cracking or other issues.

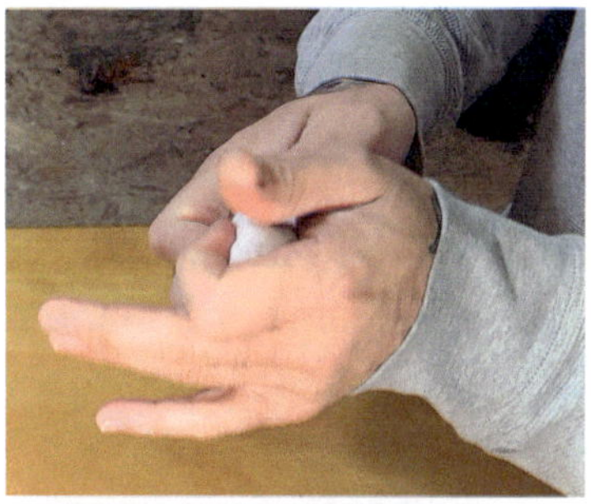

I have a reason for this, when I pour the liquid on the rag, I usually pat the rag in my palm, this allows me to feel the precise amount of padding finish I've applied, and also allows me to determine how well the liquid is distributed.

I can't make you wear gloves, but gloves are provided in every My Repair Kit™, choose your own fate.

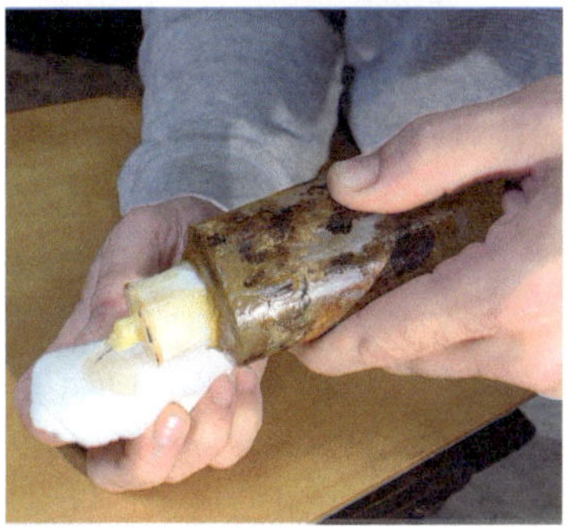

Holding your padding rag in one hand and your bottle of padding finish in the other, apply initially anywhere from a quarter ounce to half an ounce of padding finish, onto the bottom flat portion of the rag.

This is referred to as a "charge" or I may also call it a "squirt" of finish. The initial squirt will likely be the heaviest, as you need to initially saturate the rag. There's really no need to measure, just don't go overboard.

To explain the initial saturation level, I would say that there should be enough finish applied that if you slightly squeeze the rag (which is similar to the effect created by applying downward pressure), you should see the liquid start to accumulate on the surface and slightly start to seep out of the rag, but you never want the padding rag to be dripping wet.

You also don't want the finish you just applied to the rag to remain on the outer surface. After the initial squirt, pat or rub the rag in the palm of your hand a couple times to disperse the liquid evenly throughout the surface of the padding rag.

In my opinion, aside from liquid dispersion, by rubbing the pad in the palm of my hand, I feel it also slightly warms the padding finish making for easier distribution when applied to the wood surface. That may not be a scientific fact though, so don't quote me on it!

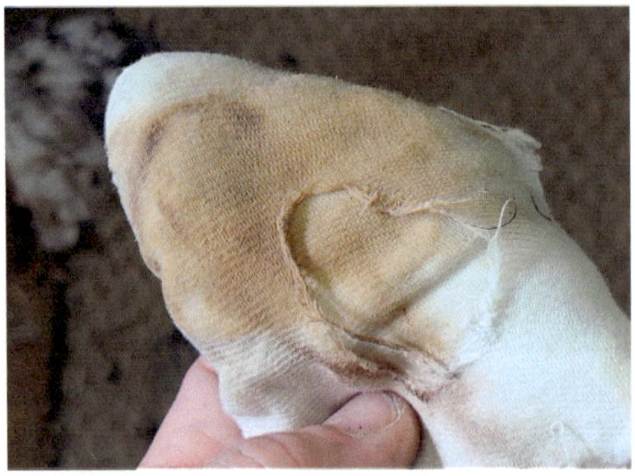

As you proceed into a french polish, the "surface" of your rag may wear down or even fray and form holes, it is often necessary to unfold, readjust and refold your padding rag so that the flat underside of the pad maneuvers to a new fresh area.

I may unfold and reposition to a new area of the rag anywhere from three to five times during a standard repair. Occasionally more, sometimes never, it's always dependent on how involved the restoration is.

Everytime you maneuver to a new area of the rag you need to apply additional padding finish, or "recharge" your rag. The rag should remain moderately damp, but not wet.

Every few minutes that you are french polishing, you may need to recharge your rag with additional padding finish. On a prepared/sanded surface, you will be transferring far more padding finish from your rag at this moment than in the latter stages of the french polish.

Think as though your rag is constantly trying to dry out. As you french polish, the finish is not only being removed and transferred from the rag to a surface, drying and evaporation are also factors that constantly remove or affect the finish within the rag. You will have to keep reinvigorating the rag at various intervals for the ability to continuously apply additional coats.

As you perform more repairs, you will begin to recognize when you may have applied too much finish to your rag. If you have applied more finish to a padding rag than desired, just rub it in your palm a little harder and the extra liquid seemingly absorbs and disperses more evenly throughout the rag.

As you progress through the building of a substantial finish on a surface, more time will pass in between recharging your rag while simultaneously the amount of padding finish used will also decrease.

You should be applying progressively less and less padding finish, anywhere from a ¼ ounce to just a quick squirt, again, depending on where you are in the process.

Reaching midway, towards the end of a french polish, you should have sufficiently built up a good base of finish on the surface, and there should be no more sanding scratches or damage visible on the surface.

Ultimately, near the conclusion of a french polish, if you can imagine, you're really just trying to keep the surface of the rag moist enough so that it glides effortlessly across a surface, while enabling the manipulation of the finish presently on the surface, so the sheen becomes uniform and defect free.

Once your task is complete, and the padding rag has fully dried out, it becomes hard, brittle and unusable and you must dispose of it properly. You may also try storing it in a glass mason jar with a lid to prevent the rag from drying out completely, if you need more time or extended breaks between the start and completion of your project.

A word of advice, don't squirt or pour the padding finish from its container onto your rag, while standing over a surface you are working on.

Any type of rogue drip or splash on the surface you are working on will definitely set you back with additional sanding and rebuilding of the finish.

The first picture to the right are some purposely dropped rogue drips. The second picture is me trying to wipe it off immediately, too late, it's already affected the finish.

Occasionally if you are building up the finish too fast, not allowing proper curing or the possibility of the introduction of an overly wet padding rag, you may see the finish on a surface start to "pull", or remove/move/damage coats of finish that were previously applied (right).

I've also heard it referred to as "pad/rag tracks". If this occurs, stop, allow the surface to dry for a half hour or more, with extreme minimal pressure, lightly sand the rough area with 600+ grit w/d sandpaper and start the french polishing process again.

If you have damage similar to the picture, after sanding, I'd advise to use less downward pressure and less padding finish on your rag to build up thinner coats, possibly allowing extra dry time between strokes, then once the sheen is similar to the surrounding surface, proceed to feather out.

Depending on the severity, you may have sanded the area, built up the finish again (french polishing), but the damage isn't quite gone yet, you may have to complete those two processes more than once to remove stubborn areas, before you can proceed over the entire surface.

This particular instance, when a finish is pulling, is also the time when a "non-crossover" pattern may be more useful than a "crossover pattern".

Let me explain, instead of making passes back and forth, constantly overlapping each previous stroke (crossover pattern), you may want to stroke over the affected area with one pass, let dry for a few seconds and continue with more singular passes in one particular direction, with a slight pause in between passes to allow additional dry time, this is a non-crossover technique.

A drier padding rag in these situations and towards the latter stages of a french polish is far less detrimental with regard to the ability to cause damage, sometimes it's better to err on the side of caution and use minimal amounts of finish.

Ultimately, there are no exact numbers as far as the amount of padding finish needed on the rag at various times, it's all dependent on the stage of the finishing process you are in, or what state the finish is in, on any particular area of a surface.

It may take you a couple tries till you get the hang of it, it's one of those "feel" type of situations literally and figuratively. Just remember, initially you need the most amount of padding finish to fill in any sanding scratches or surface imperfections, and progressively less towards the end of the repair process when you are just trying to even out the finish on a surface to create a consistent sheen.

You should be able to complete most restorations, even multiple jobs with several pieces of furniture, throughout the day, with one padding rag, but at some point with all the repositioning and use of the rag, it will become too worn to use. It never hurts to use a new padding rag if you feel necessary.

Because I've been blithering a lot, you may have forgotten, but again I want to reinforce that you **can never** stop your motion while the pad is in contact with a surface. If you do, your padding rag will immediately start to stick or at a minimum create visible imperfections to the finished surface that would have to be addressed as essentially another independent repair.

Let's get into some physics. There are a couple different arm motions that you can employ while french polishing. I always recommend applying east to west (and west to east), it doesn't matter whether you are right or left handed or whichever direction feels more comfortable, you'll have to become confident and proficient going both ways, and the main point that I'm referring to, is application parallel with the direction of the wood grain.

This side to side application will be used for virtually every repair, and the only motion you should use when finalizing a french polish. Any alternative direction or variation of motion against the wood grain will be apparent in the final finished product, possibly creating a visually sub-par final finish.

So charge your padding rag because things are about to get serious!

When starting the process of french polishing a surface, I would use the analogy of cleaning your vehicle's windshield with a gas station squeegee. Starting from one side at the top corner, we"ll refer to the top of the window as "north", you squeegee across the windshield.

For the next stroke you slightly move the squeegee south, down the window, while slightly overlapping the previous stroke (crossover pattern), to make sure you don't miss an area.

With each stroke across the window, you are slightly overlapping the previous while working your way south to the bottom, until you have covered every square inch and the window is clean from top to bottom and side to side.

Surprisingly, one of the more difficult aspects to master is picking the pad up and putting the pad down as you're stroking across the surface. Imagine a dining room table similar to the picture drawn above, as you're gliding the padding rag over a surface, left (west) to right (east), coming to the right edge of the table, you need to continue your padding motion off of the edge of the surface. You should still have the padding rag firmly in your hand, at no point should it fly away like a Wii controller into a TV!

In the same motion, after you've released from the one edge of the surface, you need to come back towards the surface, in your brisk sweeping motion, touching the padding rag down again as seamlessly close to the edge as possible while gliding the pad across the surface towards the opposite edge, and off the table again.

The padding rag needs to make contact with the surface, virtually as close and smoothly to the edge as possible. You'll need to become proficient at this task as you may seemingly repeat this process possibly hundreds of times during a restoration, or at least that's what it feels like.

An analogy I can compare this motion to may be similar to aircraft landing and taking off. We'll use an amphibious aircraft because the bottom is nice and smooth and closely resembles our padding rag.

As you would always hope on any descent is that the pilot touches down so smoothly that you don't even realize you've landed.

That should be your goal as your padding rag makes contact with the surface, touching down as close to one edge as possible, with motion, continuing to stroke through to the opposite side of the surface, and just as a pilot would take off, as you reach the opposite end of your working surface, you again continue your motion off of the surface.

Now continue to repeat that motion while slightly overlapping the last pass, systematically working your way from top to bottom and side to side, on a surface, ensuring you cover every square inch, with a near equal amount of finish applied consistently throughout the surface.

Because you are lifting the padding rag and landing the padding rag near the edges of any surface, these may be the areas that have the most "variation" as you proceed through the french polishing.

This happens because your padding rag is not in constant contact and doesn't always have the same amount of applied pressure as in the center of a surface, or you may have crash landed on one of your passes.

In some cases you may have to focus primarily on the outer 6" where the padding rag leaves and comes back into contact. Just keep working with the areas until any imperfections are removed, then extend your strokes over the entire surface to even out any variations, hopefully leaving you with a beautifully completed project.

Let's start from the beginning with this top to a decorative shelf unit, viewing from the left side.

As you can see I've sanded the top, using only 600 grit w/d sandpaper. I also did not clean the surface with a solvent prior to sanding.

Sanding removes several light surface scratches and defects, but now we need to build the finish back to a nice smooth blemish free surface. Make sure to wipe the surface clean of any sanding dust (with a clean, dry rag).

With a padding rag charged generously with padding finish, very briskly stroke back and forth across the surface 10-20 times, this is done in a matter of 10-15 seconds.

I did exactly that, quickly, on the top half of the surface to the right. You can see the difference already, from where I briskly french polished, and the area where the sanding scratches are still exposed, on the almost untouched bottom half of the surface.

This technique rapidly builds up the finish and fills/removes deeper surface scratches. You'll use this technique during most repairs, particularly on areas that you've filled and sanded.

As I mentioned earlier, it's beneficial to bring all areas of finish, on a surface, to near equal before expanding over the entire surface.

So an east to west, overlapping pattern is essentially the pattern that I recommend you mostly work with, east to west (side to side) while always maneuvering and working north to south (or south to north) of a surface.

There is no way around it, your patterns will be overlapping, it's the only way to create a consistent, even sheen throughout a surface.

There is one more useful pattern which will be circular, short circular strokes, with each stroke overlapping the previous, just like waxing a car.

This circular pattern will build up the amount of finish applied in a particular area far more expeditiously than the standard east to west pattern.

When performing this application pattern, you don't necessarily have to start from an edge, you can start anywhere on the surface you need to as long as you make contact with the surface with momentum and motion.

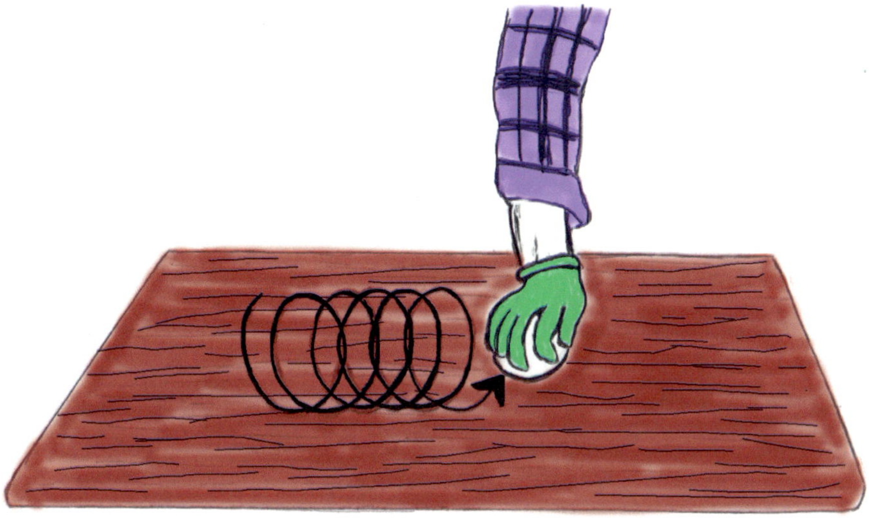

It's also beneficial to perform this pattern as expeditiously as possible, don't go slow.

Additionally, because you are overlapping your strokes, possibly a numerous amount, you may want to go slightly lighter on the weight of your hand (downward force).

This circular pattern is a crossover pattern. If you notice, we're still working our way across the surface east to west, though in actuality our pattern is covering more surface area in a perpendicular manner.

In my opinion, I feel french polishing perpendicularly over sandpaper scratches (scratches should be in line with the grain) will fill in those surface damages more efficiently than padding in the direction of the scratches.

Think of a scratch being similar to a miniature grand canyon. As you wipe perpendicularly across the canyon, the "walls" are "catching" more finish therefore filling the "canyon" (scratch) faster.

Padding in line with the scratch, which to me is "open ended", allows the finish to "escape" from the left and right ends, similar to a river running through, it flows in from one end and out the other. This effect is minimal, not a major issue, just giving a recommendation to build up a finish faster on a surface.

I primarily use the first technique (east/west), but in situations where I use this circular technique it's usually in the beginning stages of applying padding finish, mainly to assist in rapidly filling surface damages.

After you feel you have sufficiently built up a fairly even finish over a surface, you always have to finish applying your padding finish in the east to west pattern, keeping in line with the grain of the wood.

Otherwise you will notice a circular pattern left by the initial application of the finish. It may take some effort to remove the circular pattern depending on the amount of finish you've built up.

I could expand on other french polishing patterns that you may hear craftspeople refer to, examples being an "S" or figure eight pattern. In my opinion, all other patterns, other than east/west and circular, are just too difficult to keep consistent, and may lead to missing application in certain areas or building up the finish too heavy in others.

The key is simply, **never stop** your motion while in contact with the surface. I've been performing french polishes professionally for over 25 years, daily, and I can honestly say that those are the only two application techniques I've ever used.

Moving on, eventually you will notice, as you proceed through the mid to latter stages of the french polishing process, that slight surface scratches, minor gouged areas or other surface defects will fill and eventually, virtually disappear.

Continue to pad the surface till it's consistent throughout and you've reached the desired sheen level. Padding finishes generally create anywhere from a semi-gloss to a gloss sheen, if you're looking for a matte finish, I'll expand on that shortly.

You do occasionally have to let the different applied layers of finish have some dry time in-between applications. As you have built up several layers of finish, it does stay softer for a longer period of time as it cures.

That's one of the reasons you don't want to apply a lot of downward pressure (weight of hand), once you've added a significant amount of padding finish.

Let's recap, padding rag, padding finish, and initially either a straight across or circular pattern for application. You will be constantly overlapping with each pass.

Additionally, with each stroke you'll need to slightly adjust your arm north to south or south to north depending on the surface you are working on to ensure you've applied the padding finish equally over the entire surface area. It may require working back and forth, sided to side, over an entire surface, multiple times to complete.

Let me give you another repair example, either you own or I'm sure you have witnessed some kind of wood surface with white stains or rings, whether from a hot plate, casserole dish, coffee mug, pizza box, or all the above!

All those items may result in a huge white stained area in the middle of a surface, similar to these below on this dining room table.

The white marks are caused by water vapor, like the moist heat radiating off the underside of that dinner plate or hot pizza box.

Even condensation dripping off of the side of a cold glass of ice water, with prolonged contact with a surface, allows moisture to penetrate into the top layers of finish, getting stuck, and though the water eventually evaporates, the result is an apparent white ring or blotches.

There are numerous home remedies found online. One example is applying a layer of mayonnaise over the area, placing a paper towel over the mayonnaise and waiting 24 hours (I am not recommending you do this). Then clean that off and wala, the spot completely disappears (doubtful).

Other examples include the use of baking soda, petroleum jelly, toothpaste, salt, cigarette ashes, blow dryers, and the internet cures go on forever. The reality is, salt, ashes and toothpaste have a “grit” to them, which acts as an abrasive, and the paste or jelly really just acts as the lubricant.

In essence what they are trying to accomplish, whether they understand it or not, is that they're basically making a compound, similar to an automotive polishing/rubbing compound, which is used to buff out and remove scratches on your car's painted surface.

In theory, they have the right idea, just the wrong execution. I'll tell you how a professional would attack this repair, I'm just going to cut to the chase and break out some 400 or 600 grit sandpaper. There is only one true way to remove the marks, in my opinion, and that is to sand out the white stains.

Initially I assess the spot(s) in question to determine how much condensation was trapped in the finish, usually the more opaque the white spot, the deeper or more dense the moisture that was in the finish.

Often, the "whiter" the spot, may mean more sanding to remove the stain. Knowing the limits of the amount you can sand may be a little tricky to figure out initially as there are a vast array of finishes, some thicker than others.

If the white spot is more translucent and you can somewhat still see the grain of the wood through the stain then that means it's most likely just in the top coat finish, and that it should in theory sand out fairly easily.

To be more specific, if I determine the spot is shallow, I'll likely start by using 600+ grit wet/dry sandpaper, but If the spot is aggressive and there is plenty of finish to work with on the surface, I may begin with 400 grit sandpaper.

If you're sanding and you see a "light" area starting to peek through then there is a good chance that you've started to sand through the clear coat into the bare wood. Sometimes it may be inevitable, but then that's when you can employ the touch up skill that you've learned throughout this book.

This is what the surface looked like after sanding with 600 grit sandpaper, as you can see, the white areas simply sanded out of the clear coat, and I in no way sanded too much as to pass through the existing clear coats, into the actual wood.

As a general rule, when working on a finished surface, you want to preserve the original finish to the best of your ability. Using sandpaper more coarse than 400 grit would most likely leave scratches in the finish that would be too deep to be removed without significant effort.

While on the topic of sandpaper, I suggest using wet/dry, which essentially means that the paper is "waterproof".

From this point on, I will refer to this type of sandpaper as "w/d", accompanied by its corresponding grit e.g. 600 w/d, 400 w/d or similar.

Adding water while you sand is adding lubrication, which in turn will extend the life of the paper and also make smoother cuts in the finish, effectively making the abrasions from the sandpaper less aggressive.

Another alternative is that you can also just use the sandpaper dry. Using sandpaper dry may leave "corns" stuck to the sandpaper created by the excess finish that you are sanding off.

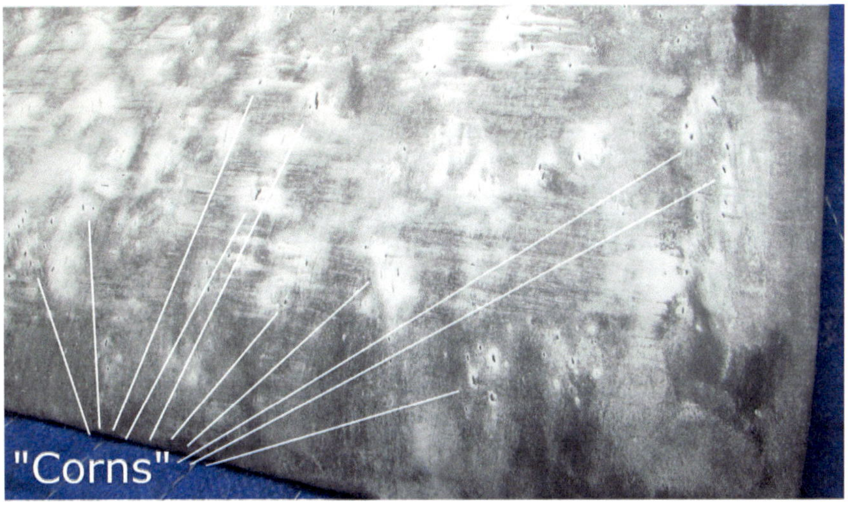

Corns may create additional scratches to a surface, and ultimately they give the sandpaper less of a lifespan.

You should also be aware of continually turning the sandpaper around to fresh, unused areas as you continue sanding. That ensures you get the most out of a single piece of sandpaper as possible.

Back to the table at hand, with medium pressure I would sand back and forth, with the grain of the wood, closely monitoring the area.

Paying close attention, you should start to see the white area begin to sand out, but don't focus your sanding primarily into one small area, it's always best to feather out, to avoid creating any apparent dips or ripples in the finished surface.

If you do use water for lubrication, sometimes you will have to stop and completely dry the area to assess if you've sanded sufficiently to remove the white stain. While an area is still wet, it may be difficult to fully see if the white stain is gone.

Once the sanding is complete, on large surfaces, like a dining room table, I may begin applying the padding finish in sections or quarters. Take your standard dining room table, for the simplicity of math, one half of a table may be 4' x 4'. I would likely work initially in four sections of approximately 2' x 2' areas.

It's easier to build up the finish in smaller areas and then as the finish starts to become consistent throughout the surface, that's when you can start finalizing the build and widen your strokes, eventually encompassing the entire surface.

In our example of a dining room table, it is possible to work on one half of the table for an hour or more of virtual continuous french polishing, how often did you recharge your pad? Hopefully several times!

Eventually you realize there is a second half of the table and you better start on that side also. So you move to the other side of the table and begin the french polishing process.

In theory, and reality, once you've moved to and started the other half of the table, assuming you go for an hour on that side also, you are giving the first section an hour or more to dry.

As I've mentioned before, be wary of working too long on one specific area, applied coats will need intermittent drying periods or the finish will be soft and you could run the risk of causing unwanted additional damage.

After you're working on the second half of the table, you realize that the table has two leaves, and you've been there two hours and haven't started those yet. So you proceed to french polish the leaves which are usually 18"-24" wide each, which means you may be looking at the equivalent of an additional, half a table.

At about the 2 ½ - 3 hour mark, you're wondering what the heck you got yourself into, but by this time hopefully you've gotten the main two halves of the table top almost done, and both surfaces have dried long enough to put the finishing touches on your french polish, possibly just having to work out any very slight variances, and french polishing one last time over the entire surface of all pieces.

When french polishing a large surface like a dining room table I suggest you perform all the finishing on each surface in exactly the same manner to ensure that the sheen and surface appear consistent throughout the entire piece.

Even though it may not be necessary for an experienced french polisher (I don't use this technique), another trick some craftspeople may employ when proceeding to the end of the process is, when reinvigorating their padding rag with padding finish, they may add a drop or two of pure oil to their pad, and rub it in. There are two basic types of oils used, non-drying oils and drying oils.

Non-drying oils will not polymerize (harden), they remain fluid and migrate indefinitely on a surface. Examples of non-drying oils are, but not limited to, olive oil and mineral oil.

Using this type of oil during the process creates additional lubrication between the finished surface and the pad, enabling the finisher to apply more finish while also simultaneously creating a smoother finish texture.

An example of drying oils are, but not limited to, walnut oil or poppy oil. Along with also assisting with lubrication, drying oil will plasticize (harden).

Once fully polymerized, the applied finish will slightly increase in solvent resistance, theoretically creating a more durable finish. A second benefit of using a drying oil is that it will increase the gloss of the surface, compared to using a non-drying oil.

As we are finalizing the french polishing of a surface, we are walking around the piece of furniture, looking primarily at a 30°- 60° angle, in the reflections of the light on the surface, to see any imperfections. Just standing back, looking randomly at the surface when any repair is complete, may not be sufficient to detect any imperfections.

Light will reflect differently on imperfect areas. If you see imperfections, you may have to go over the surface one last time to ensure everything is as perfect as it can be. If there is a window in the room, try turning off the interior lights and look at the surface using only the reflection caused by the light coming through a window.

That table restoration took approximately 3-4 hours. With some restoration companies charging $100-$200+ per hour, you can see how costly it can be to remove what may seem like some ridiculous little spot, but those are the average hourly rates of most competent repair companies if you were to hire a technician to come and properly perform the repair in your home. Basically, for the price of hiring a technician, you can buy all the supplies yourself, and learn something new.

One common issue that may arise, is that if you do not add enough finish sufficiently onto a surface with heavy sanding scratches, as the finish dries, those specific areas may slightly re expose themselves, no biggie, you'll just have to apply more finish in those areas, and go over the surface hopefully one last time.

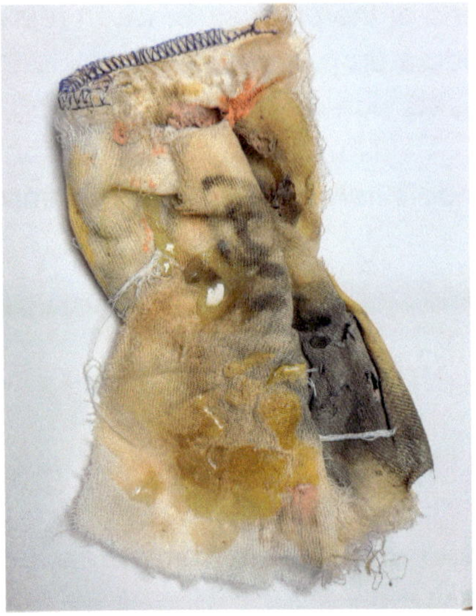

Once you are finished with your restoration, the rag will completely dry out, become hardened, brittle and unusable. Please dispose of it properly!

That's not the end of our rags life cycle though, most of the time we use these rags further to clean off excess glue or filler off from our tools, or used to clean out our paintbrushes after another completed repair. The more you can repurpose items, the more money you are saving yourself.

One other thing you should be aware of when french polishing when using either shellac or a padding finish when at the end stages, you may notice what might appear to be slight streaks, this is usually due to the oily solvent incorporated in the manufacturing process of the padding finish to assist with lubrication.

You may think you need to continue adding more finish when in reality the best way to approach this situation is to continue burnishing the surface with your almost completely dry padding rag and the streaking should dissipate, any leftover minimal haze or streaking should evaporate on its own.

Craftspeople using shellac also may apply oil to a padding rag at the end stages of the french polishing process and may cause what is referred to as a "vapor trail", which may also seem like a streak on the surface. Removal of the oil, once the shellacked surface has totally cured, is called "spiriting".

Spiriting, if you've french polished with shellac, requires a new padding rag, and traditionally alcohol would be applied sparingly to the rag and wiped across the surface to remove the excess oil.

The problem with using alcohol is that it's a solvent, too wet of a rag and you will actually damage or remove the finish you spent so much time building up. This final step is where the majority of people have been known to have problems successfully completing the french polishing process with shellac.

Instead of alcohol I recommend using naphtha. Naphtha will remove the oil without damaging the finish. Simply, ever so slightly moisten a rag and wipe over the surface. There shouldn't be any problems with naphtha, but If you remove the oil and the finish appears to be "drier" or "less rich", you can apply some carnauba wax or buffing polish to correct that.

A while back I mentioned that french polishing for the most part produces a gloss sheen. What if you don't want something glossy? Satin and matte finishes are most likely what you will be coming across the most during your repair journey.

Furniture finishes in their purest form are created by chemical companies in a gloss sheen. Gloss is the inverse of surface roughness, it is also an optical term which describes the ability of a surface to reflect light.

You should never need or use this tool, but the sheen of a surface can be measured by a small device called a Gloss Meter.

A gloss meter measures the amount of reflected light from a light beamed at a given angle onto the surface, usually 60°, which is the equivalent of looking at a surface while standing.

The gloss meter then compares this value with the "black-glass standard", which has a defined refractive index of 100 "gloss units" (GU). Gloss units can also be referred to as "luster".

There are four standard sheens in furniture finishing, each carrying an approximate gloss unit or luster percentage. Meaning how reflective the sheen is based on a scale of 1-100 GU on the gloss meter, with 100 being the glossiest or most reflective and 1 being the least gloss, or least reflective.

The four sheens are 1) flat (aka dull or matte) which usually carries a 25-35% luster (or lower). 2) Satin carries an approximate 40-50% luster. 3) Semi-gloss has an approximate 55-70% luster and 4) gloss has over 75% luster.

As you can see, there are some percentages that I did not include, like 36-39%, 51-54% and 71-74%, that's because such a fine difference in the gloss level between the standard defined sheens would not be discernible to the naked eye.

Ultimately, you can create your own sheen to the exact luster you would like by mixing your own finish, accompanied with an exact amount of flattening agent, but be cautious, I also would not suggest mixing in so much flattening agent with finish, that the luster is below 25%.

In the manufacturing process, when a finish is altered to be less glossy, the manufacturers add a flattening agent, usually silica, which is similar to a fine grain sand, almost as fine as powder. The silica is only suspended in the finish, not dissolved.

After the flattening agent is added to create the proper sheen, and sprayed onto a surface like wood, during the drying process, some of the silica rises to the top of the finish creating extremely miniscule bumps.

These bumps are too fine for the naked eye to see, but the variation (roughness) caused by the silica rising to the top, reflects and disperses light more randomly, causing the finish to become less reflective, therefore creating what we perceive as a dull/less shiny finish.

The more flattening agent there is in a finish, the more light that gets randomly reflected, creating a finish as dull as you want even to the point of having virtually no reflection or shine.

Extremely dull finishes could tend to have what appears, in my opinion, a cloudiness or slight white haze. This is from the large amount of flattening agent needed in the finish to create extremely dull sheens, silica is white, not clear.

If there is too much flattening agent incorporated into a finish, any damage like a scratch or gouge will end up appearing white, and may lead to damages being extremely difficult to repair.

There are several ways to make a finish have less of a gloss sheen, and I will explain the three techniques we use most often to create different sheens other than gloss.

If you've properly french polished a piece of furniture you have achieved the ability to create a gloss finish. If needed, one of the easiest ways to alter the sheen at the conclusion of a repair is to use Clear Toner (spray can/aerosol) in your desired sheen, and spray the altered sheen on.

I'll expand more on "toners" shortly, but a quick synopsis, I'd take my spray can of satin (or whatever sheen necessary) clear toner and spray a light to medium amount finish in a fast even sweeping pattern in the direction of the grain, with one or more passes extending wider than the repaired area, which in turn feathers out and blends a repaired area with the existing surrounding finish.

I'd estimate that I complete 70%-80% of all restorations in this manner, but there are a few precautions/exceptions to be aware of. For one, you have to make sure not to spray too heavily in one area, it could create runs if you're spraying a vertical surface, or if on a horizontal surface, you may just notice it's too heavily concentrated in one area.

Usually this is the way to go on almost any surface of a piece of furniture, except possibly for top surfaces. I say possibly not to use a spray can on a top, but that primarily depends on how "nice" the finish is.

If the finish on a top surface is minimal or not in great condition then spraying a coat evenly with a clear toner may work out perfectly well. But on a highly built, nicely finished surface, if you spray the top with a clear toner, it may leave the surface rough, or you may see a pattern if it wasn't applied evenly.

If that's the case, you may have to lightly sand with some 600+ w/d sandpaper and french polish the top again, creating an even sheen throughout the surface and try to get better results on the next try.

A second technique, If the surface is rough, is to use steel wool to smooth out the finish and to dull slightly. We use #0000 steel wool (AKA four ought).

#0000 steel wool is the "finest" (least coarse) steel wool commonly available. I also wouldn't suggest using anything more coarse on a finished surface, as it would leave noticeable scratches in the surface. This technique is often referred to as "hand-rubbed".

Wiping steel wool across the surface removes very fine layers of finish, creating a silky smooth satin sheen, with a faint pattern of "fine scratches".

Some may suggest rubbing with oil or water as a lubricant, or you can try dry, each technique creates slight variations in the appearance of the sheen. There is a special oil formulated for use with steel wool, named "Wool Lube" (right), if interested.

You always have to rub with light to medium pressure in the direction of the grain. Any rubbing out of alignment with the grain, will leave noticeable, misdirected, fine scratches in the surface.

Slowly adjust your strokes while moving north to south on a surface, similar to french polishing, with each east to west stroke overlapping the previous by at least 50-75%.

The third technique to create the sheen we require is the use of compounds. Before using compounds you should ensure that any repair has dried thoroughly and is perfectly level with the rest of the surface. Any "high area" may be ground down and removed by an abrasive rubbing compound.

Rubbing compounds are abrasives, either in powder or paste form. In powder form there is Pumice, which is an extremely hard finely ground volcanic glass.

You can alter a sheen's luster depending on how coarse the pumice is. We would recommend FF (Fine), FFF, (Finer) and FFFF(Finest), any other grade may be too coarse for a finished surface.

You can mix the pumice with oil or water, creating your own paste, and using a rag you can apply the mixture in the direction of the grain of the wood.

Once you've gone over the entire surface, use a clean dry rag, to clean and dry the surface, which should have now achieved a dull-satin finish.

One of the main differences between using steel wool and compounds is that the "hand-rubbed" effect will be minimal to non-existent with the use of compounds.

If you need the sheen to be more dull, you can continue applying the pumice, but if you need to adjust the finish to have more gloss you can use a different product called Rottenstone.

Rottenstone is an extremely soft finely ground limestone, which you also mix with water or oil and apply it with a rag in the direction of the grain of the wood. Using both pumice and rottenstone, you should be able to adjust the sheen evenly from dull to a semi gloss.

Compounds in paste form that we use primarily are all basically different forms of car wax. There are generally two types, rubbing compounds and polishing compounds. Both are going to have abrasive powders mixed into them.

Rubbing compounds will have a larger grain abrasive and is used to "cut" the finish faster to remove surface scratches.

Polishing compounds can remove any slight swirl marks and will create a high gloss sheen.

Not all compounds are graded or uniform from manufacturer to manufacturer, and can vary in coarseness.

I suggest that you try experimenting, using different types of compounds on various finishes of non important pieces of furniture or sample, finished wood boards, to see the different effects they each create.

Compounds and polishing are further expanded in the "Problems" chapter.

TONER

Rounding back, expanding more on the topic of Toners, as you proceed through various repairs, you may need to continually adjust the sheen or require assistance with further color blending.

Toners are spray cans, produced by various manufacturers, in various formulated clear sheens, also available in numerous different hues. Ensure you shake every can well to mix the contents prior to use.

Above is a good selection of Mohawk® toners available through my local supply shop, Pro Wood Finishes™, in Gaithersburg, MD. I've used their product line my entire career and I have no plans to stop. If you plan on performing repairs regularly, you should include a selection of toners, clear and colored, into your arsenal.

There are two main subsets of toners, as previously mentioned, clear and colored. As I'm sure you've figured out by now, clear is simply that, some type of translucent finish. Colored toners on the other hand contain a dye, enamel or finely ground pigment.

When it comes to clear toners, there is a large selection to choose from, each with different formulations to perform certain tasks. I'll explain a few of the varying types.

Perfect Blend® Lacquer is a nitrocellulose lacquer great for use on surfaces contaminated with wax, silicone or polishes.

Perfect Blend® Waterborne Lacquer is a water based acrylic with similar characteristics as the nitrocellulose version, but because this is water based, the spray cans are HAPS (hazardous air pollutants) free and have minimal odor.

Tone Finish® Clear is a nitrocellulose clear finish formulated for use as a "topcoat". This is the clear finish that I use at the conclusion of the majority of repairs. This one, Mohawk™ Tone Finish Clear satin sheen. Product # M102-0422

Others include Ultra-Flo Ultra®, formulated to adhere well with polyurethanes, polyesters and UV finishes.

Water Clear Acrylic is a completely translucent finish which will not yellow with time, and also could be used on certain metals.

Pre-Catalyzed clears dry very durably and are used in conjunction with catalyzed finishes. Many more clear finishes with their own special uses include, but aren't limited to, High Solids Pre-Catalyzed clear™, Finisher's Choice™ clear, Final Finish™, and others.

Sanding Sealers (in a toner can) are used to fill and level surface damages while allowing for better adhesion between an existing finish and a newly applied finish. Sealers are available in lacquer and pre-catalyzed versions.

There are also different "weights" of sanding sealers, "Heavy Bodied" contains a higher amount of solids, for faster filling of surface defects. I don't often use sanding sealer during a repair, but I do use it in almost every refinishing job. It expedites the build, is easily sandable, all while allowing the use of less "standard finish" to completion of a project.

Each type of finish, as you can see, has their use in certain restorations or circumstances. I suggest checking the manufacturer for their recommendations for each type of toner you choose to use.

Also keep in mind that each type of finish that was listed above (aside from sanding sealer) is produced in various sheens, most common are dead flat, flat, matte, satin, semi-gloss, and gloss.

I almost never use a semi-gloss or gloss clear toner because that type of sheen is often created just by french polishing alone. So after I perform a repair to some type of damage, and french polish a surface, the repair may just be complete!

I do usually keep handy a dead flat, flat or matte toner. Several types of furniture manufactured presently are finished in a flat/matte sheen.

The difference between those three is the luster percentage, I don't know exact numbers, but I estimate they are all under 25% luster, with matte likely being 20-25%, flat 15-20% and dead flat under 15% luster.

"Flat Finishes" (dead flat/flat/matte), or furniture finished with a sheen that has little to no reflection, are still probably one of the most difficult repairs to complete when needing to match such a finish.

Unfortunately most of the techniques in this chapter are not going to work sufficiently on a "very flat" finish. The only choice you usually have at the conclusion of your repair, is whether you can get away with spraying on a similarly sheened clear toner, to blend the repaired area with the surrounding surface, to appear as uniform as possible.

Often, success of a repair is determined by the location and severity of the damage. If the damage is in the center of a large flat surface, like a dining room table, I'd say, you may not even want to waste your time and effort, as these large surfaces, if they have a flat or dead flat finish, will almost always warrant refinishing or at a minimum, a complete respray in the shop.

Ideally, I try to wait until almost completion of a repair before I use any type of clear toner. This means that my goal is to not use a clear toner throughout a repair.

I know that I am going to contradict myself a few paragraphs from now and say that you can use a toner at any point during any repair, which you can, but realistically my goal is to fill any damage, sand, french polish, perform any color work to conceal the repair, french polishing again, then at the very end of a restoration, I'll spray a light to medium coat of clear toner to blend the sheen of the repaired area with the existing surrounding finish.

A word of caution, most toners could be considered dangerous products. Most will carry the www.p65warnings.ca.gov for risk of cancer and reproductive harm.

I suggest wearing the appropriate facemask, avoid inhaling any fumes, only use in a well ventilated area, and avoid use all together if you are susceptible in any way to any of the toner's ingredients.

Check the material safety data sheets (MSDS/SDS) on every product you use, always keep out of reach of children! A material safety data sheet for every product sold or included with My Repair Kit™ is available at MyRepairKit.com.

Here is the contradiction. I may spray some clear or colored toner at various stages of a repair to seal in any colorwork (pigment touch up) or to further color blend an area, under what is essentially a protective coating.

Be cautious though, if using a toner midway through a repair, you have to ensure that the surface is completely dry before you can proceed to continue french polishing. If you begin to french polish too soon, after applying a toner, you could begin to remove or damage the finish you just sprayed on the surface.

One main aspect to application is the amount of spray that you use. To give you a brief explanation, never spray a very "heavy" coat of finish, from a spray can, onto a surface.

Toner cans do not spray as consistently well as if you were using a real spray system (like a HVLP or airless), so this means that if you spray a really heavy coat, there is a good chance that you may have "trash", contamination, roughness, unevenness, or other undesired effects in the surface.

At the conclusion of your restoration, depending on how well the clear coat was applied, if you used a toner spray can to blend the finishes of a surface, you may leave the surface slightly rough and in some cases that will be inevitable.

Future use of the furniture, cleaning or having items on the surface, roughness will eventually wear down to create a more smooth surface, but that may take an extended time frame (and a client may not understand that, thinking the performed repair is not up to their standards).

If this is the case, occasionally you can take a dry paper towel, wrap it around a wood block, and gently, or with medium pressure, rub over the finish in the direction of the grain, to attempt to smooth it out.

Earlier in the chapter we also touched on #0000 steel wool, which is another way to smooth out a finish, just understand that using steel wool will leave fine surface scratches (hand rubbed effect).

Now on the topic of colored toners, with regard to Mohawk®, toners come in virtually every color that the dry pigments come in and probably even more. There are more than 100 hues available just in the Tone Finish® family, which assist us in a good percentage of our restorations.

When sprayed, the color extruded from the can comes out in a "translucent" manner, this allows you the ability to shade/blend areas even further, greater concealing your repairs.

It should be your goal not to depend on these colored toners, as it's my hope you become proficient in color blending with pigments. The more precise you can repair damages with pigments, the less you'll depend on using colored toners.

That doesn't mean that I rarely use colored toners. I do use them often, but again, I may try to wait towards the end of a restoration, just to give a repaired area that little extra bit of needed visual concealment.

On occasion, after you spray a colored toner on a surface, you may want to spray over that application with a clear toner, to seal in/protect the previously sprayed colored toner. Then when you sand a surface or start to french polish, you shouldn't be removing much of the colored toner.

Additionally, avoid spraying a lot of product in one concentrated area, you may create an unwanted area where the color may be too dark, too light or too opaque, concealing the wood grain, some of those factors may actually make your restoration more apparent.

Mohawk®, names their own colors, so you may need to learn what hues are actually produced, as the name on the toner can does not always directly associate with colors available at, say, an art store.

What hue would you imagine if I told you names like American Walnut, Pickle Frost, Tavern Pine or Colonial Maple? I'm sure you have no idea, and in 25 years, out of those four, I've actually only used Colonial Maple on a regular basis.

I've probably only used half of all hues created by Mohawk®. The reason for this is several of the hues are, in my opinion, very similar. My goal, as I touched on earlier, is to only use a minimal amount of product.

I'm really looking only to adjust the "tone", red, yellow, green, purple or similar, in the repaired area. If I need to add some red I may incorporate Dark Red Mahogany. If I need to add yellow or green I may use Dark Golden Oak or Light Walnut respectively.

A few of the other common colored toners from Mohawk® that I carry are: Extra Dark Walnut, which is useful for darkening. Orange is unique because you can obtain it in opaque or translucent, several finished wood types have an orange tone.

It is also just as important to always carry White and Black, as those toners will be a stronger concentration of color, compared to their pigment form.

Those toners I listed are just a few I normally keep in my everyday tool box. I have several other hues which travel in my work van, and even more in the finishing room of our shop (right).

With toners, different nozzles are available which create varying spray patterns. In most situations I would suggest a fine or medium spray head.

Occasionally you may need to duplicate some type of splatter or distressing. If you only slightly depress or pump the nozzle a couple times on a can of Extra Dark Walnut, black, or similar, the toner may disperse in a splatter pattern, leaving varying sized dots that appear like distressing. This will make your surface rough!

Also, you'll see a small black line on the inside edge of every spraycan near the nozzle, this is where the nozzle needs to be pointed to remove all the contents from a can as there is a small hose internally which allows you to use virtually all the product in the can. This is true for almost every spray can made, not just for toners.

Additionally, holding your spray can upside down and depressing the nozzle will clear out the spray head for future uses. Occasionally though you may have to scrape off dried finish from the nozzle tip or remove it all together and soak it in lacquer thinner to cleanse.

Also, there are specialty finishes available locally for various unique projects. If I ever ran out of clear toner from Mohawk® in emergency situations, I would go to the hardware store, they usually have a clear satin lacquer spray can that is usually sufficient to assist in completion of repairs.

If you find yourself working on an outdoor item like a piece of furniture or exterior wood panel, like a door, I suggest using an exterior urethane, which is also available at most major hardware stores.

The main benefit of an exterior urethane finish is that it's formulated to better withstand the outside elements and more importantly it has a UV protectant.

Exterior urethane is suitable for minor outdoor repairs, but brushing/spraying on an exterior urethane or "marine (boat) varnish" will likely give far superior protection to outdoor items, compared to using a spray can.

I've said this before, mother nature is undefeated, there is no type of finish that I have yet to discover that can withstand the direct abuse of sun, wind, rain, and snow indefinitely.

Even baked on car finishes and powder coatings eventually fall victim to the elements and those are some of the most durable finishes ever created.

You can also procure shellac in a spray can version, instead of the brushable version. If you're repairing furniture finished in shellac, this toner to the right will seal in and protect your repair.

Hopefully all these techniques has given you the knowledge required to go out and successfully perform some beautiful restorations and french polishes, which In theory is a simple task, but in practice it can also be very lengthy, repetitive, sometimes frustrating, but always gratifying once you've seen the pristine, beautiful, finalized project.

Keep practicing and I have no doubt that you'll have it down pat in no time flat! This was way easier than the next chapter anyway!

PIGMENTS
& THEIR
APPLICATION
TECHNIQUES

Henry Ford said; "failure is only the opportunity to begin again. Only this time, more wisely".

It's possible the outcome of your first repair attempts may not be ideal, but that doesn't mean you won't be able to eventually create beautiful, undetectable restorations in the future. Remember, there is no such thing as failure!

Robert Greene said; "the time that leads to mastery is dependent on the intensity of our focus".

For many, furniture repair or furniture refinishing is just a hobby, usually just figuring out a way to spruce up your own, families or friends' furniture.

The average person dedicates around 245 hours per year to a hobby. That's a smidge over 20 hours a month! Extrapolate even further, and it's a couple hours every other day, or a few nice Sunday mornings before the 1 o'clock kick off.

After reading this book, my goal is that you'd be able to successfully perform a basic repair, and with practice, after a year or so, possibly 245 hours, you could become very proficient at most repairs.

But it will take a lot more time and effort than 245 hours to truly become elite. I define elite as being able to satisfactorily repair or restore virtually any project that you come across, within reason.

Any man that knows anything, knows he knows nothing. I still learn new things everyday, but within my first year of work in the restoration business I became very confident in my ability to perform several different types of basic restorations.

After a few years I felt I could look at damage, internally evaluate and visualize the outcome of the restoration, before I even attempted it.

Those years of experience, accompanied with getting myself into some tricky situations also led to understanding limitations. Not every repair has the ability to be perfectly invisible.

Don't expect every repair to be perfect, I call those a "best possible" repair. Because I already visualized an unideal outcome, I can explain to the client why I think the repair will not be perfect. Possibly accompanied by a number on a scale of 1-100 on how well I think the repair will turn out.

The client then has the option to decide, 85% and a repair fee far less than a refinishing cost may be satisfactory, or we can offer our shop refinishing service for significantly damaged items, where we have the ability to remove or disguise virtually any damage through the refinishing process.

A good way to practice would be to purchase cheap, used furniture from Goodwill, Habitat for Humanity, yard sales, farmers markets, roadside finds, the list can go on.

Ultimately through practice, you'd be making these low cost items beautiful again. With each new item giving you the opportunity to practice the breadth of your new skills. When done, you may even be able to sell the item for a profit! You literally just started a business!

Not all practice is equal though. Naive practice is practicing enough to be decent at a task, becoming comfortable, but being stuck at that skill level indefinitely, never progressing to new or more challenging tasks.

Deliberate practice is structured learning, with a mentor or skilled expert guiding the way, in a predetermined process, consistently setting new, more challenging tasks to achieve.

All while the student is practicing those steps on several different items, several hours more than the average person. You really need hands-on time to gain experience.

Don't be scared to attempt repairs that may seem "unrepairable", you will likely surprise yourself. Growth happens when you start doing things you're not qualified to do!

That, in my opinion, is how one truly becomes elite. You must leave your comfort zone! The comfort zone is where dreams go to die!

Another goal with this book is to lay the foundation to accelerate your learning process. Between you and I, the process of a repair is similar no matter what you're restoring. Secure/glue (sometimes), fill (sometimes), sand (sometimes), touch up and apply a finish, that's five steps at most by my count.

Remember, quality of practice, not just quantity, is far more beneficial in expediting your learning. Don't rush, take your time until you get your project just right. The process of touch up is one in which you can theoretically adjust your touch up or color work indefinitely. You can also always remove a failed attempt and start anew.

You can be elite at literally anything by reading, watching, listening and practicing a little every day! I also suggest to always keep an open mind and an eye out for new ideas, suggestions, options, and continually look for additional and/or better information!

That's how I learned. I found people who were better than me and picked up on what they were doing by intently watching, questioning, listening and eventually trying to emulate what they did while performing my own similar tasks.

Hopefully at least I gave you some motivation! I also know that one can either find a way, or an excuse, it depends on how bad you want it. So embrace the initial suck and remember, practice makes permanent!

You're probably wondering what that spiel was about. Well, it was a round-about way of saying that mixing pigments (powdered colors) and properly applying them to a surface, will be one of the more difficult aspects of any repair.

Some artistic talent may help, but you don't need to be an artist or completely understand all aspects of color mixing to have success performing the various restorations you may encounter.

Often, once you become proficient at color matching and repairs in general, clients, friends and family will occasionally refer to you as an artist as they ponder what type of magic you used to make those damages disappear. You'll probably even amaze yourself with what your newfound talent may be able to accomplish in the future.

Learning color theory is important but it can only help to a certain extent. With regard to furniture, you'll seldomly use only primary or secondary pigments, such as red, yellow, blue, orange, etc. as your "base".

Base refers to the initial hue you choose to use, the foundation to which other colors are added, to create your targeted hue. The base hue, for furniture restorations, in most instances, will be a brown, either light, medium or dark. But just being "brown" doesn't suffice, the brown you choose needs to have the proper tone.

Remember what I told you about tone, regarding wood, on page 2? It's the "color", created naturally by the wood alone. Natural wood tones generally vary from a gray or whitish tone, to purpleish, reddish, orangeish, greenish or yellowish and those tones become more prevalent when a clear finish is applied to the wood.

For instance, the two nearly identical oak cabinets to the right have been colored with two different stain formulations. Instead of the more traditional "light oak" cabinet at the top, the bottom cabinet has more of a "walnut" tone.

If I had to perform a repair on either cabinet, the various touch up pigments I would recommend for use on the traditional light oak finish would be completely different from the recommendations I would suggest to match the bottom cabinet, even though they're both oak.

Initially, in your journey restoring various furniture, you will likely find that the "lighter" the wood or finish is, the more difficult the color blending/matching tends to be.

Some of the more difficult repairs I come across may be on woods similar to birch, maple and cherry.

Alternatively, the darker the hue or finish on a piece of furniture, the easier it may be to match.

Just keep in mind that the hue of any particular piece of furniture does not define what material it is made from. Any piece of wood could technically have any hue.

The hue of furniture has several determining factors, most notably, what type of stain was originally used, what type of finish is on it, how much finish is on it, has oxidation affected the hue, how about sun bleaching, chemical bleaching, other factors?

Was it stained traditionally (wipe on oil based stain i.e. Minwax or Varathane), or is the "stain" applied in conjunction with the clear coat (liquid dyes).

If dyes are used within the clear coat, this means the "color" is essentially sprayed on the surface and does not penetrate deep into the wood grain cavities, which may appear different than if an oil base stain was used. Most new mass produced furniture is finished in this manner.

I plan on showing you the process, but I can't always give you the exact formula or color recipes to match the target hues of all the wood variations that you will come across. Initially you'll just use color prediction, or guessing which pigments are needed.

I would initially suggest that if you're fixing a piece of light pine or oak, use a few of your lighter colors/pigments. Conversely, if you're matching a piece of dark mahogany or walnut, it makes sense to start with mostly medium to dark pigments.

Often you can narrow it down even further. For instance, you know that a piece of wood that you are looking at may not really have any red or green in it, so removing a few of the pigments with those undesired warm or cool tones should narrow down even further to which "lighter" pigments you can experiment with (which may occasionally include white).

Even if you're predominantly using light pigments, you may also need darker pigments for the same piece of wood, like a medium or dark brown to match the darker areas/grain line portions of the wood.

Ultimately, color prediction will lead to better color matching being learned through the trial with error method. It should be your goal to learn and understand the hues of various pigments, and when intermixed, what that outcome may be.

Color prediction will lead to color recipes, at least in your mind, they don't need to be written down, but eventually you'll start to remember which pigments were used for various pieces of furniture once you become proficient.

The experience of the colourist will be essential in eventually creating virtually undetectable repairs.

One good place to begin is understanding *"color bias"*. Color bias is the tendency for any particular color to lean towards its neighboring color on any color wheel.

Primary Yellow

For instance, primary yellow cannot lean towards green or orange, it must lie directly in between the two, to be "unbiased".

On an artist color wheel, the only unbiased colors will be the three primary colors, yellow, red and blue.

Does this mean that you only use a primary yellow when you need to add yellow to your color mixture?

Definitely not! Primary yellow often may not be the correct yellow to use. In certain circumstances, it will be overpowering on light woods and it may be too translucent to mix well with darker pigments.

Cadmium Yellow

It's more likely that you will need a "biased" pigment, which consists of more than one hue. You may need to adjust a color mixture with an "orangish yellow" like Cadmium Yellow, a "brownish yellow" like Golden Ochre, or even Buff which is a "whitish yellow".

Golden Ochre

There are several other yellow toned pigments, which we'll go over towards the conclusion of this chapter, but as you can see there are often "different" hues within each pigment.

The only true colors are the three primary, everything else is just a hodgepodge of combined hues, and it's up to you to decipher which hues are required to obtain your targeted color mixture.

Buff

Carbon Black Lamp Black Mars Black

Roman Black Spinel Black Vine Black

Various black pigments are a better example of color bias. If you just had one jar of black pigment in front of you, you'd think, "yep, that's black"!

But if you had six different black pigments, you may be second guessing yourself as to which is truly black.

Carbon black is obtained from the soot of partially combusted hydrocarbons. Carbon black has extreme tinting/hiding power, it's also the "blackest" black of our available pigments

Lamp black is obtained from the soot of burned tar, oil, fat or resin, and can create a bluish to brown tone. Mars black is considered a "warm" black, which means depending on the manufacturer, it may have a yellow to red tone.

Roman black has a subtle brown tone and may appear closer to a charcoal gray rather than a deep black. Spinel black is considered a "cool" black, which means it may have a green to violet tone.

Vine black is made from charing grape vine stalks and twigs, and may have the least tinting/hiding strength of the various blacks, therefore, I consider it a "translucent" black. There are other black variants, each having their own special characteristics.

Don't worry yourself too much about the different blacks unless you're into art or ceramic restorations.

For the majority of repairs I choose between lamp black, carbon black or vine black, using carbon black the vast majority of the time. Just varying the pigment to binder/medium (padding finish) ratio, to adjust the opacity.

Another thing to keep in mind is that the hue of any particular pigment may not be realized without mixing with your medium, in our case, padding finish.

In an example to the right, gray ochre, mixed with padding finish, is significantly darker compared to its dried counterpart. Not every pigment changes this significantly, or even at all.

In my opinion, pigments fall into two categories, translucent or opaque. In general, lighter pigments like yellows and white may require using a larger amount of pigment to give your mixture the proper intensity or covering power that's required.

This can be an issue while repairing white furniture, as white pigment is very translucent and takes massive amounts of pigment to conceal a filled or damaged area.

In this situation, I would recommend using a white toner as your medium instead of padding finish, because the white paint from a spray can will be much more concentrated and opaque, then you can mix your chosen pigment with the white paint to adjust your mixture to your targeted hue.

Conversely, when mixing darker pigments, often an extremely small amount goes a long way, especially with dark browns and various blacks. Usually only dabbing the moistened tip of a paintbrush into the pigment jar will get more than enough pigment for your mixture, maybe you only need a few granules.

Remember, with regard to all pigments, the more you use, in proportion to a medium, the more concentrated/strength/hiding power there will be.

Another important part of the touch up process is comprehending the different techniques of applying these products to a surface, which all play a big role in achieving a great end result to your repair.

A few of the techniques required to apply pigment to a surface, that will be expanded on further throughout the chapter, will include brush application, application with a padding rag and other techniques.

In My Repair Kit™, I keep all the pigments I use in their own individual jars. By doing that, it prevents any cross contamination of colors. An additional positive, is that I can remove from my toolbox only the jars (pigments) required for any particular repair.

If you're the type of person who stays in a shop for work, then a good alternative is to keep your pigments in a sectioned plastic box with a lid similar to the one pictured to the right.

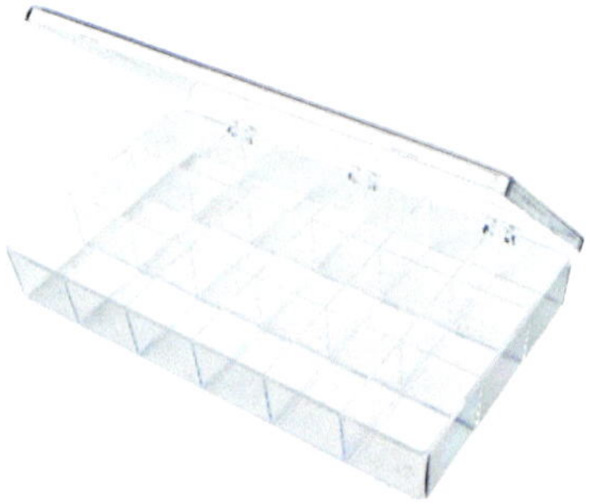

The positive associated with this is all your pigments are easily accessible. The sections have to be permanent though, you can't use one with loose dividers or the fine granulated pigments will cross contaminate.

You can find these at most arts and craft stores, it may also help to search for a "bead storage container".

I wouldn't suggest using a sectioned plastic box with a lid in your everyday travels though, the vibration from driving will cause the fine pigments to shake, become airborne within the container, and migrate/contaminate into the other pigments.

Or goodness forbid you have to slam on the brakes and your tool box takes a tumble, which has definitely happened to me on more than one occasion throughout the years.

This next statement isn't 100% true 100% of the time, but I could semi-confidently say that you should almost never use more than five different colored pigments during any particular wood/furniture restoration project

In the vast majority of restorations, I actually only use three different pigments or less. But that's only true with consideration of furniture restorations, with art, ceramics or other unique repairs, you may need to use your entire available palette.

With regard to furniture, I can't say which five or less pigments are needed, that's project dependent, but often I'm using;

1) The first pigment you will choose to use as your base will be an "earth tone" pigment. Earth tone pigments are derived from soil or minerals and fall into three categories, Ochre, Sienna and Umber.

Ochre pigments consist of ferric oxide, and clay or sand. Ochres often range from yellow to a deep orange or brown. Ochres that contain a large amount of hematite, or dehydrated iron oxide, may have a reddish tone.

Sienna is a soil composed of iron oxide and manganese oxide and can vary from warm to cool.

Fun fact, most pigments from around the world, based on minerals, soils, or clays are often named after the city or region that they were mined.

Sienna is mined in Siena, Italy. Sienna pigment derives its name from the Italian "terra di Siena", translated to, "earth of Siena."

Umber is mined in Umbria, Italy, and can also be found in great concentration in Cyprus. Umber is a sedimentary mineral (rock), which also consists of iron oxide, but has a higher concentration of manganese oxide than sienna.

Pigments high in oxides are generally more opaque with higher tinting power, resulting in deeper, darker hues than most ochre and sienna pigments.

Two of the most frequent pigments used as my base are Burnt Umber or Natural Umber, depending on whether I need to create a warm or cool mixture respectively.

The majority of the time I use burnt umber, but what is burnt umber? "Burnt" refers to when the natural umber pigment is heated/cooked to approximately 600°F.

Umber in its natural state leans more toward green, but after being heated, because of the iron oxide, it transforms to a darker warm brown. You can also achieve a burnt umber hue by mixing more red, than yellow and blue pigments.

If I were to guess, I would estimate that I probably use the burnt umber pigment in 50% of my repairs. Is it because I'm working on a lot of the same color furniture? No, I just really like to use it as my base, everyone has preferences!

Obviously burnt umber is not going to be my base if I'm repairing something light like pine or maple, but on most medium and darker, brown furniture I may use it.

Two other pigments that also work well as a base are Natural Sienna or Burnt Sienna. Natural sienna has a more yellowish tone and may be useful on woods like Oak or teak.

When natural sienna is heated, just as with umber, a slight reddish/orange tone from the iron oxide exposes itself.

Burnt sienna is also a highly used pigment and may be a good base when repairing walnut or brown mahogany furniture.

Just remember, when initially choosing an earth tone pigment to use as your base color, try to pick one closest to the hue and tone of your project.

2) The second pigment(s) that you will choose will be a primary or secondary color like red, orange, yellow, blue, green or some combination of two of them to further assist in matching a wood tone.

I find that I most often use only the orange pigment, followed by red, then yellow. Blue and green are among my least used pigments of all time, but that doesn't mean I never use them!

An example of when I would use one or two of these primary or secondary pigments, is if I wanted to adjust a base pigment to a hue that matches closer to our project, or to cancel/mute another particular hue.

For example, if using a red toned pigment, I may incorporate the pigments orange, yellow or a combination of the two, to "lighten" the red pigment mixture. If I were to use a white pigment in an attempt to lighten a red, that would turn the mixture pink, which is almost never a suitable hue for wood restoration.

It's also often necessary to use these secondary pigments as highlights when duplicating the pattern of wood during a restoration.

3) Black is the third most highly used pigment, I have it out for virtually every repair. Black is considered a shade, which helps to either darken or reduce the intensity of any particular hue.

Taking the example of a red pigment again, if I were to add only black pigment, that usually creates a near perfect match on mahogany that is dark red or some rosewood furniture.

Depending on the ratios of pigments (red and black), you can vary the hue from light to dark, allowing you to produce all aspects of the wood and grain pattern.

In that instance, it's possible that only two pigments may be utilized during an entire repair, without a "brown" pigment ever involved, but if I needed to "lighten" that mixture, I would likely add more red than black, or add a few granules of orange pigment.

So ideally, that's three different pigments or less, and often with only these few pigments, I can usually duplicate the varied tone/hue and grain pattern on any single piece of wood.

4) A fourth pigment you may need could be a darker brown pigment like Burnt Umber Extra Dark, which will usually be far darker than the pigment we chose as our base.

It is often necessary to use secondary dark brown pigment to duplicate the darker areas of grain, to recreate knots or replace distressing present in the surface.

Take this example of oak to the left, aside from having a large gouge, you can see there is a great contrast between the lighter and darker areas of wood and grain.

In this case, my initial chosen base pigment (step 1) would be something light, like natural sienna, but I'll also need a darker pigment to simulate the dark grain lines.

Even with a darker brown, it may still be necessary to mix with your primary or secondary pigments to adjust the hue or tone to match your project.

5) A fifth and final pigment could be any other random pigment that may have a special characteristic that may assist with obtaining the targeted hue.

For example, white is used often to lighten another hue. White is most often used when repairing light woods similar to birch or maple, but realistically, I may only use white in one out of fifty repairs that I complete (that isn't a white piece of furniture of course).

When repairing light furniture, a pigment I prefer in place of white, in certain circumstances, would be Buff (right).

Buff has a light creamy yellowish-brown hue, which in my opinion, also has a whitish tone.

Plum (left) or violet, could be useful for repair of purpleheart, rosewood or some mahoganies, if the wood projects a purplish tone.

There are numerous other pigments available, but the point is, no repair on a singular piece of wood furniture should ever require like ten different pigments.

Remember, subtractive and additive color mixing from the second chapter? Certain hues will offset/cancel other particular hues, and mixing too many hues together in general, often will lead to a grayish muddled mess.

My second bit of advice, if you're obtaining your own repair pigments, there are several different manufacturers, and some manufacturers may name a jar of pigment to depict a certain tree species like walnut, oak, cherry or pine.

Just because a pigment is named after a particular type of wood, doesn't mean that you will necessarily use that specific pigment for the repair you are working on, even if it is a piece of walnut, oak, cherry or pine. The hue or tone may be different in the wood, than what that specific pigment produces.

As an example, If you are repairing a piece of walnut furniture, you may not open or use a "walnut" pigment, you may use only black and orange pigments or some other combination.

Secondly, there could be several different "types" of a certain pigment, for instance, when referring to a "walnut" pigment. There could be Light walnut, Medium Dark walnut, Medium Brown walnut, Universal walnut, Extra Dark walnut, and others I'm sure, each creating a noticeably different hue.

Each example I just gave you is a different Blendal® Powder Stain, available through Mohawk® Finishing Products. So that's one manufacturer with five very different "walnut" pigments available.

As I've mentioned, there really isn't an exact formulation of pigments that I can give you, the issue is that most woods are not one uniform color. The grain of different woods can consist of dramatically different light and dark areas, or at the least, have some variation.

Additionally, stain formulations, finishes, damages, fading from direct sunlight, and a host of other variables all have an effect on the appearance of any piece of furniture or wood.

The hue can even vary greatly from the left side and right side of a single piece of furniture, so there will rarely be a one color fits all approach, this isn't an infomercial!

Don't fret though, as you've already read about a few varying pigments or pigment recipes throughout this chapter, as we proceed I will continue with suggestions on which pigments to use for repairs of various common wood types.

Let's attempt a repair on this mahogany buffet, which has a large filled gouge on the right side of the top, accompanied by some additional damages along the front edge.

After filling and sanding any damages, I recommend using your padding finish and padding cloth to french polish and apply some finish to the surface. This not only removes any sanding dust, it also begins to fill in the shallow scratches left by the sandpaper while also allowing you to evaluate the proper hue or tone of your project so you can proceed with mixing pigments.

One common issue I see when people first attempt touch ups, is that they try to mix up the perfect color and apply it with a brush in one fell swoop as a complete repair.

Keep in mind, this is a process of layering your touch up, and it may not be until closer to the conclusion of a repair that the damaged area starts to blend well with the existing surface.

The pigments I used for this repair are burnt umber, orange, red and carbon black. I usually begin the touch up process by attempting to match the lightest color of the wood. In this instance, the hue I want to match is the lighter, reddish-orangish grain.

On my palette, I mix a small amount of padding finish with a few granules of orange and red and with my first few strokes from my paintbrush, I lay down the mixture onto the surface.

Once the base color is applied, I'll add a squirt of padding finish to the palette and add a few granules of burnt umber and carbon black to darken the mixture. Then with the paintbrush, apply some darker grain lines as your second layer.

It will take additional recharging of your pigment mixture to continue painting on the layers of pigment. The third picture above may not look very good yet. There will be further blending as we proceed through the repair, you are also seeing the applied pigment start to dry out, becoming dull.

The padding finish and pigment mixture dries pretty fast once applied to a surface. This may inhibit you from seeing the intricacy of your pigment application, but once you apply some type of clear finish like slightly misting over the area with a clear satin toner or french polishing with a padding rag and padding finish, you will again see the intricacy of the varied hues and grain patterns that you've applied.

In fact, that's what I did. First, I lightly misted a coat of clear satin toner, and allowed that to dry for a few minutes. I then used the padding finish to charge the padding rag and with light pressure, french polished over the surface.

In the third picture, I'm applying additional layers of pigment with a paintbrush, alternating short choppy strokes of light and dark hues, in an attempt to further break up and disguise the filled damage.

Once satisfied with the pigment that's been applied, seal in all your hard work with some clear toner, let that dry for five or ten minutes.

Once dry you should be able to wipe your hand over the surface, it should not be sticky or soft. This is going to be the last time that I use a clear toner during this restoration, and the reason is twofold.

First, the original surface of this buffet has a semi-gloss sheen and I have the ability to complete the touch up and reproduce the original sheen to completion by french polishing alone.

Secondly, when spraying a toner onto a surface, even though you are applying a protective coating over your touch up, the atomization from the spray nozzle may leave the surface slightly rough. Make sure to never spray a toner, clear or colored, in a heavily concentrated, soaking manner.

Roughness could present itself for two reasons, first it could just be overspray, but secondly, remember, pigment doesn't dissolve in most mediums, so you may be feeling slight granules of pigment.

When building pigment onto a surface, if you feel the surface is raised or rough, you may have to use a fine grit sandpaper (600+ w/d) to smooth it out. Be sure to only glide the sandpaper over the surface or you may be removing some of your applied pigment.

The second option is to use a padding rag and padding finish, and lightly french polish the area. Be cautious not to have your padding rag too wet or apply too much pressure, as it may also soften or remove what you have already applied.

If you chose to sand the area, like I did in the pictures to the right, you'll again have to french polish the area to fill and remove the scratches created from the sandpaper.

How's it looking? I felt I needed a few more alternating grain lines both, orangish-red highlights and dark grain.

At this juncture, the applied touch up should be close to concealing the filled damage. The last color blending technique I recommended for this restoration is to apply padding finish to your padding rag, dip your finger slightly into the various pigment jars that you are using and blend the individual colors together on the surface of your padding rag.

Be sure to rub the pigments into the rag well, you don't want any highly concentrated areas, you also shouldn't want a large amount of pigment to transfer from the rag to the surface.

Think of it as though you're trying to apply the pigment in a translucent manner. Using your french polishing techniques, extend the application at least a few inches in each direction over the repaired area, while maintaining the east to west motion, in line with the grain pattern.

This last step of color mixing is not always necessary, depending how well you are able to blend your pigments with a paintbrush application. Just be conscious that the more pigment you use on your rag, the more covering/hiding power, which could lead to an opaque, muddled finish.

The repair now should be looking pretty good, but you've really only focused on the six to eight inches around the repaired area. To finalize the repair you need to ensure that the finish and sheen are consistent throughout the surface of the buffet.

Using your padding rag, padding finish and the french polishing techniques learned in the french polishing chapter, proceed to french polish the entire top.

This repair took over an hour and a half, and we were able to charge more than a few hundred bucks.

This is acceptable in most cases because the majority of "woodworkers" don't have the ability to spot repair.

You would think the two would go hand in hand, but most craftspeople/companies would need to refinish this buffet (or at least the top). You are learning a very specialized skill!

In reality, we saved the client $500 minimum, compared to refinishing the top only, which most companies would likely charge $700-$1000+. Aside from the savings, the client was extremely happy that their piece of furniture never had to leave their humble abode.

We got sidetracked from our conversation about pigments. Organic pigments may have some variation in hue or tone, depending on manufacturer or location mined, after all it's often a natural product.

These two pigments are from different manufacturers, but they are both labeled as the color Mars Yellow. As you can tell, even in their dry form, they have very different tones.

Mars yellow in general is an orangish-yellow, but as you may notice, the pigment on the right has a more orangish tone, while the pigment on the left has a more yellowish tone.

If a pigment is made synthetically it can be produced in the consistent color the manufacturer is attempting to create using a universal coloring system.

In 1925, the American Association of Textile Chemists, and the Society of Dyers and Colourists, published the Color Index, which is an international database of pigments and dyes.

The same hue may be given several different generic names depending on who's fabricating, but the standardized system created by the Color Index allows for the uniformity among all the different manufacturers, so the consumer always knows the consistency of the hue they are acquiring.

For pigments, manufacturers use Pigment Index Codes. Those codes are; PB Pigment Blue, PBk Pigment Black, PBr Pigment Brown, PG Pigment Green, PM Pigment Metal, PO Pigment Orange, PR Pigment Red, PV Pigment Violet, PW Pigment White, PY Pigment Yellow, accompanied with a number.

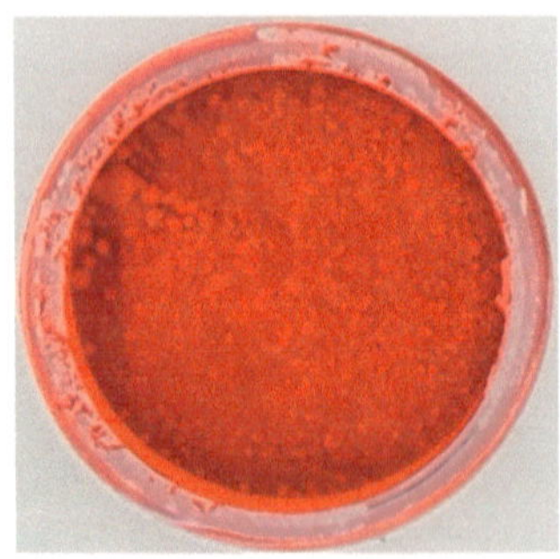

As an example, Pyrrole Red's pigment index code is PR-254. This translates to Pigment Red, and the #254 refers to two hundred and fifty fourth "red" on the Color Index list.

So everytime you see the code PR-254, no matter the name on the container, you can rest assured that you are acquiring the red that you desire.

It doesn't always work that way though. As an example, Sienna's pigment index code is PBr-7. Due to variations in the iron oxide, the hue can vary from a yellowish to reddish brown, and also can be manipulated by heat.

This means burnt sienna, natural sienna, burnt umber, natural umber and several other "brown's" may have the same pigment code (PBr-7), even though they have vastly different hues.

Some of the most useful hues, which should be considered mandatory for furniture repairs are yellow, orange, red, blue, green, black, white, burnt and natural sienna, along with burnt and natural umber.

Of the above-named pigments, I suggest having a few variations. For the yellow family I may include: primary yellow, yellow oxide, light yellow ochre and buff. That would be four variations of yellow, spanning varied tones.

There are other yellows, this is where preference comes in, other pigments in the yellow family are amber ochre dunkel, dark yellow ochre or natural yellow, among many others. You'll eventually choose which pigments you prefer.

Orange has only two options which I use regularly. A standard orange, which is almost fluorescent. The second being mars yellow, which as we talked about, could be more orangish, than yellow.

As far as reds are concerned, I suggest having a bright red, like pyrrole red, and a "dull" red like red ochre, which has a brownish tone. Other reds include cadmium red, rose earth, natural red, and venetian red among others.

Blue and green are used very rarely, in furniture restoration. I suggest having at least one version of each, but usually having a light and dark version would allow you to better match more hues.

You can usually get away with using only one black, just make sure it's clean crisp black with no gray or brown tones, my favorite is carbon black. There's also only one white I suggest, titanium dioxide.

As far as browns are concerned, the siennas and umbers listed above have light, medium, dark and even some extra dark versions. There are other browns with varied hues or tones like van dyke brown, dark neutral brown, brown ochre, and many more.

Don't be afraid to experiment and see what hue can be made when combining different pigments, I call this predictive processing, or guessing which hues are needed to hit a target color.

Once you get acquainted with the hue each pigment produces, you will have favoritism towards various pigments when used in certain circumstances on similar wood repairs, eventually allowing you to reduce the amount of pigments needed in your palette.

At the end of this chapter you'll see visual samples of all the pigments that were aforementioned, and more!

Just because you mixed pigments together, in an attempt of a repair, doesn't mean you need to use the mixture, wipe off your palette and start anew if it's going in the wrong direction.

Let's start at the beginning of one more repair project, with a little more detail about the process. We'll use the piece of oak that had a gouge on it from earlier in this chapter.

Let's say you have already filled and sanded a gouge on the surface of a piece of furniture.

Also notice that in the majority of repair examples, when the filler has been sanded level, the surface has not been sanded "through" (down to the bare wood), in the area surrounding the filler.

That's why it's suggested not to use sandpaper under 400 grit when sanding on a finished surface, rougher sandpaper will "cut" the existing finish too fast, while also leaving deep sanding scratches.

Deep sanding scratches cannot be removed without sanding further with an even finer grit sandpaper, thus creating an even larger area of damage.

It's not always possible, but it is always beneficial to try and keep the area surrounding the damage as minimally affected as possible, even if it does take longer to sand with a finer grit.

First thing, after filling and sanding damage, is to french polish the area of repair to fill in and remove the majority of the sanding scratches caused by the sandpaper.

You only need to french polish the area of sanding, there is no need to extend to the rest of the surface yet.

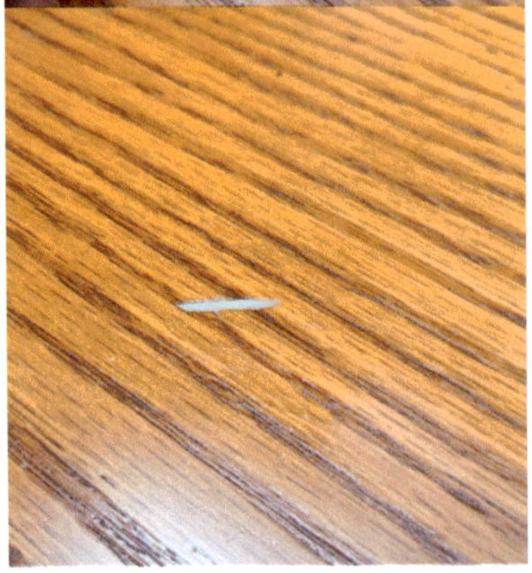

Give the area about 10-20 brisk swipes, mainly just on the sanding scratches, with light to medium weight of hand, with a light to medium amount of padding finish, well distributed in a padding rag. This should take you 10 seconds, give or take.

After french polishing, the area may be glossy, possibly far glossier than the surrounding surface. As we proceed through the repair we'll be using a few techniques to get the sheen more consistent with the existing surrounding surface.

Start with less padding finish on your padding rag until you get comfortable with the results of the varying amounts you are applying. One of the only consequences with using less finish, is it may take slightly longer to build a substantial finish onto the surface.

As you're french polishing, look at the reflections of light on the surface across the damaged area, you should literally see the sanding scratches start to fill in and begin to dissipate or disappear with each additional swipe.

Also by removing the majority of the sanding scratches by french polishing, it not only smooths out the surface, but you'd now be able to see the true color of the area you are working on.

Initially, not every single area needs to be perfectly french polished, without sanding scratches, as you will be building up more finish as you proceed through a repair. Primarily our initial goal is to remove the "white halo" around the damaged area caused by the initial sandpaper scratches.

From this point we need our "palette" that we use to mix our pigments on, we'll refer to it as the "pigment palette".

I've included a pigment palette in every My Repair Kit™. Forgive me for saying pigment palette so many times, as we proceed through this chapter.

You can reuse the glass palette indefinitely, because once you're finished with your project, you can easily clean the glass with a rag and solvent like denatured alcohol or lacquer thinner, so it's ready for your next project.

I don't suggest using the pigment palette to mix Bondo® or epoxy, unless you clean the glass palette completely while the product is still wet, as once those products cure/dry they are very hard to remove the remnants.

All of my career, even to this day, I use the rear of a piece of *used* sandpaper to mix filler and glue on.

For mixing pigments, if you don't have a piece of glass or some other non porous item, I suggest using the rear of a piece of wet/dry sandpaper. Wet/Dry sandpaper is essentially liquid proof, nothing will soak through it, making an ideal disposable palette.

Now you'll need your chosen pigments. For this piece of oak, I chose Natural Sienna (top right), Yellow Oxide (bottom right), Buff (top center), orange (bottom left) and Burnt Umber Extra Dark (top left).

Notice, that's five pigments, I'll use two or three specifically for the grain lines, and two or three to match the lighter hues of the wood.

We started with our padding rag and padding finish, chose our pigments, have our pigment palette, the other items we'll need for this repair is a can of clear satin toner and a paintbrush.

Since we're on the topic of paint brushes, any artist will tell you that a quality brush makes a big difference. If you've ever been to an art supply store, then you may have noticed hundreds if not thousands of paint brushes, so which one should we use?

Brushes come in several different sizes, ranging from #0000-#30, there are other sizes, but these will be the most common.

Brushes also will have either natural or synthetic bristles. I prefer brushes with sable hair.

With brushes, you get what you pay for. Cheap brushes work, but they will not last long and may easily fray or lose bristles fairly fast. Most of the brushes I use fall within the $10-$20 range.

There are two types of paint brushes I use regularly, I always carry a flat brush (above) in the #10 - #16 size range. Flat brushes are ideal to spread paint quickly and evenly over a large surface area.

I also carry round brush (below), usually in the #6 - #8 size range. Round brushes have a pointed tip and long closely arranged bristles, great for painting details, like simulating a wood pattern, grain, knots or distressing.

I would say that I use only a round brush on 90+% of repairs, from start to finish. Performing multiple repairs a day, a good brush may last at least four to six months, depending how well you care for it.

Hopefully, the majority of damages that you will attempt repairs on, will not be a huge area, most of the time you'll be working on damages that may only be a couple inches in diameter or less.

I would suggest trying multiple types of brushes. Use whichever brush or brushes you are more comfortable with, there is a vast array on the market to choose from.

An example of another useful brush would be a "Rigger Brush" (right), which is a round brush with extra long hairs. Rigger brushes got their name because they were traditionally used for painting the rigging of ships, in paintings.

Rigger brushes are known for their precise control. Using different sizes, you can paint even the finest detail into your repairs, like painting fine lines similar to grains of wood, or recreating detailed artwork on a damaged ceramic vase

Each brush type has a unique way of applying paint to a surface, which in some instances may be more beneficial than your standard flat or round brushes.

Now that we've determined we're using a round brush, initially squirt some padding finish onto the clean pigment palette, dip your brush into the newly poured padding finish and give it a few swirls to loosen the bristles of your brush.

Now that the tip of the brush is wet, dip it in your first pigment and pick up some pigment from the container and mix with the padding finish.

The more pigment used, the more concentrated a color will be. Sometimes you need a high concentration of pigment to hide things. This is considered opaque.

Other times you may want a previous layer to show through. Using less pigment to padding finish ratio will create a translucent/transparent paint.

Lighter pigments in general, tend to be more translucent than darker pigments. White and light yellow pigments often tend to be the most translucent.

Learning and observing a pigment's hue, tone, opacity or transparency enables you, the artist, to have greater command over techniques like optical color matching and layering.

Now swirl your pigment filled brush with the padding finish on the pigment palette. Is that the color you need/want? Remember, I usually always begin my touch up, attempting to match some of the lightest hues of the surface.

It's possible you need to modify the mixture a little, so you dip your brush into the second jar of pigment, add that to your mixture and swirl your paintbrush around to blend the two together. Is it looking closer to the right hue now?

There's no need to clean your brush between the dippings in the different jars of pigments, as the pigment generally only sticks to the wet brush tip so there shouldn't be much if any transfer of pigment from the brush into the differing pigment jars, as long as your brush tip isn't overly wet and dripping.

Maybe from here you think your pigment mixture is close and you proceed to apply your mixture to an area of damage that you are working on.

Does it look bad or is it blending fairly well? It's often better to err on the side of lightness rather than dark.

Always apply your touch up in the direction of the grain, applying color across the grain pattern may be apparent because you may see the pattern of your brush stroke going in that particular direction.

This initial application of pigment is to remove the gray hue of the filler, also, try to keep the applied pigment thin. You don't want a mound of finish and pigment protruding from the surface, or your repair will be lumpy in that area. A "drier" brush will transfer paint in a more minimal manner.

At this point it may have taken too long to mix all your pigments and the pigment mixture may be starting to dry out. Give another squirt of padding finish to the pigment palette.

Swirl your brush around to mix in the new padding finish with what you had on the pigment palette originally. Is your color too translucent now from the added padding finish?

You may then have to add some additional pigment from the pigment jars that you are currently using, trying to keep the color mixture consistent with what you need, so you can continue your touch up. Or maybe you need to tweak the color again?

You're going to be adding various pigments together all the time, often in differing amounts. For example, you may mix more yellow oxide than natural sienna, even adding a third pigment like buff.

The amount of pigment that you use from the various jars does not have to be equal. Think of it in "parts", I used two parts yellow oxide and one part natural sienna and a granule of buff, to obtain the hue I require.

Just like you recharge your padding rag when french polishing, you always need to recharge, or add more padding finish to your pigment palette, so you can continue to perform the various touch ups.

When mixing pigments with padding finish, your mixture normally may only last a few minutes till it dries out. Other mediums may stay in liquid form longer than others.

As you touch up a wood surface, your color mixture that you've applied may also tend to look "dried out". This happens because the pigment is insoluble, it doesn't dissolve in any medium.

When mixing pigments, padding finish is known as being a "binder", which means the sole purpose of the padding finish is to bind/adhere the pigment granules to a surface.

As the padding finish dries on the surface, it re-exposes the pigment granules, though this time, the pigment is bonded.

The picture to the right is a different table, but it's an example of what dried pigment on a surface looks like.

There will often be times when you pause the touch up process, so that you can add some finish over the pigment, either with a clear toner, a colored toner, or you may gently french polish the area with your padding rag.

The latter option is what I suggest most often, but it could remove the applied touch up if it hasn't dried sufficiently, your padding rag is too wet, or you're using too much downward pressure. There's a delicate balance you'll have to decipher.

If the applied pigment on the surface is too rough, it's possible to slightly sand the area with some 600 grit wet/dry sandpaper, using only the lightest pressure so as not to remove any of the applied color. Once sanded, you'll need to french polish the area again creating hopefully a smooth surface.

You can do this step at any time throughout the touch up process to seal in the pigment you've applied. Adding finish over the pigment, creates a sheen, making the area no longer appear dried out.

How's the touch up blending to this point? I'm sure the damage hasn't disappeared yet, but If the area is starting to blend in with the surrounding surface, it may be time to start adding grain to further disguise the damage.

To break up the first bit of touch up that you performed, this is where we incorporate darker pigments to match the darker grain pattern.

For this project, to match the dark grain, I chose natural sienna and burnt umber extra dark. It is possible you may also incorporate a granule or two from the orange or yellow pigment to get the right tone of the darker grain pattern.

I didn't use black pigment for this repair but often I find that matching the grain may only consist of black and either a light, medium or dark brown.

When painting in the dark grain pattern, I like my paintbrush tip to be fairly dry, so after swirling the brush in the mixture, I'll apply a few strokes from the brush onto the back of a piece of used sandpaper to remove most of the liquid off of the brush tip before I continue to touch up.

The purpose of removing the majority of liquid from the tip of the brush is to control the thickness of the grain lines. Remember a dryer brush will apply pigment more sparingly.

If a brush tip is too wet, it will apply the pigment in a thick manner and you can easily lose control of your preciseness, or I suppose you can always use a paintbrush with a very small tip.

I recommend using short choppy brush strokes, the short choppy strokes help to mimic the choppiness of the grain pattern in the wood, most wood grain does not have long continuous lines.

Numerous times, once I feel a repair gets to the final stages, I may look at it and realize it may just need one small light grain line here or there to disguise the repair even further.

Is it time to seal in your color work again? French polish or mist some clear satin toner over the repaired area.

At this juncture, your repaired area should be looking pretty good. If the color still isn't precisely right you may need to continue mixing various colors to blend the area even more.

Think about the application of the color in the same way you would if you were painting an oil painting or something similar, an artist usually has to build color up in several different layers until eventually they get it to look just right.

You may get to this point and look at the repaired area and think, "it's good, but it's just not perfect yet". First, there is no such thing as perfect, with almost anything in life, so get that word out of your head.

Like the late great Vince Lombardi once said; "perfection is not attainable, but if we chase perfection, we can catch excellence!"

There may always be room for improvement. Remember, this is a repair, the whole point is to disguise damage so well that your eyes do not notice the repaired area as you look at the surface. Basically you're trying to trick everyone into, not seeing something that is there.

For this repair it wasn't necessary, but there is another technique of color blending and that is to use your padding rag and french polishing techniques. We did it in the previous repair to the mahogany buffet.

With some padding finish applied to your padding rag, rub it slightly to moisten the tip of your finger, then dip the tip into the canisters of pigment, and rub/blend the pigments together onto the surface of the rag.

You should already know the approximate combination of pigments you need from mixing them with your paintbrush.

This is where I also would suggest wearing gloves, for safety reasons, and your fingers may be multi-colored and/or your skin may be irritated by the end of the day, if sensitive.

Depending on how translucent or opaque you need the color, that will depend on how much pigment you apply to your padding rag, but don't go overboard, you already have the repaired area looking pretty good!

Basically you're trying to not only further blend pigments on the surface, but you're also feathering out the damaged area, in an effort to conceal any line of demarcation between the repair and the existing surface.

Most often you'll want to apply the pigment to the rag sparingly as to be able to apply in a translucent manner, applying pigment too heavy will possibly lead to depositing an area of too much solid color to an area, reducing definition of the grain pattern, which may in turn make the repaired area more apparent.

You may need to add another squirt of padding finish onto the rag, in between the addition of more than one pigment. I then rub the padding rag with my finger or into my palm to ensure the pigment is evenly mixed and distributed through the surface of the padding rag.

The padding rag shouldn't be "very dry", you need it to have some moisture to easily glide over the surface, a rag too dry may not transfer the pigment properly to the surface, and of course be cautious not to make your rag too wet!

With pigment on your rag, and light pressure, begin to stroke back and forth over the repaired area, possibly only a few inches over and around the circumference of the repair, inline with the grain pattern, until blended even further.

At this moment I would think that the concealment of the damage is complete and the last issue is to ensure the sheen is consistent throughout the surface. This may be a good time to apply a clear satin toner to seal in the repaired area. Let it dry well.

If you applied the toner well, the restoration may be complete. If the surface is slightly rough, on a satin sheen surface, you may with light pressure glide over the surface with #0000 steel wool, a technique we talked about in the last chapter.

At this juncture your repair should be complete and looking very good! If this is your first time and it's not very good, don't fret, you should have at least learned some new techniques that in conjunction with practice, only leaves room for improvement!

If you're not happy with the area and think you can attempt further improvement, once dry, simply sand with 600 grit w/d sandpaper, which will remove as many layers of pigment as you need, then start the process over.

You're never stuck with an end result, that's the beauty of a repair, you can work on an area indefinitely till you get it right. Just remember to always let the area dry sufficiently before you re-attempt further repairs.

A third way to apply pigment, which is my least used method, but does come in handy occasionally is to dip the tip of your finger into the canister of pigment, collect a minimal amount of pigment onto your finger and then wipe over the surface, like finger painting

This in theory is virtually the same thing as applying the pigment with a rag, but this option applies pigment to a surface more translucent. You definitely have to french polish or spray a toner over the pigment if you use this technique because the pigment has no other way of bonding to a surface.

What has been described throughout the last several pages is in my opinion, the best techniques for application of pigments to conceal any damage.

Another way to conceal damage is if there are unique characteristics on a surface. Knots can be reproduced, or there may be "dots" or "lines", often referred to as "distressing" or "splatter". It's wise to use distressing to your advantage while performing repairs.

To recreate the splatter effect, I suggest that you use a paint brush with a larger tip of bristles. Wet the tip of the brush with padding finish or another binder, mixed with the proper pigment, then abruptly hit the paintbrush on a dowel rod, which flings the little dots everywhere.

Ensure your work area is covered or protected, as you don't want little dark spots to inadvertently land all over your carpet, floor or walls.

You may also use a toothbrush, which makes a phenomenal launching pad. Wet the head, and stroke your finger across the bristles of the brush so that the paint will fly off and land on the surface.

The more wet the brush tip is the larger the distressing and/or the more concentrated the splatter dots may be. Conversely the less wet the tip of your brush is, the smaller or less concentrated the distressing dots.

Flicking the paint onto the surface in this manner will leave rough or high areas where the new distressing is applied. After the spots have thoroughly dried, take a piece of 600 grit sandpaper and just slightly skim over the surface with very minimal pressure to knock down any high variations on the surface.

As long as you don't sand with too much pressure, the distressing will remain on the surface, and you can begin to french polish the surface again, you shouldn't remove the color work and you will be able to create a smooth consistent sheen.

It may be possible that you will have to perform this process of sanding and applying the padding finish more than once to create a flat smooth surface.

Hopefully with my guidance, I've laid the groundwork, giving you the ability to perform a satisfactory cosmetic repair, but ultimately if the repair is not turning out well, you may have to bite the bullet and refinish the affected area.

There are a lot of situations where a piece of furniture has gone past the point of being "repairable", but If you become competent at color matching with stains and/or dyes, you may be able to refinish just the affected surface in question without refinishing the entire piece.

Learning this ability is essential if you are working with insurance companies (movers and property agents), as they will not want to pay for refinishing an entire piece of furniture if, for example, just the left side panel is affected.

On a different note, you won't often be repairing items made of real metal, but you will often come across a piece of furniture or ceramic which may have metal colored accents or possibly even entire scenes painted depicting scenes from one's culture.

PM or pigment metals are basically the same as all the other pigments, but instead of being soils or clays, they consist of finely ground powdered metals, which can be mixed with a binder, like padding finish.

Other binders may be infused waxes, like Rub 'n Buff® or Treasure Gold®.

Brushable paint, like Brush 'n Leaf®, toners, or spray paint, and many other options!

From here on out, I may only refer to "gold" but that reference can be interchanged with any type of metal, silver, pewter, bronze, just to name a few.

What if that secretary on the previous page had a large gouge in the center of the lid, through the scene, and you're tasked with repairing it?

First thing I'd recommend is to take a picture with your phone so you know what the area looked like originally, before you touch it.

You know the basics, fill and sand the damage level to the surface, but try to keep the sanding to a minimum, as you want to affect the surrounding painted scene as minimally as possible.

Now to recreate the scene, good thing we took that picture, just in case there were some small details we forgot about.

Just as with "colored" pigments, you may also need a diverse collection of metal pigment hues, waxes, toners, or a combination of several products to match your targeted hue.

Just having one type of gold or silver may not suffice to match all projects.

Pigment metals, in powder form, are often combined with mica. Mica is a natural mineral which has a "glassy" shine. The mineral is mined then finely ground into a powder and combined with various pigment metals.

The "glassy" shine of the mica is what is used to try to replicate the reflection of real metal, unlike most other pigments which are inherently matte.

Unfortunately, metal hues are one of the most difficult things to match on a true metal surface. What is a true metal surface?

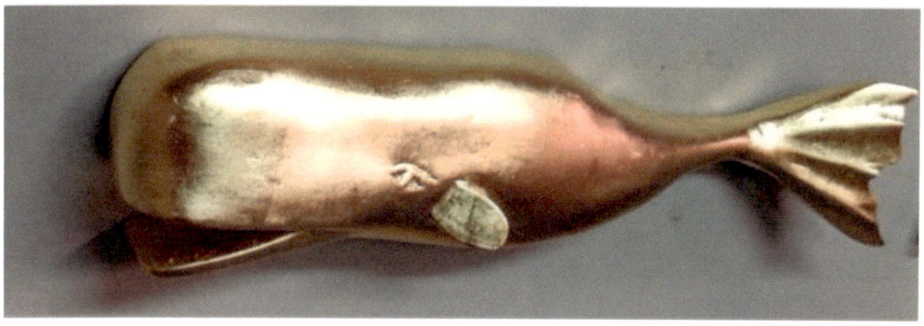

You will find some items that have gold leaf (or another metal). Using pigments, waxes, toners, or other mediums will never match authentic metal leaf.

If you have to fix something with a real gold leaf, you are going to need to replace it with a real gold leaf, or you'll just be trying to match it as best as possible by any means necessary.

Often you can tell if something has an authentic gold leaf, because other than being quite a bit more reflective than a painted surface, the leaf is generally installed in small squares, about six inches squared, give or take, with each square slightly overlapping the subsequent squares throughout a surface.

Items that have a consistent hue throughout and lack the individual squares, are most often just painted gold, and you would have a far better chance of matching those.

When it comes to actual real metal leaf, flakes, gilding supplies and metal pigments, I suggest checking out Sepp Leaf Products™. They also provide pearl and iridescent pigments.

Another item I have found that makes adding metal highlights a breeze, are metallic paint pens. They allow us to bypass taping off the entire surface, and it's easy to apply the paint in an even, consistent manner, compared to using a paintbrush or toner.

It’s also fun to add unique touches to any item by using stencils (below).

One tricky area we haven’t quite expanded on yet is painted furniture, or furniture that is a solid color, rather than wood traditionally stained and finished.

When something is a solid color, say red, turquoise, gray, etc., there is really no room for error when mixing colors to match. The color mixture has to be precise. If the color mixture is even slightly off, your repair may stick out like a sore thumb.

For instance, this dresser had the right side, rear framing split almost in half, from top to bottom. First thing to do is glue up and reinforce the broken areas, and fill any additional gouging or damage to the top.

After gluing, filling, and sanding the damage, it would be near impossible to repaint these damaged areas using the standard touch up methods you’ve learned throughout this chapter.

If there is significant damage to a solid colored painted piece, we’ll usually quote to repaint the entire item. Hopefully you have a good local paint shop that has the ability to match virtually any color, which thankfully, we do.

When obtaining custom color matches there may be additional fees to have the color mixed. Often it’s mixed, by hand, using only the eye of the master mixer. So just keep that in mind when quoting to repaint an item.

To the right is the freshly repaired, painted and delivered dresser.

Additionally, never go to the hardware store and get standard house paint. Even though they may be able to hit the target hue, house paint is not durable enough to be used on furniture.

Off white is likely the most common painted furniture color you may come across. Off white is essentially that, white with something else in it. Often it's not a primary or secondary color that is needed to be mixed with white to hit the target hue, usually it's just a granule or two of a particular brown, you'll just need to decipher which tone.

Unlike custom painted items, I can often perform repairs without completely repainting off white items,

In the pictures below, you can see the front left corner has a large section broken out. The middle picture is a close up, showing the damaged area filled.

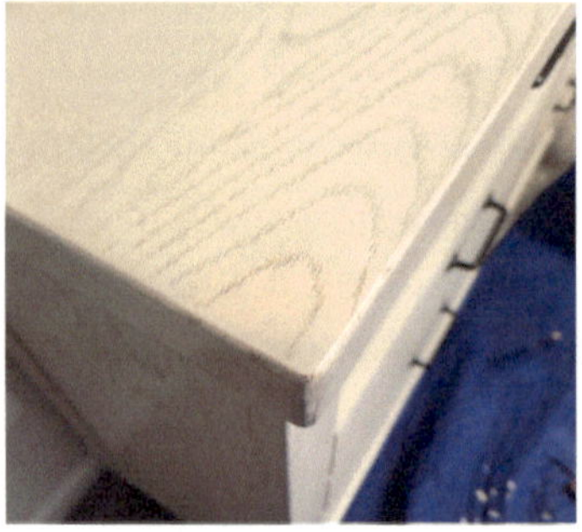

This third picture is the complete repair, which took a little over an hour. I only used two pigments, white and burnt umber, I was even able to replicate the grain using only those two pigments.

For repairs of white/off white furniture, I may substitute white pigment and padding finish with a satin white toner. Using a toner produces a more opaque pure white, which will help to conceal damage faster.

Additionally, I'll use the toner as my base/binder for my pigment mixture to hit the targeted hue because, in my opinion, the padding finish has a slight golden tint which may throw off the hue.

You may also spray a good amount of white toner onto a padding rag, blend other pigments onto the rag, and apply the color to a surface using the french polishing technique to further feather and disguise damage on a surface.

For the remainder of this chapter, I wanted to expand on all the various pigments that I keep in my arsenal. Some of these pigments are used daily, some monthly, some annually, maybe even once a decade, but all the pigments will have their time to shine at some point, during some repair, somewhere, just have faith!

I've grown to restore many more unique items other than just wood, so having all these various pigments allows me to match virtually any hue. It's beneficial to be prepared for any unique restoration that may arise.

A traditional "woodworkers" palette may only consist of ⅓ of all these pigments. For all other times you'll be wondering why the heck you're carrying around so many pigments that you hardly ever use.

My reason is I like options. Some hues may be similar or seem slightly redundant, but each hue is unique in some way.

There may be pigments added or subtracted to this palette, so this may not even be a full comprehensive list by the time you are reading this chapter.

There are legitimately hundreds if not thousands of dry pigment hues available, these are the ones I prefer to use. Feel free to discover other pigments that may be useful towards your palette, good luck mixing!

All further pictures are just approximations of each pigment's hue, accompanied with a brief description. Camera lenses, lights, pictures in books, pictures on digital screens do not always capture a pigment's hue in the same way as it would be visualized in person.

These pigments further are described in alphabetical order, and not every pigment is available in each variation of My Repair Kit™. Please check the website for a cornucopia of package details.

Pigments in containers may settle and are filled by volume, not weight. Pigments come and go and could be discontinued by manufacturers, selection and availability may vary!

	***Amber Ochre Dunkel*** A dark yellow with orangish brown undertone		***Brown Ochre*** A cool brown leaning towards an orangish-yellow		***Brown Oxide*** A warm reddish brown
	***Buff*** A cool creamy light beige		***Burnt Sienna*** A medium reddish-brown leaning towards orange		***Burnt Umber*** A medium reddish-brown
	***Burnt Umber Extra Dark*** A very dark warm brown	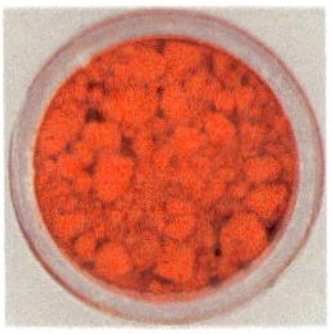	***Cadmium Red*** A bright opaque red	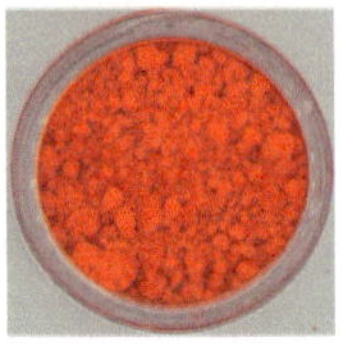	***Cadmium Vermillion Red*** Bright red with an orange tone
	***Cadmium Yellow Deep*** An opaque orangish yellow	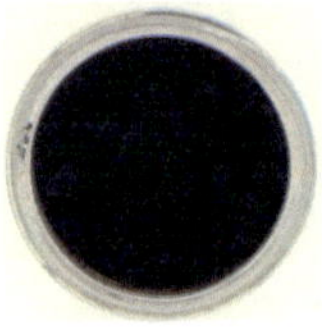	***Carbon Black*** An opaque black with extreme tinting power	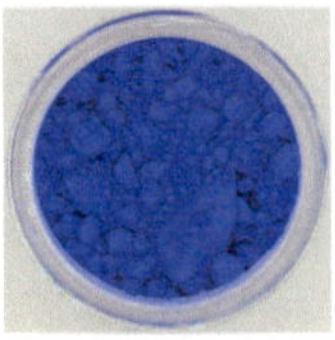	***Cobalt Blue*** A bright blue
	***Cyprus Umber Dark*** A warm deep brown, darker than most browns		***Cyprus Umber Warm*** A medium brown leaning towards red		***Dark Nuetral Brown*** Exactly what the name states
	***Dark Yellow Ochre*** A dark yellow with orange tone		***Environox Dark Brown*** An opaque dark brown oxide	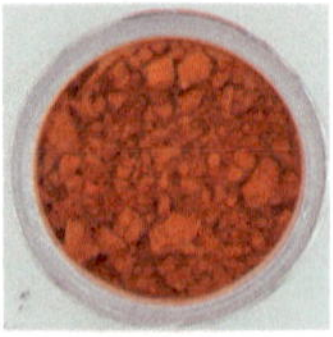	***Ercolano Red*** A semi transparent deep orange-red
	***French Ochre Light*** A very light brown leaning towards yellow		***Gold Ochre*** An opaque medium brownish yellow	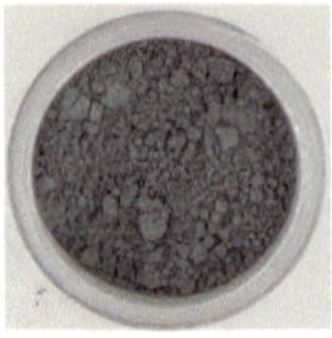	***Gray Ochre*** A warm dark gray, close to black when mixed with medium

	***Green Earth*** A light green		***Havana Ochre*** A natural yellow leaning towards orange	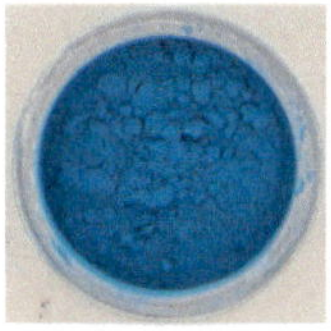	***India Blue*** A primary blue
	***Italian Umber*** A light to medium warm brown	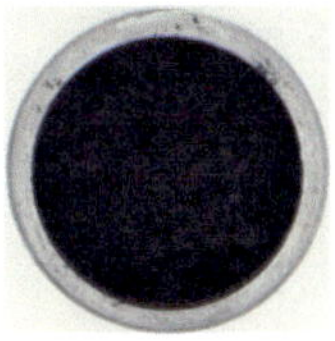	***Lamp Black*** Black with a bluish tone		***Lemon Yellow*** A light, pale yellow
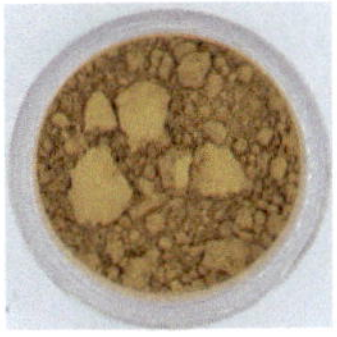	***Light Sienna*** Light brown with a greenish yellow tone		***Light Yellow Ochre*** A transparent light yellow		***Mars Black*** A opaque warm black
	***Mars Yellow*** A medium to dark yellow with an orange tone		***Mars Yellow Deep*** A medium yellow with an orange tone		***Mars Yellow Light*** A lighter yellow with an orange tone
	***Monte Carlo Green*** A mixture of green and cyan		***Natural Red Oxide*** An opaque medium to dark red		***Natural Sienna*** A semi transparent yellow brown
	***Natural Umber*** A medium brown leaning towards green		***Natural Yellow*** Medium yellow with a brown tone	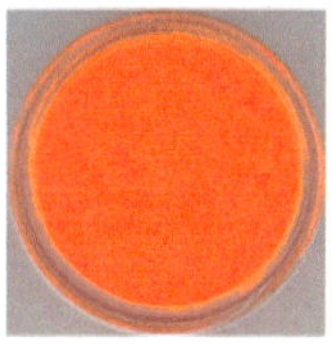	***Orange*** Bright! One of my most used pigments
	***Plum*** Semi transparent purple	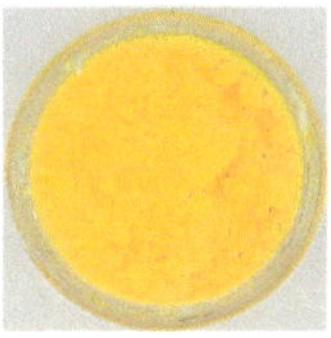	***Primary Yellow*** A strong yellow	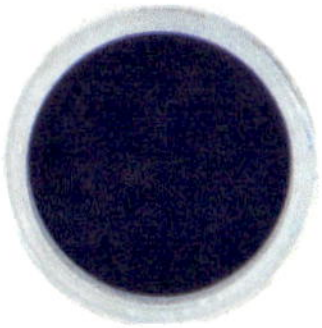	***Prussian Blue*** A deep blue pigment

	***Pyrrole Red*** A bright, vibrant red		***Red Ochre*** An earthy red with a brown tone		***Roman Black*** Black with brown tone, leans towards charcoal
	***Rose Earth*** A semi transparent red	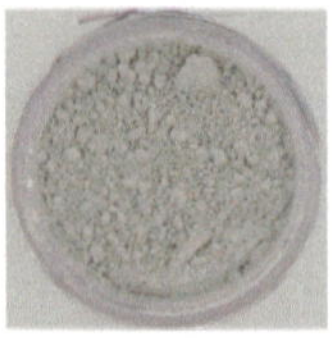	***Slate*** A bluish gray	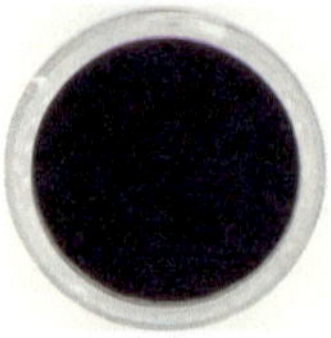	***Spinel Black*** A deep cool semi-transparent black
	***Van Dyke Brown*** A semi transparent deep, dark brown		***Venetian Red*** Semi transparent red with a yellow tone		***Vine Black*** A transparent black with low tinting strength
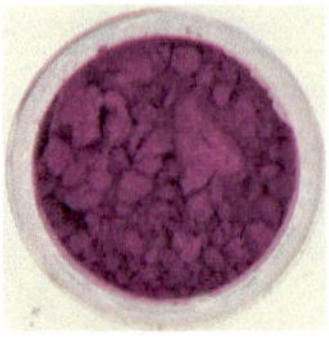	***Violet*** A bright secondary color		***White*** AKA titanium dioxide. Don't get any ideas!		***Woodland Green*** A dark shade of green and cyan
	***Yellow Ochre*** A dark yellow leaning towards orange	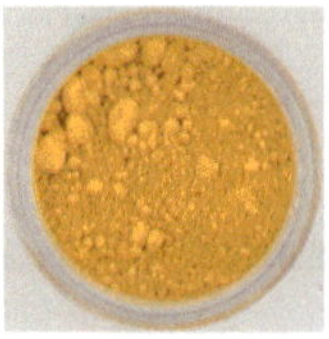	***Yellow Oxide*** An opaque earthy yellow	Visit: MyRepairKit	.com

BROKEN WOOD

During your travels, possibly in your own home, you are guaranteed to come across a piece of furniture or a unique wood item that may have some aspect broken in half.

Whether it be an arm on a chair, leg on a dresser, framing of a sofa, or the like, making that piece of furniture unusable, or at least, a safety hazard.

Whether it be a unique family heirloom or something more common like a kitchen chair which belongs with a set. You're probably hanging onto that piece of furniture, thinking, "I'll get it fixed later". Well for a vast amount of people, for whatever reason, that "later" may never come.

Throughout this chapter, I'll show you a few examples of how to fix that broken wood, so you can clear some space out of your garage and sit another family member at the dining table for the holidays.

The most important thing when repairing a piece of furniture which has a break in a critical area, is to ensure that the break is properly joined and reinforced. There may be a few ways to add reinforcement depending on the location of the break, specific to your project.

Primarily the deciding factor of where and how you will add reinforcement depends on whether the area that is broken needs to be structurally sound to bear weight, be able to withstand stress, or if it is what I refer to as a "cosmetic repair", meaning, it just needs to look good.

In general, I suggest either dowels/dowel rods, nails, screws, or hollow metal dowels (you're wondering what that is? We'll get into that soon), each having their own particular benefit depending on how or where the wood is broken.

Don't fool yourself, not everything that's broken is repairable, often things do need to be replaced. For instance, the stretcher (spindle, front cross support) for the rocker on the previous page, was obviously broken in half.

Could we have drilled a hole in the center of the broken halves and doweled it? Yes, the break is straight across the spindle, giving us a nice flat area to precisely drill out the holes needed to insert a dowel rod, but I felt the chair would be far more structurally sound if the stretcher was replaced, which required being turned on a lathe for duplication.

There are two bolts where the left and right front vertical posts attach to the seat, but other than that, the main support for those front vertical posts is that front cross stretcher.

In addition, being in the front bottom of the chair, that area is far more susceptible to being kicked or hit by vacuums, whatever the case may be. If it was a spindle on the side of the chair that was broken, I would have most likely just repaired it.

Would a doweled repair hold up? No doubt, probably at least for a little while, maybe even years, until possibly the bolts that go into the seat loosen from use of the chair, then more stress will be placed directly on that stretcher. So for us to guarantee our repair, I determined the better option was replacement.

You also may come across a chair spindle, or in our case, this front vertical post, which can't so easily be replaced, like the one below, unless you are some kind of expert wood carver, which I know that I am not!

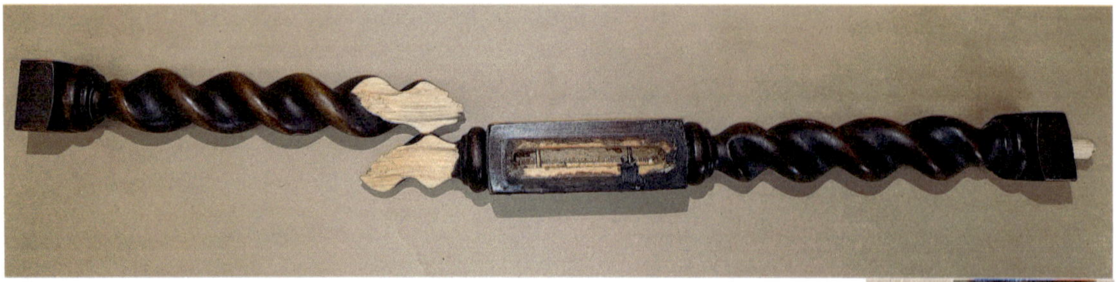

So we need to be able to perform a repair while still being capable of adding sufficient reinforcement so we can guarantee our work.

Upon closer inspection (right), you can see that the break is vertical and at an angle, instead of breaking straight across the post, as in the example of the previous rocker.

Because it's broken in this diagonal fashion, it would be near impossible to drill out and align the holes perfectly in each broken half, length wise, to allow us to insert a dowel rod. That means we will have to reinforce across the break.

This fancy arm post also ironically comes from a rocker, and on this rocker, not only is the front right vertical post broken in half, but the top right horizontal arm that attaches to this post is also broken completely in half, where it attaches to the chair's back.

In the arm, you can see evidence of where a screw is installed from the rear to hold that arm securely to the back of the chair.

Because we need to put that screw back in once the repair is complete, we know that area will inherently be weak so we'll also need reinforcement across that break.

Obviously we see the two breaks, and obviously again you see that these two sections have been removed from the chair for repair.

Part of the issue that may have played a role in the breaks, is that all the joints of the entire chair were loose, the chair required total disassembly and a reglue.

Because of all the loose joints combined, there can be an exorbitant amount of stress in unforeseen areas because those loose joints are now moving independently, possibly causing a chain reaction of stress throughout various other parts of the chair.

Just imagine that when your sitting in the chair, your body weight is pushing half of the chair downward, towards the ground, while simultaneously your back is pushing the rear framing of the chair backwards, similar to a recliner that isn't supposed to recline, but because of the loose joints, it now sort of does. When the tension is greater than the wood can handle, it has no choice but to break.

You'll see as we proceed through this repair, there's a specific process that needs to take place, and it's virtually the same for every broken piece of wood. You'll also need some specific tools, like a drill, drill bits, clamps, wood glue, screwdriver, screws, and My Repair Kit™ for the finishing and concealment of the damages.

Reinforcement of a break is extremely important if something needs to be structurally sound, you can't just assume that some type of glue will hold together two pieces of wood. You in no way want to be liable for that chair breaking apart while someone is using it.

If the chair collapses as a direct result of an improper repair, that person falls out and hurts themselves, you could be found responsible and people will sue for anything these days. So it's important to always protect yourself first and foremost, make sure you have insurance if you plan on doing this for a living!

The second reason you want to add reinforcement, is that you want to be able to guarantee your work! Someone is hiring you, possibly spending hundreds of dollars to fix something in particular, not everyone may expect your work to be cosmetically perfect but they will expect your repair to be structurally sound, after all most often a client just wants to have use of the item again.

The first thing you can do is make a dry run (left), put the two broken pieces together to ensure they fit together well. There may be loose wood particles that you need to remove to ensure the two pieces join as closely as possible. Any small loose particles of wood can be removed with your fingers or razorblade.

After you ensure that the two pieces of wood join together nicely, using standard wood glue, add some glue to the breaks of both pieces, and again, join the two pieces together and apply a clamp so the two pieces are held in perfect alignment, with a fair amount of pressure.

Use a water dampened rag to wipe off any excess glue that may have squeezed out. Once you've cleaned the glue off, you should be able to clearly see how well the crack lines up.

This is probably one of the most important aspects of any repair. You want the crack (the two broken pieces) to align as perfectly as possible, any misalignment, even by a small amount may be a detriment to the integrity of the repair.

If the alignment is off, that means wood fibers inside the break are out of alignment, which means that there may be "space" created inside the break where the glue and/or wood do not touch or at the least have a weak bond, therefore resulting in an overall weaker repair.

In addition, when a break is misaligned, you will be creating more work to cosmetically conceal the misalignment and often it may be apparent that there was a repair in that area.

Fortunately for us, the alignment was fantastic.

What you may see at the left bottom of the crack (above right), which looks like space, is not, it's actually just an area of small wood fibers that needed to be removed because they were impeding our break from properly aligning.

The next step is to add reinforcement, and I suggest using screws for this particular repair. This is where you need to get out your drill, bits and screws.

The sizes of the bits and screws are project dependent, but the goal is to determine the most ideal area(s) to install the screw(s) so that they provide maximum reinforcement.

Begin by drilling a pilot hole for the screw(s) into the top, hearty section of the wood, also use a countersink bit, so that the head of the screw is embedded below the surface of the wood.

Later we will fill over the screw heads to conceal the screw(s), and ultimately no one will even know that screws were used, if done properly.

I will be installing an additional screw, coming in from the opposite side, closer to the bottom of the break. Essentially sandwiching the crack together.

I will often reinforce from opposite sides when I have the opportunity, as I feel it will add even more support than if both screws were installed from one side, but that's just my opinion, and you may not always be able to perform this technique, as we'll see below.

After you perform the initial gluing and addition of reinforcement, leave it alone for 24 hours so the glue can dry properly, which now gives us the opportunity to work on the other part of the chair that is broken, the right arm.

As I noted earlier, it's really the same exact process that we just went through so I won't drag out the explanations, but remember, glue, screw, fill, sand and finish.

If you notice the third picture, above right, you can see two clamps and two blocks of wood. By clamping the broken wood in this fashion, from the top and bottom, we ensure that the break/crack on the top and bottom of the arm are perfectly aligned.

Remember, any misalignment is bad, maybe not the end of the world bad, but the more perfect the alignment, the stronger the bond, and the less finishing work there will be!

Don't forget to clamp the break from the opposite direction also (left to right).

If you look closely in the picture to the left, where the glue is oozing out, the wood is joined together very nicely!

Unfortunately, all the clamps are in the way of us adding reinforcement, so again, we need to leave this alone for 24 hours to properly cure. The following day when the glue has cured, we'll take the clamps off and install some screws <u>across</u> the break.

This break we will not reinforce from opposite directions, as in the previous example, because for one, the piece of wood which was broken off is pretty small, but secondly, the arm is fairly wide, so I felt there would be too much distance to cover without much benefit added in the way of additional strength to the repair.

On the arm, I may have filled and sanded the top crack prior to reinforcing, but that doesnt matter. Using your drill, bits, countersink and screws, install the reinforcement, then fill the screw holes, and sand the filler to create a nice smooth surface. At this time, we also filled and sanded the screw holes and crack on the vertical post.

Just one note on the screw that we installed at the end of the arm, the hole was drilled out at a slight angle so that we missed going through the “hollow” area which was needed to install the original screw from the rear of the back post into the arm to secure it to the chair.

At this juncture, both pieces that we are working on are now structurally sound and I am confident that under normal use and circumstances, once the entire rocker is completely reglued, these two structural repairs will last the rest of the chair's life.

From here, I recommend using My Repair Kit™ and perform the finishing work prior to reinstalling both parts onto the chair.

The first thing I will do is wipe over the surface with a padding rag moistened with padding finish. This removes any sanding dust, some of the sanding scratches and exposes the true color of the surface that we need to touch up.

Using our paintbrush and pigments first, apply some color. I used three, burnt umber, carbon black and orange. Once we get our first coat of color on each piece, we then seal in the touch up using a satin clear toner, let that dry for five to ten minutes. Don't spray too heavy, a medium to light misting is sufficient.

To blend the hues even further, I then applied some padding finish and pigment to a padding rag and lightly stroked over the surfaces to apply more pigment. This was performed on both the post and the arm.

For the finale of both pieces, once our touch up work is complete, we again seal in all our hard work with some additional clear satin toner. Remember, no soaking, I almost never use a "heavy" coat from a toner can!

Just let those two pieces hang loose for an hour or two so that the finishes that were applied can completely cure.

The most difficult aspect of the repairs are now complete. Now we're tasked with reassembling and totally regluing the rocking chair.

The process of gluing a chair should be all performed at the same time, in no way do you want to reglue the bottom half of the chair, then come back the next day and glue the top half.

If you clamp various parts on an individual basis, the different pieces of your project may not align properly or at the very least be in a slightly incorrect position. So put glue in all joints, on every piece of wood then put the chair together and clamp.

Make sure you use plenty of standard wood glue and don't worry about any glue that's running down or squeezing out of the joints as you apply clamps and assemble, that will clean off easily with a water dampened rag as you proceed.

It was the right arm and front, right vertical post which were repaired.

We were able to match the existing finish, without refinishing, the repair is virtually perfect, the client is happy and we made a few hundred bucks for a couple hours of work.

That rocker repair was fairly easy! This next example, a leg to a buffet, which was broken into two pieces, may be a bit of a doozy.

Well, it shouldn't be too bad, but often we will come across damages which a client needs repaired, but someone, not naming any names, has already attempted a repair, and it's bad! Really bad!

Gobs of glue everywhere, random nails and/or screws, multiple breaks, breaks previously glued out of alignment, what in tarnation are we supposed to do with this?

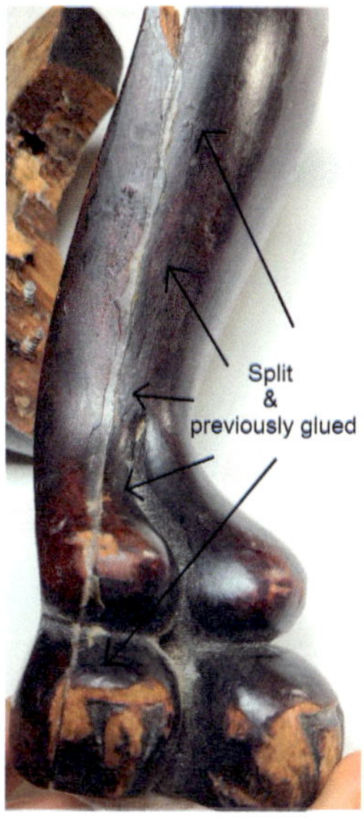

The answer is, start by removing any and all nails and/or screws, then painstakingly clean off all the old glue from the broken pieces, which usually requires chisels and/or razor blades, but it's what must be done!

Always be careful when using sharp tools, I've slipped with a razorblade before and sliced right through part of my hand, down to the bone, required stitches and it was quite uncomfortable!

It's wise when working with small items, to secure them in some type of bench clamp or vice, instead of holding them in your hands while attempting to clean the surface, it doesn't take much to slip and slice yourself, forewarned!

Also remember that as you are using these sharp instruments, glue is the only thing you're trying to remove.

It's very easy to remove large sections of wood along with the glue as you use a sharp tool, but you don't want to remove any wood.

You need the wood to stay as intact as possible so that when you join the two broken pieces together, there is a large surface area that makes contact.

Again, if there isn't ample contact, you may have "hollow" spaces inside the break, resulting in a weaker repair.

After removing all the nails and/or screws, and carefully cleaning all the old glue off, maybe you didn't remove 100% of the glue out every nook and cranny but hopefully you've removed at least 99%. Perform a dry run by putting the two pieces together to see how well they align.

After my dry run, I realized that the dowels you see at the forefront of the previous picture were causing a slight misalignment, so I removed those also. It will be very easy to drill out those holes and reinstall the original dowels at the conclusion of the repair.

Using an ample amount of standard wood glue, join the two pieces together, apply some clamps, and clean off any excess glue. Again, the clamps are impeding our ability to drill and add reinforcement, so we will let the leg dry for 24 hours to ensure the glue has fully cured.

Let me tell you why, in most cases, I don't drill the holes for reinforcement first, before I do any gluing. Some may assume that as they join the two pieces together during the dry run, that would be an ideal time to drill holes for screws and/or dowels, but the reality is that if you pre-drill your holes, when you install a screw, the simple act of the screw being tightened will often throw the break out of alignment.

It seems like the screw is straight, right? What you don't realize is that the threading on a screw is a spiral at a specific angle, some angles greater than others (that's essentially how the screw pulls itself through the wood when tightening or loosening).

As screw is installed, depending on where that angled spiral is internally, it may be pulling the wood slightly in an undesired direction, other than straight, if that makes sense.

I'm not an engineer, so that theory may be way off base, but the majority of the time I've tried installing a screw before gluing in the past, that issue of misalignment more often than not, exposed itself.

Therefore, the majority of the time, I first want to glue the two pieces together, which in my opinion, ensures that the break is in perfect alignment. Then once the glue has dried, with the two pieces still perfectly aligned, with no concern of misalignment. That, in my opinion, is the best time to reinforce.

Unless, of course, you can find a way to install the reinforcement properly while your project is still clamped, which is usually fine also, as the clamps should negate any undesired movement.

So back to the leg repair that we are working on. Now that the glue has fully cured it's time to install the reinforcement. Using your drill, bits, countersink, and screws, the next step is to find the most ideal area to install the screws.

This is now one of the best abilities that you possess, which is the ability to add reinforcement anywhere that it's needed. You shouldn't be concerned anymore about things looking bad or having screw heads exposed because you have the ability to conceal said reinforcement.

The most important determination that you are now making is, "where does the reinforcement/hardware need to be to create the strongest repair possible?"

You may not be an engineer either, but in your mind you need to figure out where the most stress is going to be in any particular break, and make sure that area is strong and secure. More often than not, it will require adding reinforcement in more than one area.

From the previous three pictures, you can see that in the first picture, I'm going directly between where those dowels are supposed to be, and also from the other two pictures, I'm reinforcing to the left and right of those dowels. The drill bit above is showing the angles in which the screws are going to be installed.

The most stress, in my opinion, is the area where the two dowels insert. That's where it looks like the crack started.

Be sure to countersink your holes so the screws are embedded below the surface of the wood.

You may see mismatching screw heads, ultimately I don't always use matching screws. I made the far right hole slightly bigger than the others so I could use a slightly more heavy duty screw in that area.

The next three pictures will show additional reinforcement from the rear of the leg. Remember to reinforce from differing sides for the strongest repairs.

Now that the leg is glued and screwed/reinforced, structurally that aspect of the repair is complete, I'm confident that this leg under normal circumstances will last the rest of the buffet's lifespan, even if we stopped our repair at this point.

We're not quite done yet though, we have to perform the finishing work to conceal our structural repair. In a picture at the start of this repair, I showed that there was a piece of wood previously glued to the rear of the leg, which was out of alignment (below).

The truth of the matter is that the section, even though slightly misaligned, was glued fairly well, there was no movement in the pieces and I would have likely caused further damage trying to remove that section.

Sometimes you need to know when to let sleeping dogs lie! Though I did add a few nails for slight additional reinforcement.

In the picture to the right, you can see where I have carefully removed some of the pre-existing glue and sliced off some of the wood. The area where I removed the wood was "high" (misaligned), compared to the adjacent piece of wood.

We always need the wood on both sides of a break to be aligned as close as possible, otherwise it may require significant sanding, causing a noticeable change in the level of the surface, often creating a visually apparent repaired area.

I chose to use a razor blade to cut the high wood away, but you could sand the heck out of the area in question, which only causes a larger area to touch up. As always, it's better to stay as minimal as possible when performing repairs.

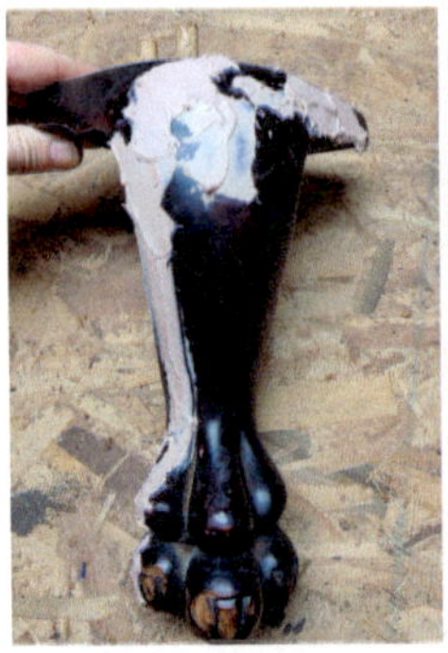

The next step is the cosmetic portion of the repair. We have to use filler to conceal the screw holes and cracks, so feel free to gob some filler onto the leg and don't worry too much about being perfect and pretty at this point.

This is just what I refer to as a "rough fill", and the main task we are trying to accomplish is to thoroughly get filler in all the required areas.

Before the filler hardens too much, usually within 4-7 minutes, I'll use a razor blade to remove the majority of the filler, leaving all the areas we need filled, filled.

When filling large areas, usually one application of filler will not be sufficient to cover all areas perfectly.

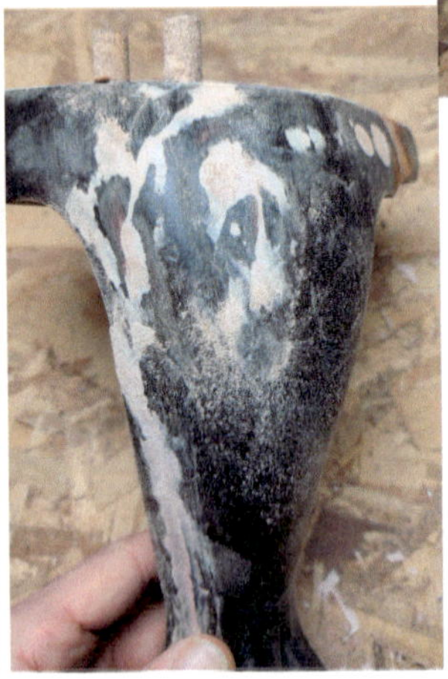

There may be "low" areas that are not yet filled level with the surrounding surface, so I usually come back and fill all the areas again, with a "skim coat" (far left).

This time applying the filler far more judiciously to fill in any nooks and crannies.

I'm also not applying the filler quite as thick, because the next step will be sanding the filler off with a piece of sandpaper, and the more filler there is, the more sanding there will be.

I was expecting to sand quite a bit to ensure all the joined pieces are all flush, so I started with 220 grit to get most of the filler knocked down, but I did finish sanding with 400 grit, to get the leg ready for touch up.

You know the routine from this point, dampen your padding rag with padding finish and wipe over the entire leg to remove the sanding dust, slightly filling in sanding scratches and showing the true color of the areas that need to be touched up.

In the first picture below left, you can see the difference in the area that has padding finish, and the area that doesn't.

Followed by the way the leg looks after simply wiping over the leg one time quickly with my moistened padding rag overall (both middle pictures below).

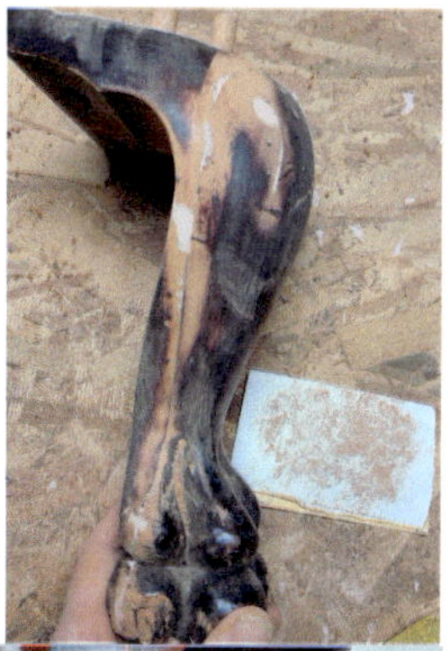

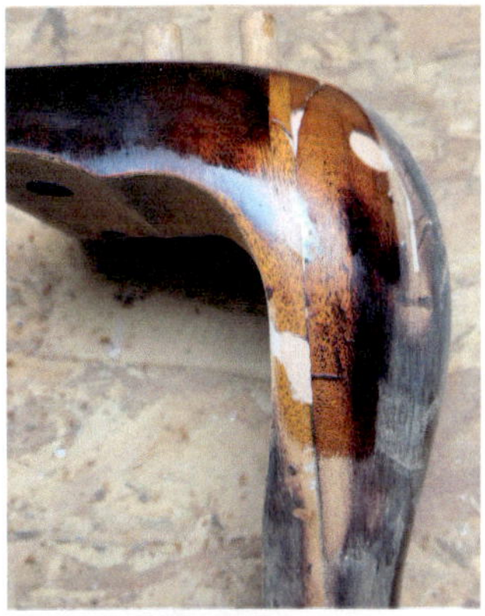

Get out your pigments, in this case I only used three (even though you may see four in the picture, I didn't use the fourth, burnt umber). I used carbon black, ercolano red and dark burnt umber.

Notice that I am using a flat brush, so I can apply pigment evenly over a large area. After the initial brushing, all the discolored areas on the leg should be covered with pigment.

Mist a coat of clear satin toner over the touched up areas, there's no need to spray the whole leg yet, the clear coat is only needed for sealing in the applied pigment. Let the leg dry for five or ten minutes and you should then be able to handle it again.

You know the routine, continue your pigment blending until the repaired area starts to blend fairly well, which may also include painting/reproduction of the grain pattern, even though this leg is pretty dark and doesn't appear to have much variation.

You've seen me mention this technique for several of the repair examples thus far, but I haven't really broken it down step for step yet. As stated recently, you may not need to employ this technique for every repair if it's looking pretty good.

Often you'll apply some pigment onto a padding rag to further blend the repaired area by french polishing. If done well, it should make the original damage have a near flawless transition from the repaired area to the surrounding undamaged wood surface.

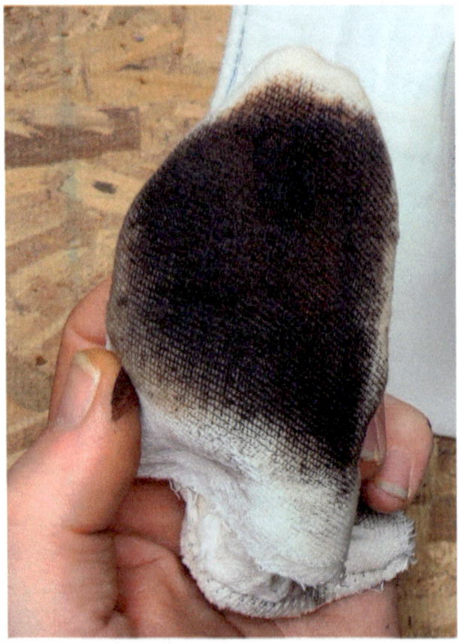

Initially I dampen my padding rag, dip my finger into one jar of pigment, coating the tip of my finger in varying amounts. I then rub that pigment onto the surface of the rag, spreading the color out evenly over the rag's surface.

Adding the pigment to the rag may make the surface of the rag feel a little dried out, occasionally, but not always, often I'll give another quick squirt of padding finish to the padding rag to remoisten the surface.

Then I'll dip my finger in the second jar of pigment I need, with a varying amount on my finger and rub that pigment onto the surface of the rag, blending the two (or more) pigments together.

This technique is essentially the same thing you're doing when mixing colors with your paintbrush, except now you're using your finger and the pallet is your padding rag.

If you don't rub and blend the pigments together sufficiently, it will likely cause uneven blending of color on the surface of the repair, possibly leaving some areas too light or too dark or too much pigment built up in a particular area. Or maybe you need one of those effects?

Though in most circumstances, you're not really trying to apply color with a rag, in an opaque manner. The harder you rub or pat the pigment filled rag in your palm, the more blended and diluted the color becomes. This is how one can adjust the amount of pigment transferred from the padding rag to the surface.

In general you want the application to be more translucent. Remember when you get to this step, the colorwork over your repair should be close to completion and you're only trying to feather out the repaired area to help with the transition between the repair and the remainder of the surface.

Otherwise, applying too much pigment could eventually lead to loss of the grain definition surrounding the repair. Darker woods are always going to be more forgiving and easier to blend than light or natural woods.

Back to the buffet leg, we're now in the homestretch. Hopefully you let the new finish dry an hour or more just so it's safe to handle. With the structural and cosmetic repairs complete, we really just need to drill out and install those two dowels that we removed initially, and glue/secure the leg back onto the body of the buffet.

Make sure you've cleaned off any old glue from the adjoining surfaces, and perform your dry run to ensure the leg fits well.

Add glue to both pieces, install the leg, and put the screws in to secure the leg to the buffet.

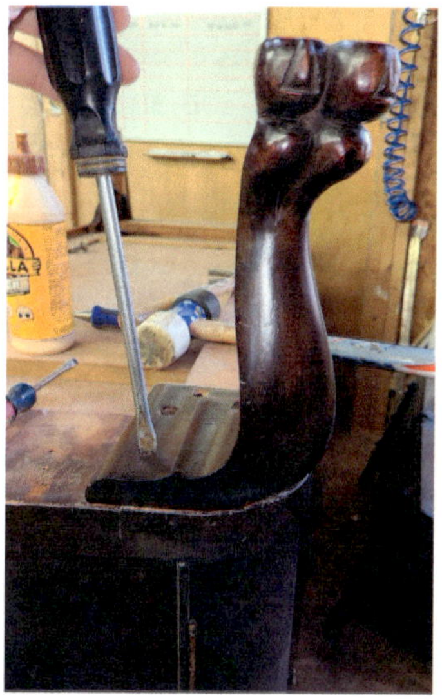

I will flip this piece upright once I install the leg so that the glue and leg can dry in the position that it will always be in, additionally the weight of the buffet is essentially acting as a clamp, as the downward force is holding the leg in place.

Leave the piece alone for 24 hours and your repair is complete, although I'll likely clean up the rest of the buffet prior to delivery just to ensure everything looks great!

Again we were able to perform this repair without any refinishing. Additionally, if the dry time isn't included, it really only took about 2.5-3 hours to complete.

If you're charging upwards of $150+ an hour, you made at least $400-$500. You may even be able to add a pick up and delivery fee since it required two people to pick up for shop restorations, and to deliver back to the client.

That should show you that even if you perform repairs as a hobby, you can still make pretty decent money!

So far, we've only used screws to reinforce, wood dowels or dowel rods are often used in several instances to reinforce broken wood.

You can probably install a dowel anywhere you think you can use a screw. I suggest gluing, securing/clamping and allowing a broken area dry, before drilling and installing a dowel, because just like we went over, with screws, joints can move undesirably while drilling, unless secured.

Joints of furniture are commonly held together by dowels, which with time and use, often become loose, or possibly end up breaking, eventually requiring replacement.

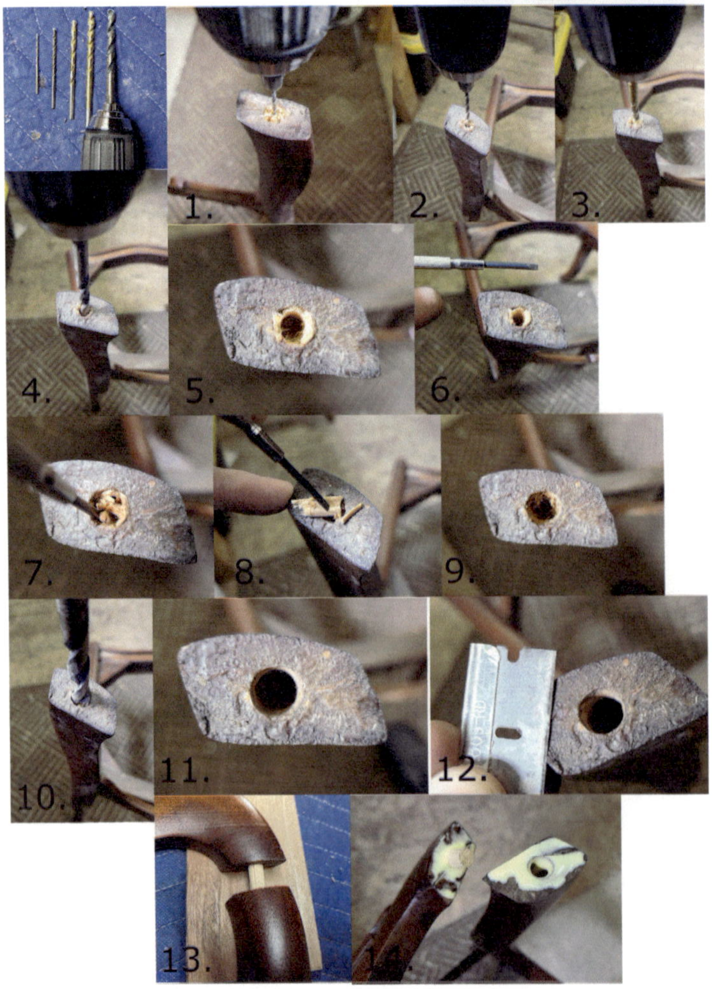

Let me start by saying, each step, 1-12, needs to be completed on both sections of the chair back, top and bottom.

Ensure you're using hardwood dowels, like oak or poplar, not softwood dowels or dowel rods, like pine.

One incorrect way to remove a broken dowel, is to initially attempt removal with a drill bit the exact size as the dowel.

Using the biggest drill bit first, it's highly likely that you will not be drilling perfectly straight. Even drilling at the slightest angle could cause the new dowel to not align properly!

Starting with a very small drill bit, try to find as close to the exact center of the broken dowel as possible, and drill a hole (#1).

This is accomplished in steps 1-4 on the previous page, ascending in drill bit sizes until the broken dowel is almost completely removed, step 5.

In steps 6-8, I use my trusty miniature pry bar to break away the remaining edges of the old dowel. This leaves an almost perfect original hole, step 9, intact and unfazed.

Now in step 10, I use a drill bit that is the exact circumference of the original hole. This will remove any leftover pieces of dowel and clean the walls of the hole from any old glue residue. Step 11, leaving a perfect hole!.

Ensure you remove any old glue from the inner surface of the joints, as in step 12. I chose to carefully use a razor blade instead of sanding. Sandpaper, or improperly sanding without a block may undesirably alter the level of the adjoining chair surfaces, creating an unstable joint.

Perform a dry run (#13) to ensure the alignment is perfect, then proceed to apply glue to all the surfaces and dowel, put the chair together (#14), and add clamps so it can dry overnight.

Screws or dowels may be insufficient in some instances for support, like possibly if the leg of a heavy sofa or china cabinet is broken. If you need far greater stability than what those provide, switch to a stronger material, like metal.

Back in the beginning of this chapter I mentioned hollow metal dowels. Well, those aren't really a thing. Basically a hollow metal dowel is just a hollow tube or better known as a "pipe".

There's a great debate (somewhere) on whether a hollow tube, aka a pipe, is stronger than a solid rod (both right).

The concept that a hollow tube is stronger than a solid rod is incorrect, or at least misleading. A solid rod will be "stronger" in almost every aspect, compared to a hollow tube of the same diameter, but we aren't necessarily worried about strength, we are usually more concerned with stiffness/rigidity.

As an example, take a half inch thick steel rod and a half inch thick pipe, in general, that steel rod will "flex" more than the pipe. That doesn't mean it's "weaker", because I would say that it's far easier to "break" a hollow tube should the outer wall become compromised.

Unlike a rod, a metal tube will not flex, it will remain extremely rigid. "Lamp pipe", or "all thread pipe" (left and right) is what I recommend. These pipes usually come in lengths of 4" to 16" and can easily be cut with a metal hacksaw.

You may even go to the plumbing section of a hardware store and get a ¾"-1" steel plumbing pipe if the job requires it.

Any movement in a structural repair could eventually degrade that repair, possibly leading to catastrophic failure.

You also don't need to change anything in your process of drilling out an area of wood to insert the pipe, just think of it as any other dowel you are replacing, it just so happens to be metal. The only thing I would change though is the type of glue that is used, I would substitute standard wood glue for an epoxy.

Be cautious when using epoxy, as the glue sets up possibly within minutes, unless you can find an epoxy with a longer cure time. If you look hard enough, possibly online, there are epoxies available with a one or two hour cure time, rather than five or ten minutes like most readily available epoxies.

Often it's beneficial to give yourself some extra time, rather than rush, that's one reason I prefer standard wood glue during most repairs in the shop because I have the luxury of time.

The last type of reinforcement that is recommended are nails. The good old fashioned, tried and true way to connect two pieces of wood that's been around since at least 3400 B.C., in Egypt.

In our case, nails are almost never used for a structural purpose. The thin nature of most nails aren't sufficient when something needs to be weight bearing. But nails are ideal for cosmetic repairs, when we just need two pieces of wood to stay together (also using glue of course).

Nails can vary in size from long to short or thin to thick. In general we use what are referred to as "brads" or "finishing nails", we're never using nails that are over a couple inches long, thicker than an ⅛", or nails which have a large flat head.

I also recommend using a "nail punch" (right) to countersink the nail heads. Most finishing nails will also leave a smaller footprint when it comes to the filling and touch up required to conceal as compared to a screw.

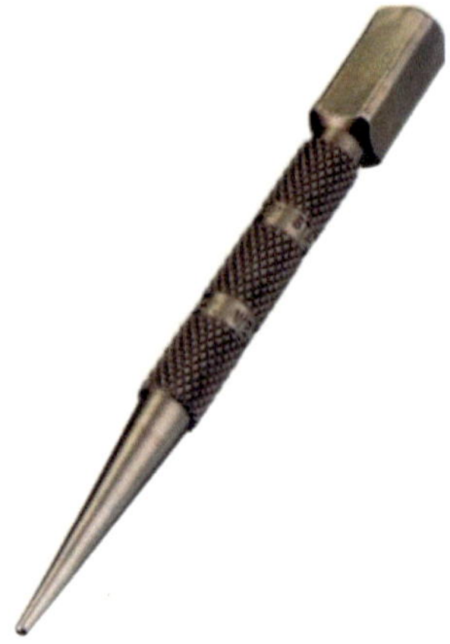

Pro tip: cut the tip off the nail to stop wood from splitting. It's called "blunting" the nail. Simply take a pair of cutter pliers and cut off the tip, then hammer time!

A sharp nail point will "chisel" its way through the wood fibers which forces the wood fibers apart (splitting). But a blunted nail simply breaks the fibers as it penetrates, greatly reducing the chance of the wood splitting.

So as you can see from the few examples in this chapter, the process for repairing broken wood is virtually the same for all repairs. I hate to be repetitive but clean the surfaces, glue the pieces together, add reinforcement, fill, sand and use MyRepairKit™ to conceal the damage.

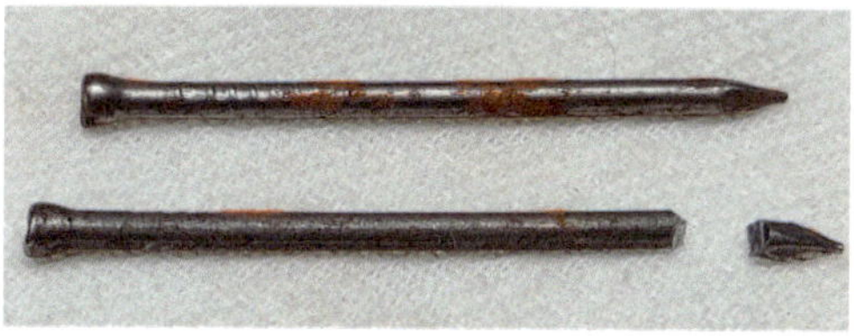

I'd like to show you one more thing and I'll try not to drag it out too much. This chair's right arm was broken in half, at a joint, with a large section of wood broken out and missing.

As of now, I've glued the break back together, but the original dowel that you see is really only going into the right side of the arm less than a ¼".

In my opinion this arm would easily break if I were to just leave it as is, so how should we reinforce?

I couldn't really add a longer dowel due to the curvature at the front of the arm. I also can't really add any screws due to the thin nature of the wood, and we just said that nails usually are insufficient for a structural repair.

I used a pneumatic cutting tool to create a channel so that I could fashion a piece of wood which extends through the break, into both sections of the arm. In my opinion, this is the most ideal way to reinforce this type of break.

I used epoxy, glued and clamped the wood spline in place. Once dry, we can remove all the clamps and shave off any excess protruding wood.

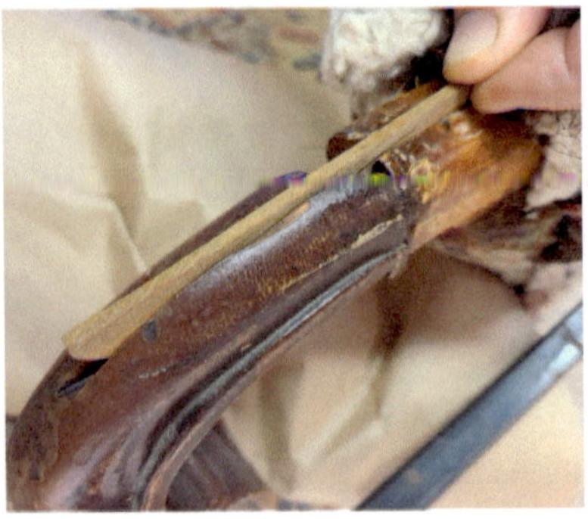

There's also another trick I like to implement when there is an excessively large area that needs to be filled.

I will install some screws, but I'll leave the heads of the screws sticking out slightly. I may also shoot a few small brads (thin, small nails) into the area with my brad gun.

Is this for additional reinforcement? It is, but it's not reinforcement for the wood, it's reinforcement for the filler.

With nails and screw heads protruding in different directions, once the filler encompasses the area, the nails and screws give the filler additional area to hold onto, giving more strength when bonding to the surface, in my opinion.

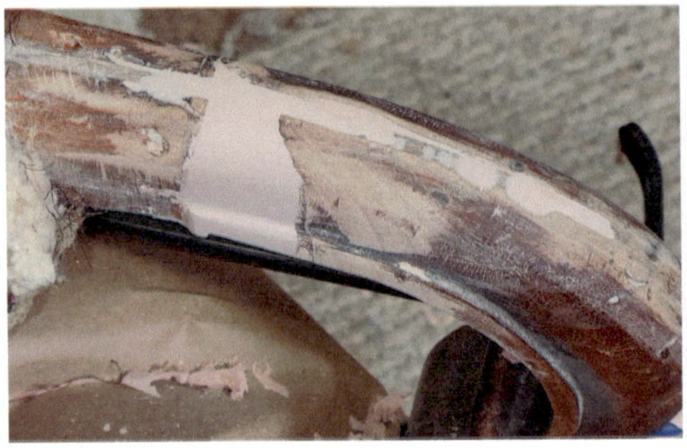

Then, as with all the previous repairs, fill, sand and proceed to touch up. Once the touch up is satisfactory, we then needed to re-stitch the upholstery and properly reattach it back onto the arm. Finito!

There is a second type of filler that I use occasionally, when I run across areas that need to be filled, but require even more stability than standard fillers can provide.

I'll just refer to this filler as an epoxy stick. Mohawk™, Gorilla™, JB Weld™, among others make these fillers.

They are sold in most hardware stores, and there are even formulations for repairs to metal, plumbing, fiberglass, and I'm sure many more applications.

To use, cut off the desired portion and knead it together till its uniform in color. In most cases, you probably have about ten to fifteen minutes of workability time prior to curing extremely hard.

Don't fill something, walk away, then come back in an hour, you'll be kicking yourself if you have to sand this fully cured material.

Wiping the epoxy stick as its curing with a water dampened rag helps to smooth out the surface of the epoxy. The epoxy, like Bondo®, also has a sweet spot during the curing process, when you can easily trim with a razor blade if needed.

You may not get this epoxy filler perfectly flat with the initial filling, but often with any low areas or imperfections, the second time, and all additional times, I will fill the area in question with Bondo® to complete the process, it's just easier to work with.

Let's just get this understood up front, an epoxy based filler will be far stronger than an automotive body filler, but there is no filler that can be a substitute for proper reinforcement of a critically broken area of wood, which requires structural stability.

One could argue the semantics between a gouge, scratch, knick, ding, chip, dent, scrape, cut, abrasion, gash or some other descriptive word for any particular type of damage.

In reality, the primary characteristic I look for, is whether the damage in question is strictly in the furniture's clear coat, or if the damage has broken through the surface of the finish, and extended into the wood.

I'll refer primarily to two types of damages, a "scratch", which I would consider the damage to be longish, and fairly thin in nature.

The second being a “gouge”, which may appear as an area of direct impact. Both types of damages could vary in length, width and could either be shallow or deep.

Deep damage, in my opinion, is anything that has broken the surface and extended into the wood, similar to the gouges in the center of the previous picture. That type of damage most often requires filling and sanding to level the surface.

Shallow damage refers to only surface damage, similar to the scratches pointed out in the previous picture.

Often you’ll barely be able to feel shallow damages, sometimes your fingernail may be able to catch in the scratch as you rub across it, but the damage hasn’t broken completely through the finish.

The bookshelf to the right only has shallow surface scratches, which has only been sanded with 600 grit wet/dry sandpaper.

By lightly sanding the surface, you’ll see that often the shallow areas of damage will begin to sand out and disappear.

Even if the shallow scratches don’t fully disappear, like in this picture to the right, you still probably don’t need to fill them.

Get out your padding finish of choice, apply some to your padding rag, and proceed to french polish the area in question.

In the picture below, you can see where I have begun the french polish on the top half, and you can see the sanding marks and remaining surface scratches on the bottom half.

Soon after beginning your french polish, look in the reflections of light and you should begin to see the surface scratches and sanding marks start to fill in and dissipate.

The padding finish is being deposited from the rag into those scratches, while simultaneously leveling out the surface.

Make sure to check out the "Hand Applied Finishes" chapter, if you haven't already, for more information on proper french polishing techniques.

Often it's necessary to stop french polishing and let the newly applied finish dry for a few minutes. After a few minutes, and a fresh charge to your padding rag, continue french polishing, which should remove most of the remaining sanding scratches, while eventually working your way over the entire surface, ensuring that the sheen is consistent throughout.

Occasionally some specific areas of damage can be stubborn. Once dry, you may have to gently come back with some 600+ grit w/d sandpaper, and softly sand the area(s) in question (pictured right), then french polish again.

It may take performing this process several times before your surface is complete and void of all damage. The restoration to this top surface took about thirty minutes.

One of the positives regarding repairing scratches in this fashion, is because you are not using filler or pigments, you are simply adding a clear finish, which acts as the filler and removes the majority of the scratches without altering the appearance of the surface, aside from the sheen level.

Deep scratches or gouges, damages that break through the surface of the finish and extend down into the wood, the majority of time, need to be filled.

If you try to sand and feather out deep damages without filling, you will most likely see a low or dipped area in the surface as you begin to build the finish up, rather than being perfectly flat.

Filling a deep scratch or a gouge is essentially the same process, the only difference is really just the shape of the damage.

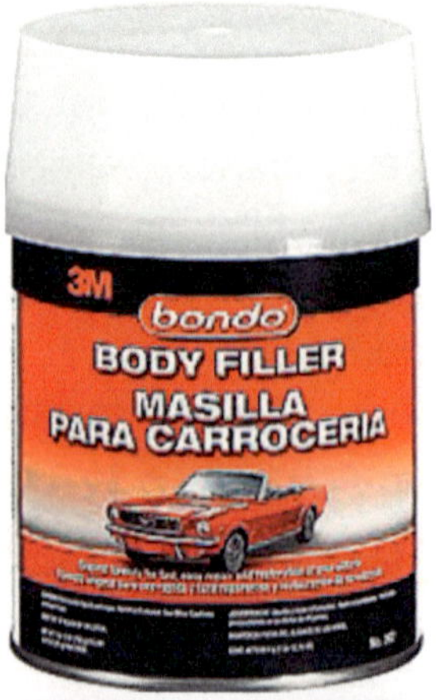

The filler I recommend is Bondo®, manufactured by 3M®. Bondo® is a polyester resin and talc mixture, which needs to be combined with a hardener/activator (second picture) to begin curing.

Standard Bondo® has a gray hue, and the standard activator hue is red. Combine those and you'll notice that the filler you mix up, in general, is pinkish.

Some technicians prefer not to have the pink hue, especially when filling areas of a natural, light finish like on maple or white oak.

Personally it doesn't matter to me that it's pink, as I've still managed to conceal the repairs without much difficulty, but Bondo® does make a filler that is golden in hue, named Professional Gold®.

Hardener/activator can also be purchased in a white hue, negating all pink hues. The trade off is that the golden filler is slightly more costly.

The truth of the matter, in my opinion, is that the pigment you apply to conceal the damage during the finishing process will be covering the filler in an opaque manner anyway, so in most cases it shouldn't matter what color the filler is.

There are a few specific reasons I prefer using Bondo® as my primary filler, for one, it cures fast. Time is the name of the game when you're out performing repairs in clients homes.

When mixing the activator provided with filler, you only need to add a small dot, usually less than the size of a pea. If I had to guess, I usually mix it at least 10-20 to 1, but I do tend to waste a lot.

A ratio of more activator to filler will make it cure faster but if you add too much, it may not cure properly at all. A smaller amount of activator will slow the cure time

The filler, once mixed, is usually workable within four to seven minutes, pretty hard after ten to fifteen minutes, and fully cured and more difficult to work with after about thirty minutes.

Bondo® cures very hard. Ultimately it was formulated for use on a car's exterior metal body so it doesn't really shrink or expand with extreme temperature fluctuation.

The filler bonds extremely well to a prepared surface, bonds to itself remarkably, you can tint (color) it with pigments or dyes, it's waterproof, easily workable, highly resistant to shock and vibration, and most importantly, it accepts paint or pigments well without causing any type of reaction or contamination when coated with a host of various finishes.

All fillers may have one or two of these fantastic properties. But there is no type of wood specific filler that I've ever come across that possesses them all like Bondo®. In fact, I'd be fine with this being the only filler I ever use in any non-structural restoration for the rest of eternity.

Most other fillers either take too long to cure, never cure (wax fillers), shrink, won't get hard enough (rigidity), get too hard to be workable (epoxy), and probably a host of other reasons.

I'll expand on some of those "other" fillers later in this chapter because they all may have their place for use, depending on case and circumstances.

The last reason I love Bondo® is because it's available virtually everywhere there is an automotive department, your local hardware store, auto parts store, Walmart, Target, and others, so it's easily obtainable, rather than being some unique filler that needs to be ordered from a specialty company.

The filling of scratches and gouges will most assuredly be one of the easier aspects of any repair. Just understand that most often it will require more than one application, in my opinion, to fill the vast majority of damages.

Next, I'll show you a restoration of a pretty significant gouge on the top of a buffet (below). From far away it may seem like the damage isn't that big, but realistically the damage is approximately 3 ½" x 1 ½". This I would consider a significant area of damage, especially being on the top of a very large surface.

If a repair isn't performed as close to perfect as possible, on a large flat surface, the damage will most likely be apparent when viewed from particular angles. If the damage is still apparent once completed, you may not satisfy your client, and you might not get paid for your work, even if it took you several hours to complete!

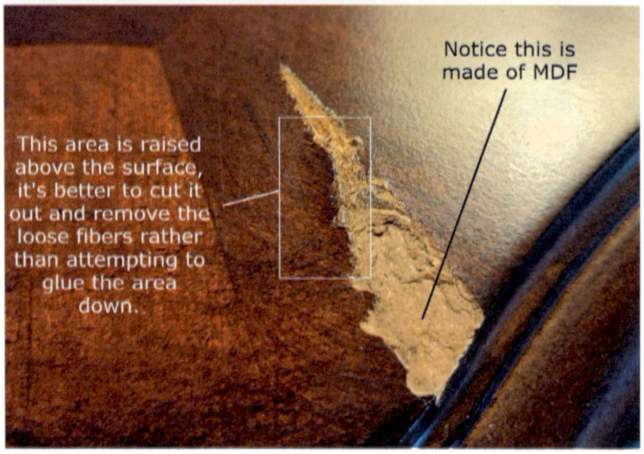

Let's assess the damage. Upon closer inspection, we know immediately we are working with a veneer, because due to the depth of the damage, the MDF (medium density fiberboard) has been exposed.

This tells us that even if we wanted, we could not refinish the top to remove the damage.

Technically, we could refinish the top, but the damage extends deeper than the veneer so even in the refinishing process this damage will need to be filled and touched up.

In the picture to the left, one of the initial things that I want to do is remove any loose fibers from the damaged area.

Using the edge of a razor blade, hold the blade at an approx 15°- 30° angle, with the blade squarely on the surface, sliding across the damage to remove any loose particles.

This technique will remove any "high" areas, and I also scraped out any loose fibers in the center of the damage (right).

The initial fill that we perform is to fill the damaged area as close to flat as possible. Using an application tool, Bondo® and hardener, I will initially fill the damage (right).

After the filler has cured for around four to seven minutes, I will use the razor blade once again to cut off the excess filler and begin to level the surface (below).

Normally I try to cut the filler off at a slight angle, <u>across</u> the surface of damage, not with the direction of the damage.

Cutting the filler in the direction of the damage, runs a higher likelihood of pulling the filler out of the groove.

I find that there is a sweet spot during the curing process, where the filler has cured hard enough to be permanently attached but still soft enough that you can easily shape it with a razor blade. That sweet spot is determined by the ratios you mix, and your experience working with the material.

After the initial trimming, you should see that the damage is not perfectly filled. There will likely be some low areas (bottom right) or trapped air bubbles, but there shouldn't be any high areas because those should have been removed by the razor blade initial trimming.

This is when I'll come back with some additional filler (below left). Applying the Bondo® with the edge of a tool, making sure to use the most minimal amount of filler possible to fill the remaining low areas, while creating a thin, flat, even layer over the damaged area.

You've heard this several times already, but It's usually key to keep the repaired area to a minimum. The larger the area of damage, the more difficult it can be to properly touch up and finish.

The picture to the right, shows after the second razor blade trimming. At this moment you can tell that the filled damage is now fairly level with the surrounding surface, but as you can see below, I filled it one more time.

This third filling (right center), if you notice, is extremely thin. You can fully see the majority of the outline, of the filled area, beneath the skim coat.

With this hopefully last filling, I'm just making sure there are absolutely no low areas or imperfections, that if left, without addressing, would likely show themselves in the final product, possibly inhibiting you from creating a truly undetectable repair.

Notice that we haven't used any sandpaper yet, and because we haven't sanded anything, we're still keeping the size of the damaged area to the bare minimum.

These three fills and two trims may have taken a total of 15 minutes, now I let the third fill dry for about 10 minutes. It's a good thing there are other repairs on this same job so I'm not sitting there twiddling my thumbs.

Now that the filler has cured well and is as near flat as possible, it's time to sand the area of damage perfectly flat. I used 600 grit w/d sandpaper and a sanding block.

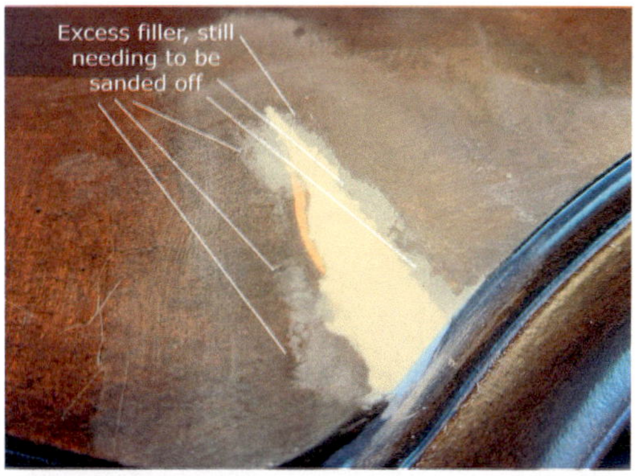

As you sand you will see that the excess filler will start to be removed, leaving only the original damaged area filled.

If you see any excess filler around the repair, you have not sanded it completely flat and you need to sand more.

These areas will be "high" if you stop sanding at this point, and will appear as a "bump" in the finished product. Filler should only be present in the original damage, and nowhere else on the surface.

Now that the damage has been filled, sanded and is perfectly flat, it's time to start the finishing process and complete this repair.

Also notice, with all of the sanding, I still haven't broken through the finish of the surface surrounding the original damage.

At this point, I was probably a half hour into the repair. The process of filling and sanding properly is extremely important, it is the basis of the entire repair. If any damage in question is not perfectly level prior to touching up, you will notice variation in the level of the surface, possibly creating a visually subpar restoration.

Use a padding rag and padding finish to start building up the clear coats and filling in some of the sanding scratches.

Begin your touch up using all the techniques you've learned so far. I'll try quickly to run through the rest of this repair for you.

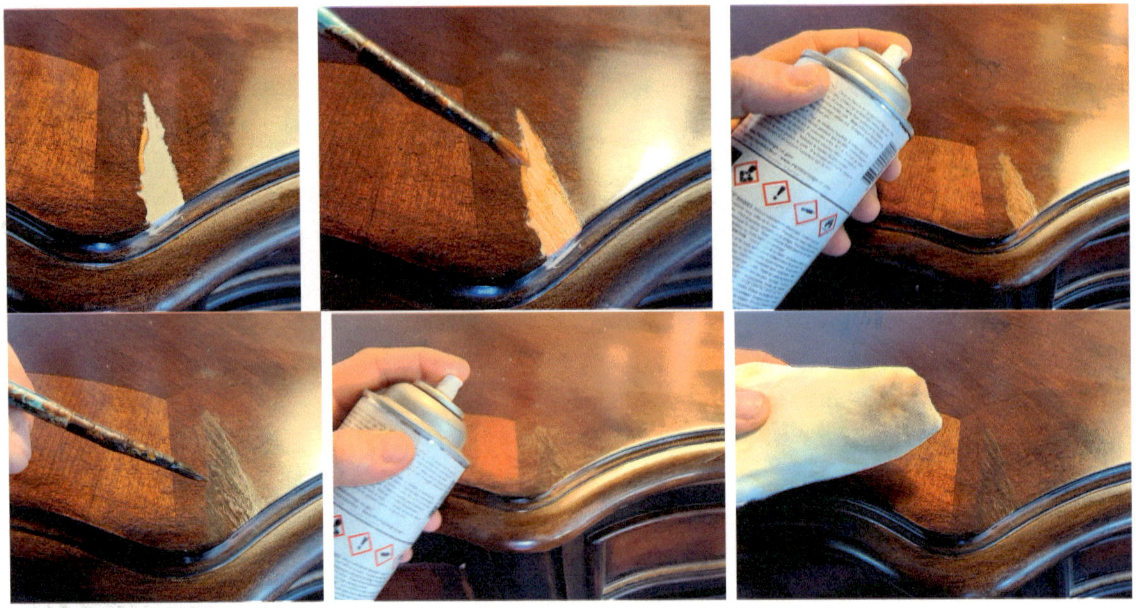

So far after properly filling, slightly french polish, touch up, seal, touch up, seal, lightly french polish again, then proceed with additional touch up.

One aspect you need to be conscious of, is that as you are building up your touch up paint onto the surface, if you apply it too thick, you may be leaving high areas on the surface.

A nearly dry brush will leave less build up of product, leaving a flatter surface, but occasionally you may have to sand with 600+ grit w/d, with extreme lightness of hand, just to level out the surface. We've gone over this technique a few times already.

Notice that my touch in the center picture above, I'm using short choppy strokes to try and simulate the grain, additionally the grain pattern I'm trying to replicate is on the lighter spectrum rather than matching the dark areas.

I alternate between the lighter hue and darker grain lines, while also simulating some of the distressing which represents themselves as dark lines or splatter.

I gave it another very light sanding to try and knock down the high areas of pigment, then proceeded to french polish the damage, eventually extending over the entire surface to ensure the sheen is consistent throughout.

This repair was pretty tricky, it will take time and practice to be able to perform a similar repair, but stick with it, I have no doubt that you will be able to eventually perform similar tasks.

This repair took slightly over two hours, and the only pigments I used were orange, carbon black and burnt umber.

There is another type of filler that I don't use during any repair for a client, those are colored wax sticks.

That doesn't mean they are bad, they are useful in a lot of circumstances, like plugging nail holes, especially on finished crown or base molding, or things of that nature.

Wax sticks may be available in several different stores, but there usually won't be a large selection of hues, this one stick (to the left) is supposed to match five different hues, according to the packaging.

Different stores may carry varying brands and hues. You can see from the display to the right, there is a vast array of hues available, and those shown in the case are all likely manufactured by Mohawk™ Finishes.

Our company doesn't use wax sticks because we feel that applying colored wax into a damaged area is not a permanent repair that we can guarantee.

Wax never hardens, and it can easily be scraped or rubbed out with future contact or cleaning. You also can't manipulate the color of the wax enough to replicate a complex grain pattern

Unfortunately though, wax sticks may be popular amongst other unnamed repair firms. If you hire a technician to come into your home to perform repairs and they show up with these, kindly turn them around and find someone with more experience. A truly talented, reputable company will not perform repairs in this fashion.

If you must insist, I suggest using wax sticks mainly in areas that are not highly visible, like side panels or base moldings, never use on a top surface unless you're not concerned with the appearance. Wax fill will always have a slightly matte sheen.

One of the only abilities wax sticks carry over other fillers is speed and ease of use.

You're basically just grinding some wax into an area of damage and trying to make it as level with the surface as possible. That means you can potentially fill a gouge in seconds and move on with your life.

If you have My Repair Kit™, you can take it a step further without a lot of additional effort. Once you've ground some wax into an area of damage, you can ever so lightly wet sand the area with 600 w/d sandpaper and water, dry, touch up and french polish or spray a clear toner over the damage, which will hopefully make it look close to invisible, for the near future anyway.

Essentially, the repair just described in the paragraph above, has the same process as any other repair, except you are only substituting Bondo® (a permanent filler) with wax (a non permanent filler).

What I have described since the start of this chapter is, in my opinion, the most ideal, expeditious, damage minimizing, best possible way to fill damages.

When I first started performing repairs, I was taught to fill damages using the "burn-in" method.

In fact, I still have and use them, they're literally in my tool box right at this moment. My first two burn-in knives, the main tool that I started this journey with, they're older than all my kids and now they've been retired to only mix and apply epoxy or fillers.

Before I even get into describing the burn-in method, I'm telling you not to use this method in the way I describe, consider it only for the perseverance of the technique for historical documentation purposes. Plus, I don't want to get sued for someone burning their house down trying to fix a gouge on a piece of furniture.

The burn-in method may also be referred to as shellac stick patching. This method started well before my time and it was the only way I witnessed my mentors in the industry filling the majority of surface damages until probably shortly after the 2000's, though some craftspeople still use the method to this day!

I probably stopped using this method 99.8% of the time in the late 90's, because it was laborious and I realized I could complete similar repairs way faster by using Bondo®, while completing repairs with similar satisfactory results.

There is one circumstance where I do prefer using a burn in method, and that is when there are damages on a mahogany, walnut or similar surfaces, which have a high gloss finish.

The reason is twofold. For one, there is usually great clarity through the finish to the grain of the wood, and using a translucent amber (right) or "crystal clear" burn in stick allows you to "see through" the filled area to keep that perceived depth of the finish.

In this repair process, you want to complete your touch up with pigments prior to burning-in (filling) the damage. If touched up, filled, leveled and finished properly, it's possible that damages may become virtually invisible.

The second reason is that if a surface has a truly high gloss sheen, you likey won't be able to replicate the gloss reflection, if you have to perform repairs using a padding finish and french polishing techniques.

Gloss surfaces really have to be buffed out with compounds to keep the sheen consistent with the original sheen level. One positive thing about the burn-in method is that because you applied your pigment underneath the translucent filler, you cannot "buff/compound/polish" the applied pigment off the surface, it's protected by the filler above it.

As you buff the burn-in and surrounding areas, you should be removing faint sanding marks and the filled damage should become level with the surface, while creating a sheen as glossy in the filled area, as the surrounding surface.

As you can imagine in the method's name, burn-in must have to do with heating something. More precisely it involves heating your burn-in knife, to extremely high temperatures, and melting a stick of colored synthetic thermoplastic resin (yes, the "sticks" are no longer made of shellac), into the damages.

Now that I look back on how I was taught, and the method we used to heat our burn-in knives, I realize now how naive I was to the fact that I could have easily burned someone's house down, or at the least started a fire, I was fortunate.

To heat our burn in knives we had to create our own homemade burner. We took a new, small, empty metal oil applicator can, and cut the nozzle two thirds of the way down.

We then tore off a section of a rag to create a wick, which we put through the spout and extended the remainder of the cloth into the bottom of the oil can.

The can was then filled with denatured alcohol and the lid back was put back on the oil can loosely, so that air could enter inside the burner. If no air enters through the threaded area of the cap, it may explode.

Denatured alcohol would seep up the nozzle into the wicking cloth, and I would light it with a lighter. At this point OSHA would not approve.

Notice first, the "burner" is sitting on a folded piece of sandpaper. I slide my burn-in knife across the sandpaper often to clean any excess filler off throughout a repair.

Remember with the burn-in method, we perform the touch up first (below).

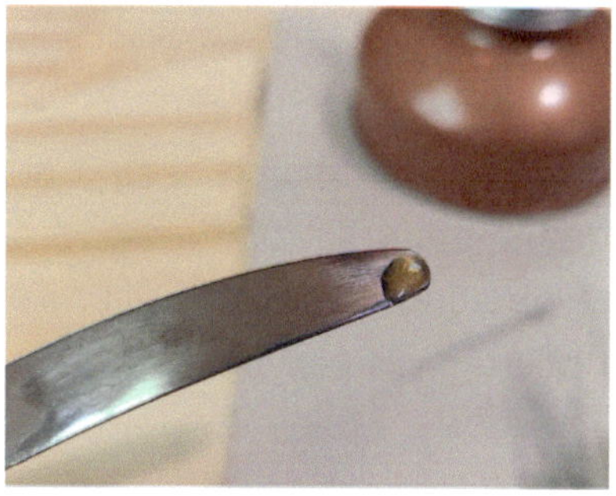

After the pigment application, get the tip of your burn-in knife sufficiently heated over the flame, then push the hot edge of the blade into the fill stick and remove a little molten ball of filler (right).

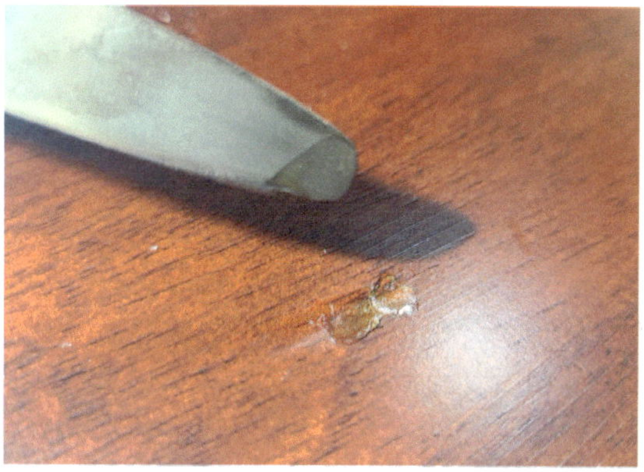

Take that molten filler on your heated knife blade and transfer it into the damage (right), you can try slightly dripping or smearing the filler into the damage.

Clean off the excess filler from your blade by scraping across the sandpaper. Keep heating your blade until you're prepared to level the surface.

The temperature of the blade is of great importance at this moment because if your blade is too hot you could blister the finish surrounding the burn-in which would cause the need for additional repairs and touch up.

Notice a little puddle of water on the surface of the filler (left), this water will act as a slight lubricant and will assist in keeping the surrounding finish from blistering as we slide across with the hot curved underside of the knife's blade.

There is a product called burn-in balm that acts in the same fashion as the water just described. I don't like carrying a lot of extra products so water does the job just fine for me.

Heat your knife, sometimes 15-30 seconds, err on the side of less time till you get used to anticipating the temperature of the blade.

Using the curved underside of the heated burn-in knife, begin to wipe across the filler in differing directions. Just make sure to keep the knife moving.

During this process, it's alright to go against the grain of the wood, think of it as you are pushing the excess filler from the damage outward in all directions until you feel that the filler appears fairly level with the surrounding surface.

It may take several repetitions of heating your blade, adding water to the surface and leveling the filler before the surface is sufficiently leveled.

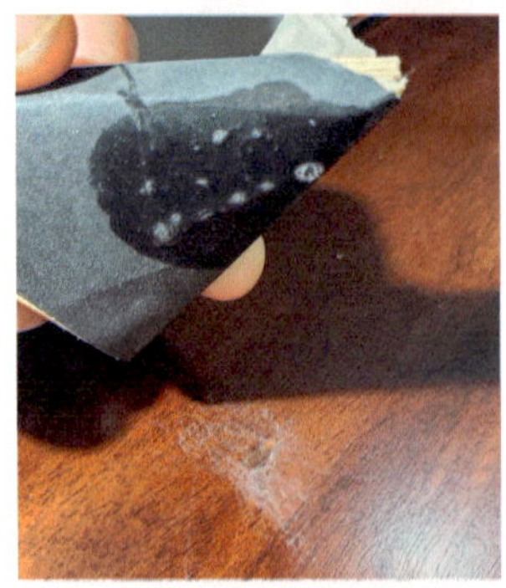

Once the filler has been leveled sufficiently, blow out your burner, twist the cap on tightly and you're done with that aspect of the repair.

Using a piece of 600 grit w/d sandpaper, a sanding block and some additional water for lubrication, lightly sand to continue to remove any excess and to further level the surface.

The picture to the right shows the sanded and leveled surface. Notice, I have not sanded through the surrounding finish to the wood or removed any of the color from the filled area.

Use your padding finish and padding rag to french polish the area to remove the sanding scratches and build the finish up, as in the picture below.

Finish it off with a medium misting of a clear satin toner (sometimes), and admire the finished product.

If you're not quite satisfied with the colorwork or grain pattern, simply continue to touch it up, on the surface, till you get it just right.

That right there is the reason I switched to Bondo®, as often I still had to touch up over the filled and sanded area.

I figured that if I was going to need to add additional touch up to the surface after the burn-in anyway, I might as well just use Bondo®.

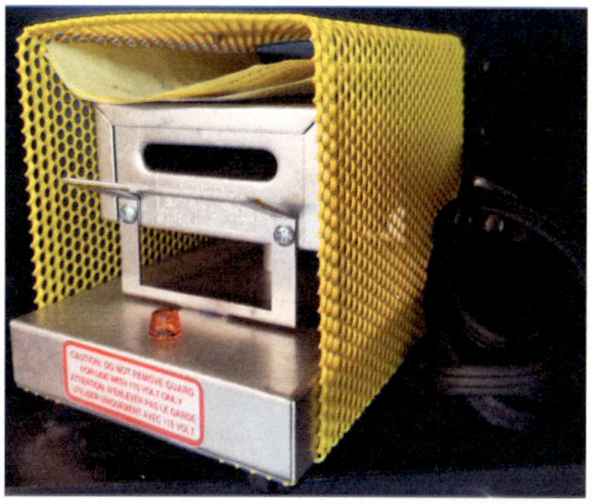

I could mix up a batch of Bondo® and fill numerous gouges at one time. I no longer had to melt a stick over a fire to fill, then level each individual area of damage.

For anyone else interested in performing the burn-in method, there are two other options to get the heat you need to perform the task. One is to carry around a large contraption that is strikingly similar to a miniature pizza oven (right).

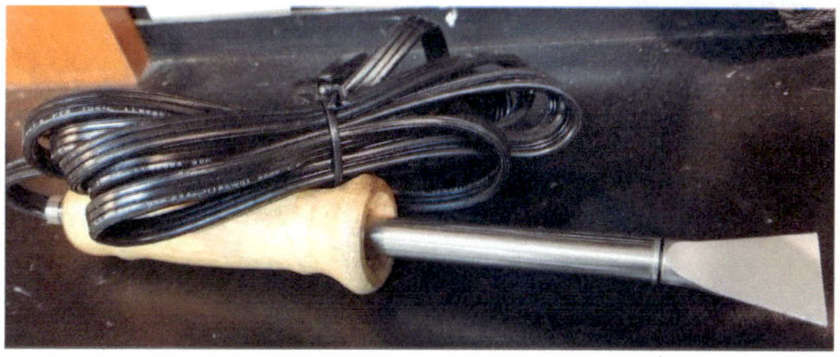

The second contraption is an electric burn-in knife, which is a long tool with a power cord coming out of the rear, and at the opposite is a metal tip that would heat up, similar to a wood burning tool.

This tool is cumbersome, it could be almost a foot long and you are still tied to an extension cord or an outlet.

Both tools need to be plugged in for them to function and heat up the knives. I often found that this option would not heat the burn in knives to a high enough temperature, that I preferred, or at the least I felt I had more control over the temperature of my blade when using an open flame.

That's all the information I can muster with regard to filling surface damages, have fun with your new found talent on a plethora of exciting projects!

A section of veneer broken off and missing is an extremely common type of damage when restoring an older piece of furniture, and can be prevalent with newer furniture also.

If you have just a loose bit of veneer, you may be lucky, the only thing you may have to do is get some glue underneath the loose area and secure it down. Often though, there may be quite a bit more that you may need to accomplish.

I don't carry any veneer with me while working on the road, for one, older veneer is far thicker than today's veneer, sometimes as thick as a 1/16". Plus, in my opinion, it's far quicker just to fill, touch up and repair the damage.

Even if I did have a piece of veneer, and glued it on, the area still needs to be filled, at least on the surrounding edges where the new piece was spliced in. Additionally, the new piece would still need to be colored to match, and most likely the grain pattern of the new veneer will not match the pattern of the existing piece of furniture.

In my opinion, splicing in a new piece of veneer is often more time consuming and could be more apparent than simply filling and touching up the surface.

So save yourself the headache, unless new veneer is specifically requested by the client, then charge accordingly. The restoration will likely take longer and maybe even two trips if you have to obtain a particular type of wood.

But if you're experienced enough with repairs, you should be able to replace that missing veneer with filler, and be able to replicate the hue, tone and look of the grain pattern with your pigments so that any unwitting person would have no clue that a repair was ever performed.

In the close up picture to the right, which is the same as the title picture, you can see there is a large section of veneer pulling away from the frame of the drawer face, along with an approximate 3" x 2" section of veneer completely missing.

One of the most important aspects to be aware of when needing to fill a veneer chip, is to ensure that all the veneer surrounding the missing chip is secure with no loose areas.

If there is loose veneer around the edges of your filling, a crack will likely develop where the unsecured wood meets the filler. Ultimately causing the filled area to chip out in the future, or at least your restoration will be apparent.

If there are any loose areas of veneer, mix up the proper amount of epoxy (I use epoxy while making house calls and standard wood glue in shop, in general, due to time constraints), insert some glue to the rear of the loose veneer, and to the frame, basically both surfaces where the veneer contacts.

It is then wise to use a clamp and a block of wood to hold down the loose veneer, but as you can see in the picture (below right), tape can be useful as a clamp also.

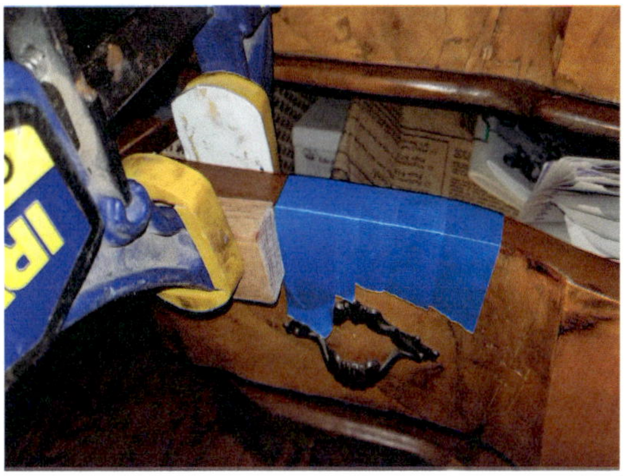

Be careful not to use an excessive amount of glue and be sure to clean off any excess prior to clamping.

If you don't clean off the excess and a large amount of glue seeps out onto the wood block, you could have glued that block to the surface and removing it could cause even more damage to the veneer.

Pro-tip: If you're not sure how much glue you've used, put a piece of wet/dry sandpaper, waterproof coated side down, and clamp the block over that. It's far easier removing extra glue and paper rather than an entire adhered piece of wood.

Any excess glue that does seep out, once dried, I will use a razor blade to clean off the surface.

Also do not let extra glue migrate into an area that needs to be filled, as filler may not bond well to the smooth surface of glue.

Once all the veneer is secure you can mix up the proper amount of filler and apply into the area of the missing veneer chip.

The main lesson that I hope you take away is that all the surrounding surface needs to be secured, before you address the actual missing veneer.

From here it's essentially the same process that we went over with most of the previous repair samples, so I won't bore you with dragging out all descriptions, but I'll quickly try to walk you through the rest of the repair.

Remember, you may have to fill the damage at least two times before it's perfectly level, then wipe over the sanded surface with your padding rag, padding finish, and begin to perform the touch up.

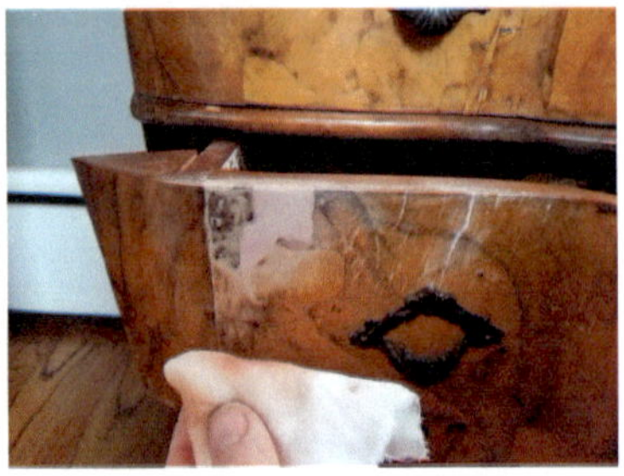

This is the type of repair when using the surrounding characteristics of the wood is a good idea. If you notice the grain pattern, it's erratic. I'm going to use a lot of those erratic lines to conceal the repair even further on the next page.

I then come back with some pigment applied to my padding rag, so that I can blend the area of damage in even further, seal all the hard work with a clear coat, and this repair is complete.

This repair took about an hour, and the pigments used were orange, buff, yellow oxide, burnt umber and carbon black.

There's a pro-tip that I want to tell you about, even though I probably won't use it anywhere in this book,

For damages that are filled, if the surrounding wood, for instance, oak or teak, has deep or prominent grain cavities, you may use the sharp corner of a razor blade and cut tiny lines in the filler to simulate the deep grain pattern.

The key is to cut a consistent transition from one side of the surface, over the filled area, to the other side of the surface in the pattern of the surrounding grain.

You could cut a grain pattern deep, shallow, jagged or long and straight, but I find I do this far and few inbetween as I've come to realize that a "grain pattern" is often created simply through the various levels of pigment application as you perform your touch up. Strokes from a paint brush may create small variations in the finish, which if applied properly can often be perceived as the original grain of the wood.

There's a term that you've probably never heard, or knew existed, but have unknowingly admired its visual effects in the surface of virtually every finished piece of wooden furniture, wood wall panel, instrument, wood carving, the list could continue.

"Chatoyance" is derived from the French word "Chatoyer", meaning "to shine like a cat's eye". It's a term used to describe the effect that makes a finished wood surface appear three dimensional.

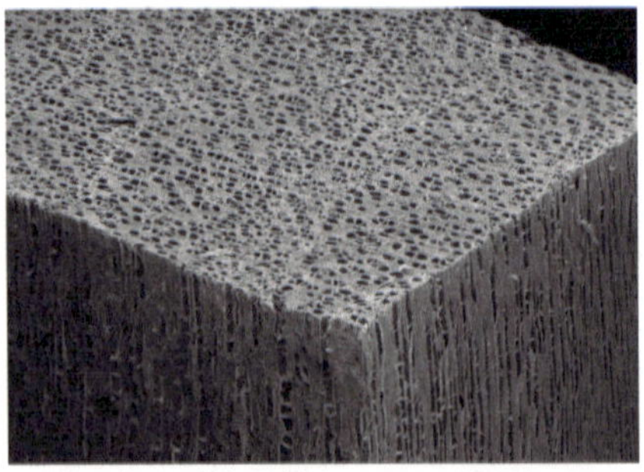

Virtually every piece of wood that has a clear finish, you may notice light and dark areas of the wood and grain start to shift, and possibly dance as you walk around a surface, changing the angles from which you are viewing.

It's caused by light reflecting into the various cavities of the grain/wood cells. The picture to the right is a microscopic photo of those grain cavities, from a piece of American Beech. Differing woods will have different appearances.

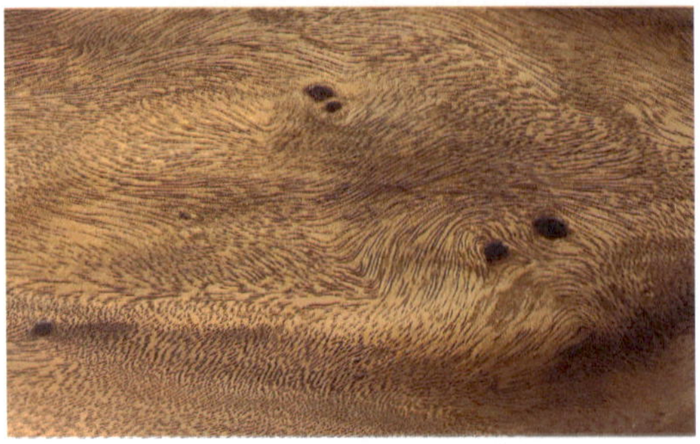

You can also notice the phenomenon around knots, or where abrupt changes cause the reflected light to change dramatically based on the grain's orientation.

It's very easy to observe what appear to be three dimensional patterns in what is essentially a flat surface.

Almost all finished wood will have some chatoyancy, but it's usually not pronounced enough to become an issue during the majority of repairs.

Additionally, the amount of chatoyancy may also depend on how transparent the finish is. Some manufacturers color/stain their furniture by adding dye into their clear coats.

Therefore the color from the dye stain, mixed with the finish, dries on the surface, and doesn't penetrate deep into the grain cavities.

Thus making the finish less translucent, which in turn decreases the perceived depth of the grain, negating a good amount of chatoyancy.

Unfortunately, chatoyance could potentially be one of the most difficult aspects to overcome while performing repairs.

The first picture is a close up of a dining table that has a fairly large gouge, which I began to fill. The affected area is approximately 8" long by 2" wide.

I did this repair as a sample, there was other significant damage which warranted refinishing of the table, just fyi.

The second picture shows the gouged area filled and sanded. Please note that I did not sand through the finish to the bare wood. The "whiter" halo is just sanding into a different level of the clear coat.

The majority of time during any particular restoration, you remain in one location, in front of the subject, near your tool box, performing the repair. Basically looking at the damage from one angle as you work.

Towards the conclusion of the repair, you get up, walk around to the other side, and oh my goodness, the beautiful repair you thought was just about finished, looks way too light, or in some cases way too dark, as you can see in the third picture

In the fourth picture, as I walk around the table, the light reflects into the grain cavities differently, so the repair has now appeared to change hues and become lighter.

Often it requires using a combination of different techniques, learned from various chapters, which include the use of varied color pigments in an opaque or translucent manner, painting with alternating colors to match the existing wood hue and grain pattern as closely as possible.

Possibly adding some padding finish and pigment to your padding rag in an attempt to feather out and further blend the repair.

Even using dyes from toners, either by misting some on the surface, or actually spraying the colored toner on the back of a piece of sandpaper, and using that specifically for touch up with a paintbrush.

There are many ways to attack the problem, and the more you practice in general, the better some of these more difficult repairs will turn out. To the right is the freshly refinished table.

Occasionally though, during a particularly tough repair that may have a large amount of chatoyance, you may just have to find what is considered a "happy medium".

From some angles the repair may be completely invisible. From other angles the repair may be slightly noticeable. Without the option for refinishing initially, you may consider repairing the damage, to as near perfect as possible, from the angle it would be viewed most.

It may take some experience to know, prior to starting a repair, what the end result will be, but if you're worried the issue of chatoyancy may arise, I would suggest speaking with your client about the effect prior to starting.

It's far less stressful to explain initially that a repair may not turn out well, rather than to explain what went wrong at the conclusion, to an unhappy client.

My axiom is to never over promise how well a repair will turn out initially. In fact, I usually try to undersell what I feel would be the final result. Then, when repairs are complete and the client comes back and can't find the repair at all, they are pleasantly surprised, but because I forewarned them that the end result may not be ideal, the client already is possibly expecting to be disappointed or to see a poor repair.

Don't scare the client too much prior to the restoration though, you should always appear confident in your abilities. It's also a far easier conversation to have regarding the next steps needed to correct the unresolved issue, like deciding with the client that the surface may need to be refinished to create the perfect restoration.

As you become more proficient in restorations, you will have a good grasp of what a completed repair may look like prior to even starting the process.

Another disappointing fact, if you are not successful with a repair, you may not be able to charge for it. The whole reason you were hired was to fix the damage, nobody wants to pay for a job that wasn't completed to their satisfaction.

Again, there may be limitations to how well a given repair may turn out, based on numerous factors, even if you are the most talented furniture repair technician the world has ever known. Some damages just refuse to become hidden/disguised/invisible, those stubborn damages get reclassified into "character".

If all else fails, you now may have found the perfect opportunity to start perfecting your refinishing techniques. Refinishing could easily triple or quadruple your repair cost/earnings.

Refinishing a dining room table could easily range from $1000-$3000, depending on numerous factors, the size of the table (including leaves), the "nicer" the finish has to be, the more work involved, the higher the repair cost.

There are usually several determining factors in play when it comes time to differentiate whether a particular type of damage may be able to be repaired, or requires refinishing.

Some of those factors may include the antiquity value, the customer's desire to keep the original finish, ability to perform the required task, whether it's more work involved than the value of the item, along with a host of other possible factors.

The majority of the time, it's actually the piece of furniture that makes that determination for you, usually based on the characteristics of the existing finish.

I'll explain a few of the varying issues with finishes that you may come across. Most of the issues are a direct result of historically poor or inconsistent environmental conditions, or care over the life of an item.

"Alligatoring" is a term for the appearance of an aged finish, often appearing as a pattern of tiny intersecting "cracks" or "micro-voids", the size and depth of the cracks can also vary from small to large.

The phenomenon may also be referred to as "crazing". Wood is constantly shrinking or swelling in direct relation to the atmosphere, placing stress on the clear coat finish, eventually causing it to crack.

There is a process used to reverse "alligatoring", called *amalgamation* (you may see it written as, reamalgamation), which in short, means to combine or unite to create one structure.

Amalgamation requires the use of a solvent. For shellac, the solvent required is denatured alcohol. For nitrocellulose lacquer, it's lacquer thinner. Any finishes harder, like urethane, varnishes or epoxies cannot be amalgamated.

In this case, you are combining the aged finish and a solvent to create a "new" finish, though the finish technically isn't "new", consider it, renewed or at the least reinvigorated.

Applying the solvent by brush or padding rag will soften (or seemingly melt) the finish, filling in and/or removing the small hairline microscopic cracks/voids, and once the solvent evaporates, the finish will harden again without defects.

Everything works in theory, though it may not always work out that well in practice, but try it to see. Maybe it turns out you are able to preserve the existing finish instead of needing to totally refinish a particular piece.

Another way we can correct this issue is with MyRepairKit™, a lot of patience, sandpaper, padding rag and padding finish. After cleaning the surface, sand it well with 220-400 grit sandpaper.

You will notice the sanding powder will be fairly white in color, that's normal due to the old dried out finish. Sand the existing finish as much as possible without sanding completely through the original clear coat, to the wood surface. After the initial sanding, the finish should be pretty smooth, void of any substantial roughness.

I then suggest using the circular french polishing technique and begin to build the finish back up. This will expeditiously fill any microvoids/cracks left in the surface from the alligatoring. Eventually french polish in the east/west motion, in line with the grain, to remove visible circles from the circular technique.

Continue to french polish until you have obtained a beautiful, nearly flawless finish. Pay attention to all areas of the surface, there may be occasions you have to let the applied finish dry, re-sand, french polish again and/or touch up an area additionally to remove stubborn finish defects.

More significant cracking can be very pronounced in thicker finishes. These cracks can open or the finish can begin to lose adhesion from the wood surface. If this is the case, the existing finish cannot be salvaged. At some point the finish may degrade further and begin to flake or chip off.

These next two pictures show significant cracking of the finish. Both pictures are of the same exact location but from different angles and lighting so you can see variation and the extensiveness of the cracking/crazing.

This piece below would need to be refinished to correct this type of cracking.

This type of cracking can also occur over time, when any finish type is applied too thick. Finishes in general shouldn't be thicker than 3 mil (except for possibly epoxy or self leveling finishes which are specially formulated to be "thick" and most common on restaurant tables or bar tops).

I know there is no way for you to really measure that, just don't spray an excessive amount of coats. I find the finishes we apply are perfect or near perfect within approximately 4-6 applied coats, with a conversion varnish, and sanding in between each coat.

Today, most mass produced furniture is coated in a ***conversion varnish*** (right). Conversion varnishes contain an alkyd resin, in addition to several other solvents, and requires an acid catalyst to cure.

One coat of conversion varnish can equal up to four coats of other single coat finishes. That is why it's possible that slightly more "coats" of applied finish is allowed when using nitrocellulose lacquer(left).

Nitrocellulose lacquer does not have the same amount of solids, and does not build up quite as fast.

Those approximations may also vary depending on how heavy or light the various coats of applied finish are. In general, I suggest applying "lighter" coats initially, and "heavier" coats of finish towards the conclusion of the spraying/refinishing process.

Shellac and nitrocellulose lacquer are known to be a "non-conversion" coating, meaning the coatings are formed by solvent evaporation alone, there is no chemical reaction involved in the curing process.

Conversion varnish usually consists of between 40%-60% solids. Alkyd resin is a thermoplastic or a thermosetting polyester resin, so yes, that translates essentially to most furniture being coated in plastic.

Conversion varnishes require to be sprayed on, and usually will need to be done by a professional unless you have the proper equipment yourself, like an HVLP (high volume low pressure, or other) spray system, spray booth, the various finish ingredients, and just as important, personal protective gear, especially a respirator.

Ingredients include the finish, an activator/catalyzer, thinner and possibly other chemicals which are precisely measured and introduced/mixed prior to spraying. There is a shelf life, as once the ingredients are mixed, the curing process begins, and the finish will need to be used in a certain time frame, usually within 24 hours.

Some may refer to these finishes as a "two pack coating". These types of coatings are not reversible once the chemical activation/conversion takes place.

Once mixed and applied the molecules in these chemicals grow larger in size, begin to overlap, causing the cross-linking of the molecules to take place, resulting in an extremely durable finish that will last significantly longer than lacquer or shellac (non-conversion varnishes).

We use a conversion varnish for most of our refinishing projects. The finish is ideal for high use environments like desks, dining tables, kitchen and bath cabinetry, or any other surfaces that see considerable use or moisture.

The finish is not impermeable, but far more water/liquid, scratch and solvent resistant than the majority of other finish types.

Most of the time, what I notice most is how thick the finish is, or are there any depressions in the finish from the grain cavities? The surface of a piece of furniture finished with conversion varnish will likely be almost perfectly flat due to the high amount of solids filling the grain.

Secondly, I take into consideration how much damage is there overall on a surface. Usually conversion varnish is highly resistant to most scratching, and generally would require a significant impact or abrasion to cause damage.

There is also a "look", in my opinion. The finish appears to glow with a seemingly whitish reflection and more often than not, the majority of furniture nowadays is produced in a satin sheen, which makes that "whitish glow" even more evident, at least from my perspective.

What I feel I see as the "whitish glow", is a direct cause of the high amount of solids and flattening agents used to create the finish. The solids are not always translucent, they are white, which causes the finish to appear to be cloudy in the container.

The trick to minimizing this whitish effect is to build up all your coats with a gloss finish, then for a final coat, alter your mixture to create any desired sheen less than gloss.

A word of warning, if you start spraying with satin/flat and continue to build several coats of satin/flat finish, each coat will increase the appearance of the solids, making the surface even "whiter" and/or more opaque with each additional coat.

There are different finishes available that are "crystal clear" (water clear). Once applied to furniture, it's not always easy to distinguish between finishes, especially high gloss.

One other telltale sign that the finish is a conversion varnish, is when sanding, the finish turns into a fine white powder.

For the most part, using My Repair Kit™, we can complete the majority of repairs to perfection on furniture that has been finished with a conversion varnish, but one area that I would consider difficult, or at the least, not ideal, is on large top surfaces like dining room tables, buffets, a large triple dresser top, or the like.

Repairability often depends on the location and extent of the damage. If there is significant damage as far as multiple gouges, impressions, or large scratches, located near the middle of a surface, we may find it a far better option to refinish that surface, rather than repair.

One issue I feel is durability of the finish. Padding finishes are "non-conversion" finishes, they will never harden to be as durable as an existing conversion varnish.

That doesn't mean that you can't create a near flawless repair, that just means that your "repaired area" may not be as durable, scratch resistant or colorfast as the rest of the surface, and may wear differently with time, possibly making the repaired areas slightly noticeable in the future.

"Water damage" is often a common occurrence with furniture. Spilled water on your dining room table, left a water cup on your nightstand, had a plant on an end table?

The range of damage that can be created by water/liquid could be minimal, as small as just a slight white discoloration(left), to disastrous, like cracking wood, flaking finish, buckling veneer and swelling grain.

You can usually create successful repairs on most minor damages, treating and attacking the repair as if any other small defect or gouge.

If liquid permeates through the finished surface and the wood grain has become swollen, the surrounding finish will lose adhesion to the wood and eventually begin to crack/flake and/or chip off.

One thing to always keep in mind when repairing surfaces with water/liquid damage is that the finish that you apply over the surface is only as strong and secure as the existing finish underneath

Meaning if the existing finish has already lost adhesion to the wood, don't expect your new repair to be permanent unless you take proper steps to ensure all the surrounding finish is secure to the surface.

There really is no way to repair the water damage in the picture to the right, that would look decent and be permanent. Once the finish starts flaking substantially, your only recourse for a good outcome would be refinishing.

"MDF" (medium density fiberboard) is similar to a dense, thick, paper type material. Any introduction of water or liquid will severely swell the affected MDF.

For that matter, similar damage may happen also when liquid is introduced to plywood or pressboard/particle board material, but may seem even more significant with regard to furniture consisting of MDF.

Once a liquid is introduced, the MDF wicks it up like, well, paper, it will swell, even causing veneer to swell and become raised or uneven.

Attempting to sand any "raised" area flat, will only burn completely through any veneer into the swollen material.

Sanding alone doesn't always make a water swollen area perfectly flat. Once the internal fibers begin to swell and become dislodged, it creates an unstable area.

These fibers will never become as stable as they were when the MDF was fabricated, that's why it generally makes for a better repair if the damaged area is simply cut out, filled and touched up or replaced.

"Chemical Damage" is another popular type of damage seen on dressers and nightstands, which for the record, is definitely not caused by careless women (remember, it's never a woman's fault, you're welcome gentlemen!).

But usually caused by poor design of a product's packaging and by solvents commonly used in products like nail polish remover, oil scents, perfume/cologne, and countless beauty products.

These products can contain alcohol, acetone, oils or numerous other chemicals that have the ability to dissolve a finish.

A telltale sign that the finish was damaged by a solvent, as seen better in the image to the right, is that the edges of the affected area will seem “melted”.

More often than not, the finish has also been melted/removed all the way down to the bare wood, in the shape of the bottom of the container.

The affected area is noticeably different as compared to an abrasion or gouge, if you pay close attention to the characteristics of the damage.

There are two options for repair using MyRepairKit™, the first is to simply sand the affected area and try to gradually feather out the damage. One issue with this method is that once you start applying the touch up and building the finish up, you will likely see a “dip” or unevenness/waviness in the surface.

More often than not, you will need to fill and sand the damage, so that the surface would be perfectly flat, then proceed with touch up. Keep in mind, the larger the damaged area, the more difficult a repair may be, usually anything over 4”-6” squared will warrant refinishing, or at the least be considered a “best possible repair”.

“Climatic damage” can appear in several forms but there is one factor that causes it all, you guessed it, the climate! Wood in general, even after being made into a piece of furniture, consistently shrinks or swells with the surrounding atmospheric conditions, which creates issues like warpage and cracks.

Wood is a *hygroscopic* material. This means that wood releases moisture in a dry environment (shrink), and absorbs moisture in a damp environment (swell), until there is an established equilibrium.

This concept is known as Equilibrium Moisture Content (EMC). Moisture content (MC) of wood will come into equilibrium with the relative humidity (RH) of the surrounding air.

For each level of relative humidity of the air, there is a matching equilibrium moisture content of wood. The way to find the moisture content of the air is to use a hygrometer.

Some professional hygrometers (right) have attachments, invasive and non-invasive, that can also test the moisture content in the actual wood!

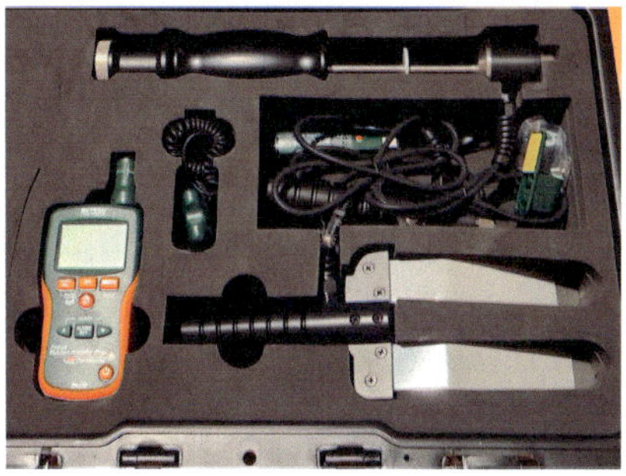

Here are a few numbers for perspective. If the relative humidity is 30%, the moisture content in wood is 6%. RH at 45%-49% has MC in wood at 8%. RH at 58%-63% has MC in wood at 11%, and one more, RH at 75%, has MC in wood at 14%. Ideal moisture content of wood should be between 7%-8%.

It's also pretty apparent, by the adjacent map, that the closer you are in proximity to water, the higher the relative humidity.

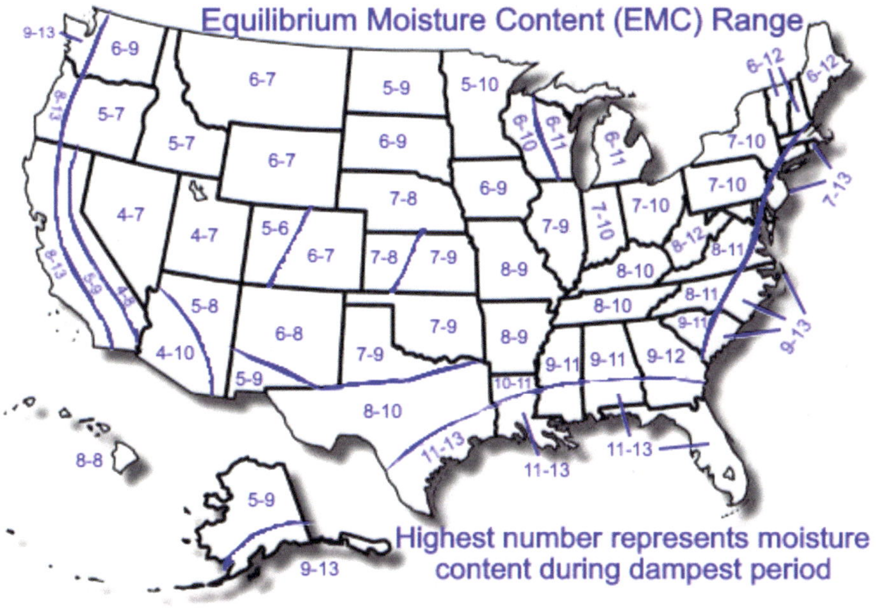

From the map, it looks like Hawaii is the most ideal place to live year round for the health of your furniture, pack your bags!

Seriously though, if your environment is too moist or too dry you should incorporate a dehumidifier or humidifier respectively. Try keeping your furniture in a stable, temperature controlled environment, with the relative humidity somewhere around 35%-45%, this should minimize any climatic damage that would ever have the possibility of occurring.

Climatic changes may not always be visible, slight shrinkage or expansion will likely not always be noticeable to the naked eye. In some instances, with particular types of finishes, like epoxy finishes, if the wood is sealed well on all sides, the atmosphere may not have an effect on the wood greatly or even at all.

Wood is also *anisotropic*, which means wood has different properties depending on the direction of the grain, it's not the same in all directions, therefore wood does not shrink or swell in a perfectly uniform manner.

Wood shrinks/swells across three planes, the radial plane, tangential plane and the longitudinal plane. Combine all three of those together and you get volumetric shrinkage/swelling.

With solid wood, warpage and cracking could happen within hours of exposure or gradually over time, acclimation to a new climate for a piece of wood or furniture could take a few days to a couple months.

Once acclimated, the expansion or contraction should never change as long as the environment stays the same.

To put it in numbers, approximately one percent dimensional change takes place with each three percent change in the moisture content of the wood.

One of the most obvious types of climatic damage is cracking.

You may often notice small cracks on the ends of tables, or separation beginning in glue joints of two or more solid wood planks.

Splitting the edges of solid wood furniture is a phenomenon most frequently seen with antique or older furniture which may have been stored in an unheated/unregulated area, maybe a basement, garage or shed, and are then subsequently brought into a heated home.

Moisture content of wood furniture stored in unregulated areas may be up to 12% higher on average, and as soon as these pieces are brought into a heated home, they immediately begin to dry out, shrink and proceed to have the possibility of cracking or warping.

Moisture movement is much more rapid from end grain than from side grain, the edges of furniture begin to dry and shrink, but the core usually retains its original dimensions, thus resulting in the unsightly splits on the edges, which may extend onto a surface.

Wood doesn't always have to crack though, warpage is another major issue. Once wood decides to "bend" in a direction it's not supposed to, it's almost impossible, without significant modification to remove the bend/warpage.

Warpage may happen more often with long flat panels that are not supported on most sides, like doors of cabinets or edges of a table, as seen to the right. This type of warpage is called "cupping".

As a contractor who assess damages for the military (to all past, present and future military members, I thank you for your service!), we often see families moved from overseas to the states.

A family's contents/belongings are usually brought by ship, in metal shipping containers, which are not climate controlled. These containers can reach in excess of 150°F degrees during summer, or -20°F degrees in the winter depending on where the ship is coming from or going to.

Combine that with constant moisture/humidity from the ocean and you have yourself the possibility of disastrous repercussions concerning your furniture.

Climatic damage is one of the most difficult things to explain to a client, while also explaining that it was not caused by an action of the mover. The only thing the client will say is; "it wasn't like that before the move!"

Technically they are not incorrect, in fact, it's such an issue that to protect yourself, you need to purchase insurance specifically for climatic damage. In the moving industry, this type of damage is considered "inherent vice", or in other words, unavoidable, therefore not covered by insurance without the additional specific climatic coverage.

So if you are moving overseas, or coming home, though expensive, it would be wise to have this type of additional protection, particularly if you own several antiques or solid wood constructed pieces of furniture.

Since we're on the topic of insurance, it's also wise to never accept or purchase the minimum insurance which is .60¢ per pound. This means if your damaged piece of furniture weighs 100 pounds, the insurance liability is $60.00.

That amount of money will rarely cover any type of repair, as the average restoration company may charge $100-$200 per hour.

Also, remember earlier I mentioned a dining table refinish may be $1000-$3000. Very few dining room tables would weigh more than a couple hundred pounds. Even if a piece of furniture weighs 300 lbs, that still only adds up to an $180.00 liability for the insurance company, and that amount of liability will rarely cover the cost of repair on most items. To cover yourself, I suggest obtaining "Full Value Replacement" Insurance.

An additional liability that may be wise to carry is called "pairs and sets". This coverage is for items which belong to a set, for instance, a bedroom set, could consist of a bed, triple dresser, tall chest, two nightstands and possibly more. This type of liability will account for the entire value of the set, instead of one individual piece, which should provide additional money to cover any expenses incurred.

Similarly a "pair" could be 2 matching lamps. If one lamp is shattered, and you have pairs and sets coverage, then you should be compensated for both lamps, not just the individually damaged one. This type of liability is also good to have when dealing with large sets of fine china, crystal glassware, or the like.

Back to the topic at hand, when we do come across climatic damage, we have to tell the shipper (client) and the carrier (moving company) that we cannot guarantee a repair. There is no amount of glue or filler that will stop a climatic crack from shifting again (which will expose the repair products if the crack opens or closes further).

You can attempt to sister a new plank of wood to the rear of the climatic crack to add stability but that is still no guarantee the crack wont continue to move and may even cause additional cracks in unforeseen areas because not all wood changes at the same rate. You really have no idea what type of pressure any particular piece of wood is under.

With veneered furniture, the damage may seem even worse than a simple crack. The problem that may occur is that the veneer is glued to a wood subframe. Often the grain pattern of the veneer and the grain pattern of the wood subframe under the veneer are not aligned in the same direction.

Meaning that the veneer and wood framing are fighting against each other, expanding or contracting in opposite directions, which will most definitely cause the veneer to buckle and/or detach from the wood subframe.

This may happen often with a crotch veneer, as the grain pattern is going in multiple directions, creating a large amount of stress for the veneer to stay attached.

In the picture to the right, the veneer's grain pattern is applied vertically, but the wood subframing underneath the veneer is positioned horizontally.

The wood subframe under the veneer, and the veneer has shrunk, both changing at a different rate and direction.

The veneer and older glue could not take the stress, so it buckled. In the case of this desk, similar damage was consistent throughout all sides, the top and legs.

We considered this desk to be "non repairable". It's not that we couldn't repair it, it's just that the amount of work that would be involved to properly remove and reattach all the buckled veneer and fill all the cracks would be extremely time consuming.

Additionally, to create a flawless restoration, the desk also requires refinishing. We're talking about a repair cost in the thousands based on the time it would take to properly restore.

Moving adjudicators/insurance will always consider what would be the most "cost effective" avenue, taking into consideration if the piece is cheaper to pay out (cash settle based on its value) or repair?

That is usually the determining factor in most restorations with regard to moving damage and insurance work, although if someone is willing to flip the bill, you should never deny the work!

Another issue that you are guaranteed to run into at some point while performing repairs is what I refer to as ***"too much damage"***. Which means exactly that, there is just too darn much damage to realistically restore without refinishing.

At some point, with every piece of furniture, there comes a decision as to whether it's a time commitment, expected outcome and/or a financially viable option to perform a repair or determine something is better off refinishing.

If damage is extensive, a repair could conceivably take more time to perform than actually refinishing the area/piece. Additionally, if there is that much damage that requires your need to make this decision, then you should probably expect that any repair you perform will likely be noticeable in some areas.

In the following pictures of a dining table, the damage may not appear that extensive from afar, but upon closer inspection, with varied lighting, you can see an inordinate amount of damage throughout the surface.

In my opinion, “it’s just too darn much damage to fix”, the only option from my perspective is to refinish this table, which we did.

“Contamination” of a finish, is a catch-all term that can be presented in several different forms.

Contamination is usually caused by oil based or silicone products being used for cleaning throughout the life of a piece of furniture.

These products imbed themselves deep into the wood cavities and could be very difficult to completely remove during the restoration process. Most often, contamination will arise during the refinishing process, not always during a “repair”.

Proceeding we will touch on some of the various problems that may come about during either the repair or refinishing process.

“Blushing” may occur during both the refinishing and repair process. Blushing is a term that is used when moisture gets trapped on or in-between various coats of finish, appearing as a milky white, cloudy, defect in the clear coat.

Moisture can penetrate into the finish by long term exposure to humidity. There could be too much water in the atmosphere when you are finishing/spraying a piece of wood/furniture.

There may also be water in your spray equipment or air lines which feed your sprayer.

If you're using a spray system other than an HVLP, you should incorporate an air regulator with a water trap and/or filter similar to the one on the right, which will remove any water or contaminants from your airlines before it gets to your spray equipment.

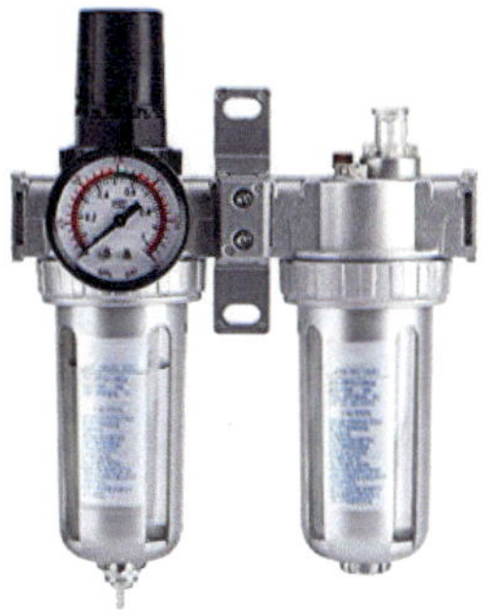

For that matter you should have a regulator at the end of every airline in your shop, you do not want water flowing into any of your air tools.

If it's a rainy day, you may want to hold off on applying a substantial amount of finish to a surface. If the problem persists there are products called "no blush", or "blush retarder" that you can apply to the finished surface or incorporate into your finish mixture that will remove or greatly limit the white haze/blushing.

"Blooming" is similar to blushing (I don't know who makes up these terms), it's when the applied finish appears to have an iridescent or bluish haze. This will not occur during a "repair" but happens during refinishing.

Usually caused by incompletely cured oil stains trapped under the clear coat of a surface, which means the applied stain on a wood surface may not have properly dried before beginning the application of clearcoats.

There is a possibility that if this particular problem occurs you may have to strip the finish off of the surface because the oil incorporated into the stain has migrated into the clear coat. When the finish dries, the oil will still be trapped.

"Streaking" will only happen during a repair, and is usually caused by contaminants on a surface that has not been properly cleaned, prior to french polishing/applying a new padding finish.

The contamination is caused by cleaners or polishes previously used, leaving remnants of particular chemicals or silicone on the surface, which reacts negatively with our padding finish.

If streaking occurs, the previously applied padding finish would need to be removed, either by solvent or sanding, then the surface will need to be properly cleaned.

Streaking/reaction will happen almost immediately when performing a repair. Don't confuse it with the end process of a french polish where you may see some variation in the finish from the oils incorporated into the padding finish.

Those oils may cause what appear to be faint streaking, but usually as the padding finish cures, the oils evaporate, leaving a streak free finish. This aspect is also covered in the chapter on french polishing.

"Fish Eye", may also be referred to as "cratering", or "crawling", doesn't always occur when performing repairs, unless you apply a "very heavy coat" from a toner can. More often this problem presents itself during the refinishing process.

Liquid silicone is oil based, noticeably "slicker" than most other oils. The slick qualities cause a finish to "pull away", rather than stay in place, once a clear coat is sprayed onto a surface.

Fish eye is caused by silicone or oil on the surface which has also proliferated deep into the wood grain or wood substrate.

Several of the most popular furniture cleaners/polishers may contain silicone, and silicone may be more commonly found in their aerosol versions.

Have you ever polished a surface and wiped your finger across it, leaving a streak? That streak, usually, is a direct result of silicone being present on the surface.

Needless to say, silicone is bad for furniture. As it builds up on a surface, and seeps deep into the pores, it eventually closes/blocks the pores, causing the wood and finish to dry out prematurely which may eventually cause a host of issues as furniture ages.

Silicone's slick qualities also may make repairs more difficult. Be sure to clean a surface properly before starting a repair if you feel there is a heavy build up of product. You can minimize fish eye initially by cleaning a surface well with Naptha, denatured alcohol and/or lacquer thinner.

There are also several other products formulated to assist with this issue, which could include sealing the surface initially with shellac or sanding sealer, and/or adding in specific additives into your clear coat prior to the application, like "fisheye remover" (right).

If all else fails, you can usually defeat this issue simply by building up the finish and sanding well in between coats. At some point you will sand the high areas of the surface to become level with the craters caused by the contamination, eventually creating an even, uniform finish, though it may take numerous coats and extensive sanding in-between applications to remove this type of contamination.

"Orange Peel" describes a particular type of textured imperfection on a finished surface. The imperfections appear slightly "bumpy" or "pebbled", similar to an orange's skin/peel, hence the term "orange peel".

This effect could be seen during a repair, but more often during the refinishing process. The phenomenon could be caused by a host of variables, like applying too heavy of a clear coat, incorrect spray gun set up, old finish, unwanted expeditious evaporation of thinner, spraying at an incorrect angle, or other factors.

As similar with fisheye removal, sanding the surface, in conjunction with correcting what may be the underlying issue, will remove the orange peel, followed by the spraying/application of additional coats.

Persistence is usually key when dealing with "finish problems". Often inexperienced wood workers may assume that a surface which has fisheye or orange peel is a disaster, and the only option to remove the "damage" is to strip off the finish and start over.

I would say 95% of the time, building up several coats of finish and sanding well in-between the coats will correct the majority of these issues, without any evidence that the issue ever occurred. I've also been refinishing items for over 25 years too, not just performing repairs, I speak the truth!

"Runs or Sags" on the finish of a surface is easy to determine the cause.

This issue can occur in both repairs and refinishing. With refinishing you may have sprayed too heavy/much finish on the vertical surface with your spray gun and gravity took over from there.

Similarly, during a repair, you can apply too much finish from a toner can that creates the same issue. The majority of the time when I use a toner finish, more often than not, I am only applying a light to medium misting of a surface.

More information on the proper techniques to apply toner finishes are explored in the "Hand Applied Finishes" chapter. It will require sanding and recoating to correct/remove the runs.

"Imitation Wood" is very popular with regard to heavily carved areas on newer, mass produced furniture. Most of the time carvings consist of a polyurethane, dense foam or hard plastic/resin material.

These "heavily carved" pieces are actually cast in a mold, then installed on various pieces of furniture and painted to match during the finishing process.

Often it may be very difficult to determine that what you are seeing is not actually wood, there may even be a grain pattern in the cast along with variation in color as it's painted to replicate real wood.

Almost this entire leg is fabricated out of a plastic resin. In the second picture I have sanded the surface, which removed the paint to show the plastic resin it consists of.

Also looking carefully at the top of the leg, you can see a rectangle in the center, this is a block of wood that was placed inside the mold prior to cast so that nuts/hardware could be embedded to secure the legs to a table.

Otherwise, the resin itself is not functionally strong enough to secure the hardware and too much stress would shatter the resin. If this leg were to break in half, it wouldn't be repairable because you cannot add support or reinforcement through a break, the resin is too brittle.

"Sun Bleaching" can cause permanent discoloration and is a direct result of the sun's visible light, harmful UV and infrared rays.

Sun bleaching is like watching your kids grow taller. You don't really notice because the daily miniscule incremental change really isn't apparent, until one day you're like, "wow you got taller", or in regard to a piece of furniture or hardwood floor, "wow, it got lighter".

Not all woods become bleached, there are woods that get darker with sun exposure like cherry. Cherry's rich copper tone is a direct result of exposure to UV light.

With varying degrees of exposure to the sun and its rays, darker woods tend to lighten, lighter woods mostly become even lighter (or darker as with cherry), and brighter (colored) woods, like mahogany, bloodwood or purpleheart, will become more brown, losing their colorful tone.

This drop leaf table was directly next to a window sill, apparently for a long time. The bottom half of one leaf and the opposite side of the table was protected from the sun.

Often the line of demarcation between the unfaded portion and sun damaged will be significant and there is really no way to blend the two, to create a flawless uniform hue, without refinishing.

It's not only the sun that bleaches, lights do it also. The picture to the right is where a sign <u>used</u> to be. A light from above faded the exposed wood, leaving the unexposed areas under the metal sign, unaffected.

We had to fabricate a new panel to cover the existing, as you'd never be able to blend these light and dark areas to become uniform. This will inevitably happen again!

"Piano Finish" most often is a polyester finish. Polyester finishes are used when a "wet look", "mirror-like" gloss finish is necessary. You will not often see this type of finish on regular furniture, mainly just on pianos.

It may be most common to see this finish in a gloss black, often called "ebony", but there are pianos available in various colors or finished over a stained wood surface.

Also not every piano has a polyester finish. Pianos could also be finished with lacquer, acrylic or conversion varnish, but if you see a super shiny, "wet look" finish on a piano, 9.8 times out of 10 it will consist of a polyester finish.

Older grands or upright pianos, may tend to have more traditional lacquered finishes if manufactured pre 1970's.

A polyester coating is so hard and durable that the most common type of damage that you may tend to see will only be superficial surface scratches.

If your only issue is surface scratches consider yourself lucky! Surface scratches can be removed, just like buffing them out of a car.

We even use the same types of rubbing compounds, polishing compounds and waxes that an automotive body shop would use when buffing out a freshly painted vehicle.

My preferred products are 3M® Perfect-It polishes, but I do also use Mirka®, turtle wax or other similar products, most of which are sold in automotive supply stores.

There are a few other tools you will need to complete the task of removing surface scratches from a polyester finish. Sandpaper (maybe), a variable speed rotary buffer/polisher (right), and polishing pads.

Due to the extreme effort required when polishing, I wouldn't suggest attempting to remove large areas of surface scratches by hand polishing alone, only if the area in question is minor or small.

In most cases, you likely will not be able to remove the piano from where it stands, so you must make sure you take preventative measures and cover your floor, walls, and furniture.

When using a variable speed polisher, drops of compound will fly everywhere.

On the piano to the right, I am not going to use any sandpaper during this repair. To begin removing surface scratches, simply begin by using a rubbing compound.

Rubbing compounds can be thought of as the equivalent to "rough" sandpaper.

There are abrasive powders incorporated into the polish, considered "grit". If you rub the compound between your fingers, you'll feel it.

Rubbing compound could completely remove most surface imperfections, even scratches that are slightly deeper (which you may be able to slightly feel with your fingernail).

If you find a scratch is deeper than average (fingernail definitely catches in the scratch), you may actually need to use sandpaper.

I would not suggest using any sandpaper less than 1000 grit. In fact, after using 1000 grit, you should continue to sand with even finer sandpaper, using anywhere from 1500 grit up to 3000 grit.

You may also want to incorporate water while sanding as lubrication. The "finer" the "sandpaper scratches", the easier they will be to remove with your compounds.

As you are applying the rubbing compound with your variable speed polisher, you should notice most if not all of the sanding and/or surface scratches disappearing. This may take several different applications.

Nearing completion of this step, the finish may still appear slightly hazy. This is a standard result and caused by the grit of the rubbing compound. If you've removed the majority of the scratches, after you've reached this juncture, switch from using a rubbing compound to a polishing compound.

A polishing compound still has a slight amount of "grit" incorporated, but if the rubbing compound is considered "rough", polishing compound can be considered "fine".

Using a polishing compound after the rubbing compound will remove any "swirl marks" or haziness created by the previous, while also enhancing the gloss to the "wet" look.

More often than not, this should be the end of a repair, all scratches should have been removed and the finish should be extremely glossy.

Occasionally, if deemed necessary, I'll use even finer waxes, like carnauba wax or a fine swirl mark remover. For black pianos, there are specially formulated waxes that are dark in color, made specifically for black/dark finishes.

There are three primary types of pads to use with your polishing machine. Foam, wool and microfiber, with each type used at various stages.

Foam pads could be used for compounding, polishing and waxing. Most foam pads are color coded, based on their "aggressiveness" of the pad, which may also be referred to as "correction" or "cut". The "stiffer" the pad, the more aggressive the cut.

Wool pads are usually more aggressive than foam pads, they "cut" faster. Wool pads may come in two variations, twisted wool, or untwisted, and each may consist of 100% wool or a combination of wool and synthetic materials. Twisted, 100% wool, will be the most aggressive pad in terms of cutting ability.

Microfiber pads and towels are used at the end of the polishing process, often opting for hand application rather than a machine, to apply and remove waxes.

Just to recap, the order is, rubbing compound, polishing compound, then waxes. Start the process with a wool pad to cut as much as possible, graduate to a foam pad to remove any remaining superficial areas of scratching or swirl marks, and finish with a microfiber pad to create an extreme gloss.

We've talked about this in other areas, but remember, the "smoother" the finish, the glossier it will be.

As light reflects on a surface, any roughness or variation in finish level, will reflect light differently making less smooth areas visually apparent.

If you have chips or gouges in the glossy polyester piano finish, well that's a whole different beast to repair. There are three ways to repair chipped areas, the right way, the easier way and the last is to use a polyester finish repair kit.

The first two options require using spray guns and a refinishing shop, and the latter is considered the "best possible" repair.

Some of these pianos can be valued up to $30,000 or more. Due to the need for perfection, we always fix polyester finishes the "right way".

The right way is also the most involved with regard to the time it takes to perform the repair. Take this black piano in the next few pictures, the legs have multiple deep gouges, and also the front left corner of the piano was crushed, along with a few other areas of damage.

Obviously the first step is to fill the gouges and crushed areas to bring the damaged locations back to an appropriate level, consistent with the surrounding finish, and yes, I am still using Bondo™!

After the damage is filled and sanded, next comes the paint. We are using a spray system/gun and black polyester finish.

After spraying a few coats on the piano, the areas that were filled and sanded are no longer visible, except for variation in the paint level (may look slightly bumpy or have minor low areas) from the application. From this point we need to block sand to level out the paint.

Keep in mind, even though on the body of this piano, the damage is only on the front left corner, we have to spray with finish, block sand, and polish the entire outer body of the piano to ensure that the finish is consistent throughout the entire circumference of the piano.

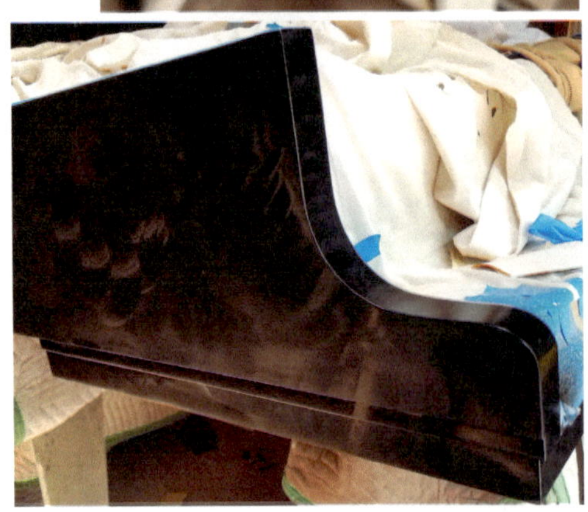

If we were only addressing the 6" surrounding the initial repair, there will be a line of demarcation where the existing finish and the new finish meet, but because we went over the entire body of the piano, you cannot see any line of demarcation.

After you've sanded the new finish perfectly level, it's time to begin to polish out the finish to remove any scratches caused by sandpaper, to create a mirror-like shine.

Again, you will have to buff out the entire body of the piano. It may take literally several hours to properly buff out the finish, you may not even finish it in one day.

One area of concern that I would like to forewarn you about when using a high speed polisher/buffer, is to be cautious at the edges and corners. It's extremely easy not to realize how much the buffing pads can actually cut through a finish.

If you're not paying close enough attention, you could literally buff through the newly applied paint. This is often referred to as "burning through the finish", and if this happens you're back at square one, effectively ruining the repair that you probably have already spent days trying to accomplish.

I said there was also an easier way to perform the repair, which is true, but it's not ideal, like the "right way", which was just described.

Basically you can follow every step that was just listed, but instead of spraying the piano with a polyester finish, you can simply use gloss nitrocellulose lacquer. Nitrocellulose lacquer is an easier medium to work with and you will likely not have any "reaction" when applying the new finish over a polyester finish.

The main thing that differentiates the two repairs is the hardness or durability of the finish. You can use the nitro finish, sand and buff out to a mirror-like shine, and no one will ever really be able to tell the difference (except maybe a professional).

The difference is, the nitro finish will scratch easier or will be less durable, but it could cut your working time possibly by ⅓.

These repairs will be expensive either way you look at it. We hire piano delivery companies to pick up and deliver the pianos to our shop and back to the clients, that is usually $400-$600 per trip.

Performing a repair the correct way may take 20-30 hours, which at $150 per/hr could be $3,000-$4,500. That may be on the low end for time with some repair shops charging $5,000+ for a similar type of restoration.

Add that all together and you could easily be looking at a repair cost of $5,000-$7,000, just for a few gouges, seems ridiculous right?

That is probably, for this reason, that polyester repair kits were invented. The kits that you will find available can vary greatly when it comes to contents, and can also vary in price from a little to a lot.

One kit may only include a 2 part polyester resin which you mix together and fill the damage (and that's it).

Other kits may include polyester resins, hardeners, tools, sandpaper, sanding blocks, compounds, UV light (which aids in curing) and instruction booklets. Kits can range from under $100 to over $500, remember, you get what you pay for.

Some repair companies may even be upfront and tell you not to expect a repair to be invisible, that's usually dependent on their level of expertise, anything can be restored to virtual perfection with the know-how and proper restoration products.

The reason I don't suggest using polyester repair kits is because there will usually be a line of demarcation between the filled area and the surrounding finish, that is, unless you paint over the repaired area which brings us back to either the right way or the easier way of repair.

Additionally, not every black hue is the same, which may be because a piano was near a window and has faded or the black may have more of a green tone than a blue tone or the like.

The same can be said for a white piano, black isn't always black and white isn't always white, there can literally be endless varied tones with regard to any solid color.

Basically, trying to perform a "spot repair" on a polyester piano will almost never be completely invisible. Additionally, when using a high speed polisher over a "repaired" area, the repair products do not create a "thick" enough finish and could be "burned through" easily, or the high speed polisher will "remove" some of the filled area just by friction alone, causing a dip or waviness in the repaired area.

Often a repair is more dependent on the location of the damage (you've seen that statement several times by now). Based on this small chip on the bottom corner, lower edge (right), I would suggest that a repair could be virtually perfect with a polyester repair kit.

For that matter, you may even just dab a small amount of gloss black finger nail polish in the area and save yourself a few hours. That repair likely wouldn't be perfectly invisible, but it might only cost you ten bucks.

Another issue that may arise is most polyester repair kits are only made for colored (black or white) pianos, not necessarily pianos that have a "clear" finish, with the wood grain apparent.

Take this mahogany piano lid as an example, if there was a large gouge in the center, in my opinion, it would be virtually impossible to perform a "spot repair" and have the repaired area invisible.

My advice when dealing with these high end finishes is to temper your expectation of repair, especially for a novice repair technician.

Even I do not look forward to performing any restoration when dealing with pianos that have polyester finishes, and I've been performing repairs for over 25 years. There is no easy way!

"Mold Damage" is caused by moisture condensation from humid air, which is attracted to cooler surfaces. Mold spores can settle on these surfaces and begin to grow. This is a common problem in damp basements, attics, garages or any other structure with similar characteristics.

We see a lot of mold damage with moving shipments, such as those in metal containers which travel from overseas. The ocean, a leak in a container or atmospheric conditions can make for a perfect breeding ground.

Mold spores if caught early, on solid surfaces, can easily be cleaned/removed, possibly with the use of specialized cleaners. But if not caught early, the spores can embed themselves deep into the grain cavities which could ruin the finish on any particular piece of furniture.

An example of a mold cleaner is Concrobium. Concrobium is a non toxic cleaner which (is claimed by the manufacturer to) encapsulate and crush the mold spores down to their root structure, stopping any regrowth.

There are other similar products, if you have a mold issue I advise you to research the use, safety and effectiveness of each product before using.

I never recommend using bleach, ammonia or other similar products, because not only will they not completely kill all the mold, especially if it's deep down in the grain cavities, but the harsh products will further damage the finish of a wood surface.

Mold spores, even when cleaned and killed, will most likely leave spots or defects on a finished wood surface (right).

No matter the instance, I always suggest using a respirator when dealing with mold. Even if you think the mold is completely gone, because during a repair, to correct the surface defects, it requires sanding, and you do not want to inhale any mold spores, dead or alive!

At this point if the mold is dead, you can treat the surface as if performing any other repair. Sanding the affected area with 400-600 w/d sandpaper, touching up any particular imperfections and proceeding to french polish which should remove any evidence of the mold.

The final picture below shows what the completed surface could look like. This repair was done in a client's home in less than 2 hours.

One caveat with regard to mold, on upholstered furniture, often if left unchecked mold spores can grow and embed themselves into the upholstery, even deep down into the padding and inner wood framing of a sofa or the like.

Only if the damage in question is really miniscule, and you're positive that the mold damage is specifically on the surface, then you may be able to clean.

But heavily water stained items or items covered in heavy mold will almost without question need to be either thrown away, refinished and/or reupholstered. It's wise to seek a certified professional opinion when dealing with mold.

There was, what I considered, significant mold on these pews. We stripped all the upholstery off and completely refinished 17 of them, now they're used at a farm house, barn wedding venue.

The last example I'll give of problems that you are assured to come across, is referred to as "***Pre-Existing Repairs***".

The problem is that someone has previously, poorly executed a repair, creating additional issues that have an effect on how well our repair may turn out.

Take for example this chair, which had a loose back that needed to be reglued and secured.

I could determine, from the picture to the right, on the edge of the seat, someone had previously tried to repair a break/crack by drilling and inserting two dowel rods.

The problem lies in what I couldn't see. Neither of those two dowels are installed near or in the direction of the rear right post of the chair back.

There was no evidence of any other dowels or hardware installed around the edge of the seat which would lead me to believe that there was anything else holding the back post to the chair seat.

But the back was loose, I could wiggle it in all directions. The back's right post just wouldn't free itself from the seat portion, so just like any other fine woodworker would, I get out my mallet and start whaling away.

Gently of course, initially, until you get slightly frustrated and give it one good blow from the mallet and.. Snap! Just like that, you find out why it was so hard to get apart, there was a hidden screw!

I came to the conclusion that, A) at one point the right side of the chair seat was broken completely off. B) at that time, the back was still in place, so C) someone ran a screw into the base of the back post, prior to D) reinstalling and doweling the broken/detached, right side of the seat.

Because the screw was hidden, it caused me to break out a large section of wood. Was it my fault?

If not for the pre-existing (previous) repair, that back post and all its spindles would have easily been removed, allowing us to perform what should have been a quick, simple regluing.

We also could not charge any additional money, even though there was an hour added onto the total repair, because we now needed to fix the big piece of wood that broke off the seat.

It's not usually worth the effort to explain to a client that it wasn't quite your fault, it was really the previous repair person's fault. Sometimes you just have to suck it up and pick your battles wisely.

Every piece of furniture you encounter will likely be unique and you would rarely ever see two of the same items, that aren't from the same job. That also means all damages you come across will also be unique.

There will never be identical repairs on two different pieces of furniture. You may have to do similar things on similar items, but nothing is ever exactly the same. There will be numerous challenging situations and circumstances that you will encounter through your journey in furniture restoration.

Hopefully, if and when you eventually run into problems, you can refer to some of the techniques and problem solving in this chapter to overcome some of the more difficult aspects of furniture restoration.

OTHER COOL STUFF

Marble & Stone

Do you know the difference between a rock and a stone? Some may think those two words are interchangeable, but in reality they are quite different.

Rocks are typically found in the earth's crust and cannot be "moved". A rock only becomes a stone when a portion is cut or broken off, creating a smaller "moveable" piece.

There are three classes of rocks. Igneous rocks are formed by the cooling and solidification of magma. There's a good chance you have granite countertops in your kitchen. Granite is magma!

Sedimentary rocks consist of organic and mineral deposits on the earth's surface, which with time and pressure creates cementation. Examples of sedimentary rocks are travertine, limestone, sandstone and others.

Metamorphic rocks were once either a sedimentary or igneous rock that has been transformed chemically and physically due to intense pressure and heat over an extended period of time. Marble, slate, quartz, soapstone and others are all forms of metamorphic rocks.

Once these rocks are cut into stones, they may be shaped and formed to create top surfaces on a wide range of furniture types, dressers, nightstands, end tables, coffee tables, dining tables, buffets, bars, the list could go on forever.

One of the best characteristics of stone is its durability, you almost can't scratch or gouge it, and liquid usually has no adverse effect (except for possibly staining porous sedimentary rocks).

That's why kitchen countertops, furniture tops, bathroom vanities and countless other products are commonly made of this almost impervious product. Not all stone that you see on furniture will be marble, and not all stone products are made equally. Just as with wood, stone could either be "solid" or "veneer".

Most often, higher end or older furniture will have one solid piece of stone. While lower tier furniture will most always be veneered to replicate the stones' look, but reduce costs for the manufacturer and consumer. So how do you tell the difference?

Veneered stone will have multiple different "pieces" applied to a surface, usually in the form of various sized rectangles, applied in a "brick" pattern, glued to a wood subframe, then sanded and polished out by the manufacturer.

You can also tell that a piece of stone is veneered because just like wood, stone also has a grain pattern. You would see abrupt halts in the grain pattern accompanied with a line (joint) around the circumference of each individual piece of stone.

Those white lines in the picture to the right, reveal several joints. In this example, each stone rectangle may be 2" x 6" approximately.

A veneered stone will usually be less than a quarter inch thick, compared to a solid stone top which is usually almost always a minimum, three quarters of an inch or most often, thicker.

Whether a piece is veneered or solid, both can still acquire damages, have sections broken off, or maybe even be broken in half if it takes a hard enough impact.

If an edge or corner is chipped or broken, we can usually repair that damage almost to perfection using My Repair Kit™, by simply filling the chip, sanding and touching up the surface just as if you were repairing any piece of wood.

The next few pictures are close ups of the stone top that we were tasked with repairing, in a client's home.

There was an approximate 3" x 1" chip broken from the top center, near the front edge, along with the front right corner having a large section of stone cracked with pieces missing.

This is obviously not a solid stone top. Do you see the wood panel exposed in the middle of the broken corner?

In the picture seen below, in some cases, filler may not adhere well to a smooth surface. I find that using a razor blade to "scratch" the surface creates minor "channels" for the filler to seep in, helping to adhere better.

It's possible to have the same issue on a wood surface too, as there could be dirt, oils or cleaners in the damaged area which might inhibit the filler from adhering properly. If the filler does not bond well, it will likely break out at some point, most often as you begin to sand.

Once the areas have been properly prepped, just like you've heard numerous times throughout the various chapters, the process is pretty much the same, fill, sand and touch up.

When sanding stone, the material is usually extremely hard. In reality, it takes diamond sanding pads to really "cut" through stone, so hopefully if you glued any pieces back on, you ensured that the surface is as level and flat as it can be.

You may be able to start sanding with sandpaper as coarse as 220 grit, but you should always finish with at least 400-600 grit.

The hardness of the stone will likely wear out your standard sandpaper pretty fast. Make sure you keep turning the paper on the sanding block so you can use all available areas on the piece of sandpaper.

With both areas sanded satisfactorily, using your padding finish and padding rag, french polish the sanded areas to fill in any slight surface scratches, remove sanding dust and show the hue of the area.

Proceed with your touch up! I used several techniques to imitate the stones appearance, which included pigment application with a brush and a padding rag.

Using some satin white toner, slightly misted, to replicate some of the small whitish splatter pattern in the stone.

Also using a clear satin toner in between application of various coats of pigment to seal in all my colorwork.

The good thing is that most stones appear heavily distressed with veins and other unique characteristics, so the repair doesn't always have to be visually perfect in every way!

As long as someone's eye doesn't go right to the repaired area, then you probably did a pretty good job!

If stone repairs are not feasible, you may need to take a sample to your local marble/stone shop to see about having a new top fabricated, it won't be cheap, trust me.

Clay & Ceramic

Clay and ceramic vases, decorative dishes, Lladro's, Hummels or other artistic pieces don't always hold up well during moves, giving us the opportunity to work on some pretty unique items.

It shouldn't seem possible, but the value of some of these items may be very high, often several hundreds of dollars or more.

Below is a vase that has a pretty large hole in the bottom. It must have been placed down too hard, but I'm no detective!

The first thing we need to do is to piece it back together (without glue), to make sure the majority of the broken pieces are available, while simultaneously figuring the order the pieces need to be installed so they all fit back together properly.

There will be some pieces which need to be installed before others, but once we're confident that all the pieces are accounted for, it's time to glue them back onto the body of the vase.

It's not like this vase is used to store grains, it's just a decoration for someone's home. For this project I choose to use standard wood glue. I would suggest using epoxy if your project will spend most of its time outside.

Epoxy would only allow me to glue one or two pieces prior to the glue setting. The real reinforcement will be incorporated a little later in the repair process.

Make sure to wipe off any excess glue that squeezes out as you assemble your project.

The tricky part of something shaped like this, is that it's hard to clamp all the pieces together. You can't really use standard clamps because none could reach around the circumference of the vase, so often you'll have to improvise.

I find using ratcheting strap clamps (aka tie downs) often work well on oddly shaped items. As you can see we also incorporated "movers rubber bands" to hold everything together nice and tight.

If you're wondering why there are few random pieces of wood under the straps, it's because I needed some additional pressure in a specific area, to ensure the various pieces lined up properly and were flush.

There was a pretty big chip and crack around the base that I wanted to fill with Bondo™ to ensure nothing would seep out during the reinforcement stage of the repair.

You can easily trim off most of the excess filler before it hardens too much, but for the rest of the cracks, I would use a filler that is easily sandable.

The crack is aligned well, allowing us to keep the sanding to a minimum, ensuring we do not disturb the natural aged patina of the vase, which will be beneficial as we proceed.

I chose to use Minwax™ Color-Matched Wood Filler. It doesn't get as hard as Bondo™, but it does the job, dries fairly fast and sands into a fine powder with sandpaper that doesn't need to be very coarse.

You can even clean the filler with a water dampened rag to remove any excess to require even less sanding. You can choose to sand the filler at this point, or wait till a little later.

I like to perform all structural type repairs to completion before I concern myself with the cosmetic stuff, just in case something doesn't go right.

We've done a good amount of work to the outside of the vase, now it's time to flip it over and install what I referred to earlier as the "reinforcement".

Reinforcement includes the use of a fiberglass cloth, the accompanying resin, hardener, mixing container, stir stick, paint brush and scissors.

Looking inside the vase (right), you can see the outline of the crack. You may also see a little excess glue and a few minor chips missing.

No need to worry about filling the chips or removing the excess glue, as the fiberglass and resin will be covering and filling those areas.

The next step would be to cut your strips of fiberglass cloth. I cut four strips, each strip was approximately seven inches wide and twenty four inches long.

Follow the instructions on the can for mixing the resin and hardener. Initially, pour some of your mixed resin into the bottom of the vase and use your paintbrush to coat the entire area that will have fiberglass attached, it must be thoroughly coated.

Put your fiberglass strips into the vase, make sure they're centered properly, and place the layer onto the resin covered bottom.

Take your brush and apply more resin over the layer of fiberglass you just layed down. I chose to lay two layers of fiberglass in the bottom prior to coating with my second layer of resin.

Continue that process with the remaining two fiberglass layers and ensure all the fiberglass and the entire bottom is coated well with the resin.

This whole process has to be done within a short amount of time as the resin cures in ten or so minutes.

The second picture has four layers of fiberglass and is thoroughly coated with resin. I did remove the excess puddle you see.

As the resin cures, in conjunction with the woven sheets of fiberglass, the reinforced area will become harder than the clay.

I feel this repair would last quite a long time, or at least it wouldn't crack or break where we fixed it, under normal circumstances.

Even though the resin cures fast, I still like to leave it alone for at least another day. Who else likes dragging stuff out?

The structural aspect of this repair is now complete so we can move onto the cosmetic portion.

After sanding off the filler, treat it just like any other repair that we've gone over, proceed with the process of touch up.

Wipe over the surface with your padding rag and padding finish to remove the sanding dust and expose the hue of the area that needs touch up.

Applying pigment, using a combination of a paintbrush and padding rag, I was able to cosmetically conceal the broken areas.

Keeping on the topic of vases, check this one out below! Almost all the same concepts that we just went over with the clay vase, apply to this repair, minus reinforcement.

I would also tell the client that once repairs are completed to something that's clay, ceramic, a vase, china plate, coffee cup etc., that it should only be used for decorative purposes.

I wouldn't suggest eating off of a repaired plate, drinking from a repaired cup or putting flowers and water in the vase to the right.

I'm not necessarily concerned about the structure holding up once glued together, the main issue is the finishes we apply will never be as hard or durable as a glazed and fired piece of ceramic, and we don't want to drink coffee with padding finish and pigment in it!

To be honest, we're not fixing regular dinnerware anyway, so almost anything ceramic related that we fix, is already most likely going to be used for decorative purposes only.

Keeping in line with the first steps of the restoration, you must make sure that all (or majority) of the pieces are available by piecing the item together without glue, while simultaneously finding the order in which the pieces need to be installed.

It is possible that some broken pieces may need to be glued together prior to gluing them to the body of the vase. I'm also going to use epoxy for all ceramic repairs.

When gluing ceramic, the key is to apply the most minimal amount of glue possible. That may sound counter intuitive, but the glue itself, if applied too thick, will act as a barrier and you may not be able to align the pieces together perfectly flush, which we all know by now is the most important rule when repairing broken items, ensuring the alignment is as perfectly flush as humanly possible.

The way I apply the glue is with the tip of my finger. I mix up a small amount of epoxy, dip the tip of my finger in, then proceed to wipe off 95% of what is on my finger, back onto the sandpaper.

Then I would just dab the remaining 5% of what's on my finger onto the broken edges of both pieces that I intend to stick together, and only those areas! Do not apply glue to any area that you do not intend to stick a piece to.

To make sure there is no heavy build up of glue in any particular area, just keep dabbing your finger (or use a dry finger to remove excess glue) over the broken edges, then stick the two pieces together and give them a little pressure to ensure they are properly seated.

Yes, sometimes you may have to sit there perfectly still while your hands are cramping because you have to hold those two pieces together in perfect alignment for 10 or 15 minutes.

You don't want to move because you're not sure if the epoxy is quite dry yet, and you can't reach over and touch the glue mixture to see how close it is to curing because your hands are full, but often this is what must be done!

Pro tip: Create a miniature sandbox, which is perfect for holding glued pieces in certain positions or particular angles, so as not to put any stress on the glued joint while it further cures.

It could literally take hours or days to glue back together badly shattered items. So let's piece together this vase!

As you can see, the vase is now fully glued together. You may also see that there are a few very small chips that I did not glue in.

In some cases it's easier to fill those small areas rather than try and glue in those microscopic pieces.

From here, I'd use a razor blade, sliding over the surface to remove any excess glue, then proceed to fill all the cracks with Bondo™, keeping it minimal!

Ceramics are very forgiving with regard to the amount that you are able to sand.

Technically, there's usually a pretty thick durable clear coat that was applied and fire hardened in a kiln during production.

I would usually recommend sanding the filler with 600 grit sandpaper, maybe 400 grit to start but always finish with at least 600 grit.

This is where some artistry will come into play. When sanding there may be some areas of the "scene" that you sand off, using your padding finish and pigments, you should be able to paint in and recreate anything that was removed.

As you proceed, you can treat this touch up like any other, after applying some color, you can seal the colorwork in with your clear toner finish.

You can also french polish on padding finish to create a nice gloss sheen. Ceramic repairs are one of the limited times I will use a gloss clear toner to seal in all our hard work.

The two pictures to the right are the complete vase.

Think about all the different pigments required to match all those various hues! It was several more than the five or less pigments I recommend with wood repairs.

Here are a few honorable mentions. I used all the same processes for repair that we just went over, glue, fill, sand, touch up!

FABRICATION OF MOLDED PARTS

Another topic, which in my opinion is truly unique and definitely one of my favorite things to do, is the making of molds to create missing items. The catch is there has to be an exact area or item available that you can use as a sample for duplication.

I often use this technique in circumstances where a heavily carved area is missing, or to replicate a missing part, like this small knob to the right. You can essentially clone and reproduce whatever is missing!

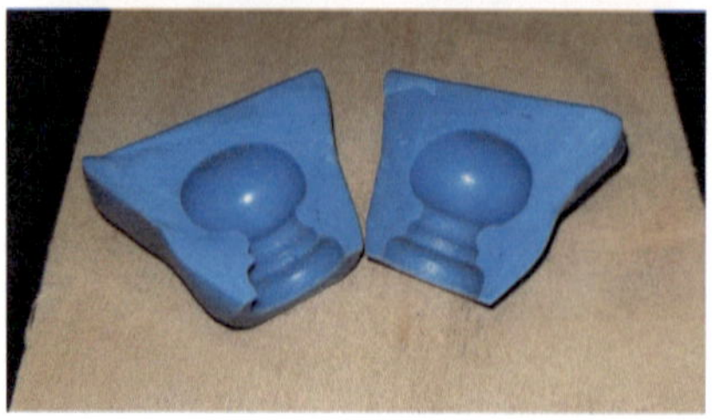

You can obtain casting materials from several resources, but the material we use for molds is actually manufactured for the dental industry.

The manufacturer may vary but the product is Polyvinyl Polysiloxane (not included in MyRepairKit™). Referred to from here as impression putty (or just putty). Similar products could vary in "weight" (viscosity) and cure times.

This material is used by dentists to make extremely precise negative imprints of a person's mouth, along with the surrounding structures of their oral cavity to create bridges or crowns.

The picture to the left is a panel to an oak chest.

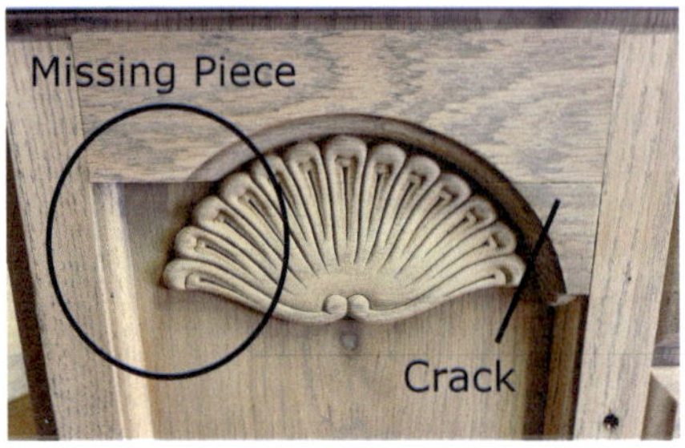

As you can see there is a fairly large section of wood missing from the left side (and the right side is cracked, but that's an easy reglue and fill to conceal).

We can't give the chest back to the client nicely refinished without replacing this missing section, so how do we go about replacing it?

I could spend a few hours trying to whittle down a piece of oak and glue it in and fill the crack and nobody would ever know that it was replaced, but the client doesn't really want to pay two or three hundred dollars extra for the time that it would involve to fabricate the missing piece.

This is where our impression putty comes into play. As long as there is an exact area somewhere else on the piece of furniture that I can use to create a mold, I can easily reproduce the missing area with Bondo™.

Lucky for us there is an identical panel on the other side of the chest, which ironically has the same area of wood cracked, but hasn't broken off and is not missing (top right).

Once that area is secure, I will mix equal parts of our impression putty, which consists of an "activator" and a "base". Once mixed and uniform in color, apply the putty over the sample (right).

Make sure that you push the putty well into all the crevasses, nooks and crannies. The more attention that you pay to this aspect, the more precise your mold will be.

Once the putty has cured, after ten or fifteen minutes, it turns into a solid rubber and you should be able to easily peel or pry it from the sample (below).

What we are left with is an almost perfect negative. Do you see that I even included, in the mold, a portion of the wood carved decorative piece from the center of the panel?

That area of the mold will encompass the same carved decorative wood piece on the panel that we need to do our fabrication, it will assist with our alignment.

Now that we have our mold, apply a generous amount of Bondo™ to both areas, the missing area on the cabinet, and in the mold (right).

Below left, firmly apply the filler, filled mold onto the surface, make sure the alignment is correct and firmly hold the mold in place until the filler has cured.

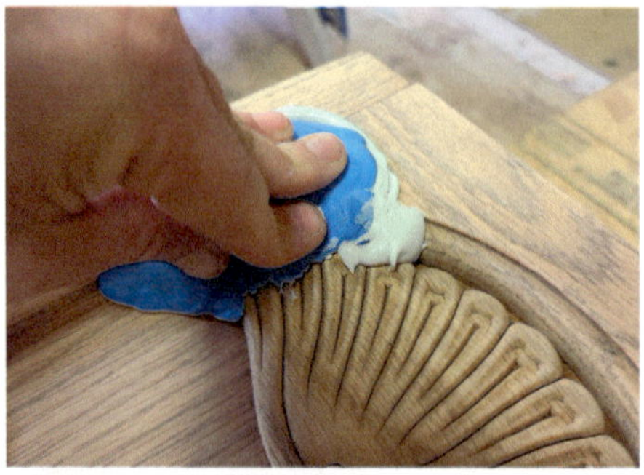

Dont worry too much about excess filler spilling out, that will easily be trimmed or sanded off.

Once dry, gently pry the putty off from the surface (below left). The filled area will look a little rough and may not be perfect immediately (right), but you have the beginning stages of replacement of the missing part.

From this point, you may also notice that not every small area of detail is perfectly filled, so we'll again want to apply more Bondo™ to fill in any slight imperfections (right).

I'm not too worried about putting a large amount of filler onto the area, since the panel is flat I will easily sand off the excess filler with an orbital sander and then trim and hand sand the inner routered edge.

Once the area has been properly sanded and contoured (below), you can consider the fabrication of the missing part complete!

This chest was in the process of refinishing, so after it was stained, and as we were applying our clear coats through the finishing process, we used pigments, mixed with the finish that we were spraying, conversion varnish, to blend and touch up the filled and replaced area.

The entire process, (other than refinishing) took maybe 30-45 minutes to fabricate and replace the missing piece of wood, rather than a few hours to actually carve the missing portion out of real wood.

There may be another thing to keep in mind, and this next technique doesn't really apply to the piece we just fabricated, but it's often a good idea to keep the "rear" area of the mold as flat as possible. I'll attempt to explain what I mean.

We were tasked with replacing these tiny little wood pyramids for a bookcase. They are only about a quarter inch squared, even though the picture may make them appear larger.

You can see that one is apparently missing. That's just the picture I placed here, there were actually almost ten of those little pains in the a.., I mean, decorative pyramids that were either missing or damaged that needed replacement.

Because they are so small, it would be almost impossible for me to hold them and perfectly sand or cut all four sides of the pyramid to create a perfect point in the center.

I need these pieces to sit perfectly flush onto the surface of the bookcase, therefore I cannot have a lumpy or uneven "bottom" (rear) surface on the new pyramid.

Taking a sample off the bookcase, we mix up some impression material and insert the sample. Then I'll squeeze it slightly between two hard surfaces, to properly seat the sample.

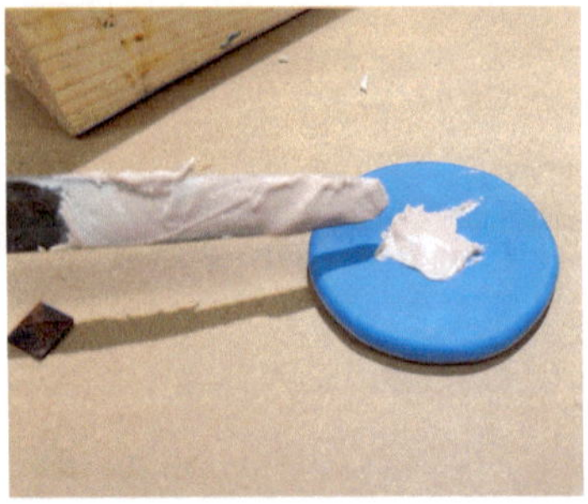

As the putty hardens, this will ensure that the "rear" surface of the putty is "flat" (left).

I can then easily apply filler into the negative cavity (right) and use a razor blade prior to the filler curing, slicing across the surface to create a "flat" bottom/rear of each pyramid (left).

This technique negates any sanding on the rear side of the fabricated parts, allowing them to sit flush onto the bookcase surface.

In fact, I didn't have to perform any sanding on these pieces, I was able to proceed straight to the touch up.

I was able to mass produce these pieces in a fairly short time frame, and once the pieces were fabricated, all I needed to do was glue them on. Bada bing bada boom.

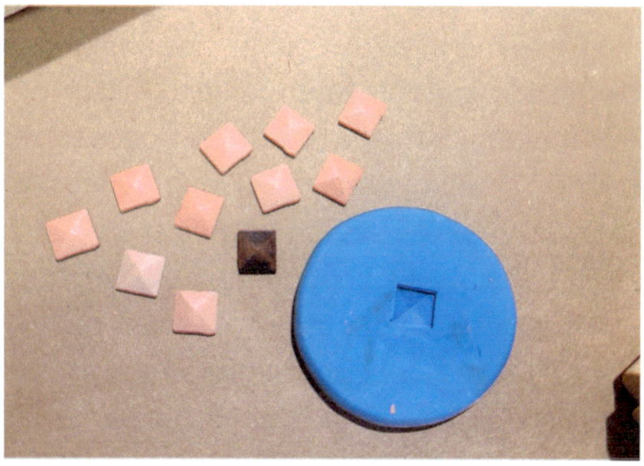

The pyramids that we fabricated were pretty small, but there are a few minor details to keep in mind when creating larger items when using mold techniques.

The first thing to keep in mind, if you are putting a large amount of filler into a big mold, is that you could inadvertently be trapping air bubbles/pockets in the filler as you goop it in.

I find that aggressively tapping the mold, once full of filler, onto a hard surface numerous times, prior to the filler curing, will cause most trapped air pockets to travel to the surface and escape. This "tapping" may also assist to help the filler travel more efficiently into the tiniest of detail.

Another thing to think about is you may not always have an exact match to use as a sample, but there still may be an area available to use the impression putty to assist in the fabrication of missing parts.

In the case of this mirror frame (right), there is a sample area on the right side bottom of the frame but the problem is that the sample area is the complete opposite.

I can still use that area to duplicate the missing parts, I may just have to modify them so that they appear to be in the proper orientation.

I also had to hand make some of the parts needed by simply filling the area and using a razor blade or Dremel™ (carving tool) to shape the areas.

Once everything is shaped, filled, sanded and secured to your liking, the next step is to paint the area to match. I used various golds, like toners, Rub-n-Buff™ and gold powdered pigments to assist with matching.

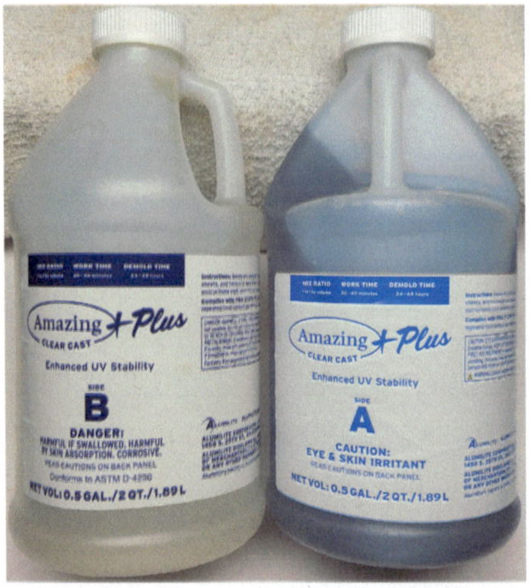

What I've shown is the process to easily fabricate missing parts, but I also wanted to mention a product that we use on occasion as our "filler" in lieu of Bondo®, when it comes to filling a mold that you've created out of the impression putty.

This material is created by a company called Alumilite™, more specifically we use Alumilite Amazing Clear Cast Plus™.

Alumilite Amazing Clear Cast Plus™ is essentially a resin that is mixed in a 1 to 1 ratio, which allows more than ample cure time, and is well suited for filling large intricate molds. Once cured, this material can also be easily tapped, machined, painted and dries extremely rigid.

We've created numerous items like missing handles, knobs, moldings, carvings and we recently used it to create this heavily carved piece to the right, which is called a "capital". A capital attaches to the top of a column, a column may also be referred to as a pillar.

This capital, aside from having some damage, has an identical piece missing for the opposite side column on an old shrunk (European china cabinet), spelled "shrank" in Europe.

You can see that this capital is fairly large, heavily carved and over 6" squared. We were tasked with obtaining an identical matching capital, to replace the one which was lost in a move.

It's already been determined that I am not a wood carver and I couldn't find a craftsman willing to make one out of solid oak.

Additionally, computerized CNC carving machines that I have access to are not quite up to the task to reproduce this capital.

The only alternative I have to create a new capital is to create a mold of the existing sample I have. In fact, this is the largest single item that I have ever created using this process, which we will go through.

The first step is to repair all the damaged areas on our sample (right), otherwise we will have an incomplete mold.

There were multiple areas chipped or broken off on each side, and as usual, the process is to fill and sand to recreate the missing areas.

Now that our capital is whole again, I used impression putty to cover the sample (left). It required mixing several different batches to eventually encompass the entire unit.

Some items you put the impression putty on can easily be removed, but this piece has too many nooks and crannies to easily detach the impression material from the sample, so I had to slice it with a razor blade in a few areas to assist with releasing the capital (right middle).

You may now wonder how we will repair the mold material where we cut it. Well, nothing sticks to this material, except more impression putty.

To the right, I mixed up a little more putty and applied it over the cut areas ,to make the mold whole again.

The picture on the left is a close up of the inside of the mold. Just to show the detail that the impression material creates, even recreating the precise grain pattern of the original wood sample.

Amazing Clear Cast Plus™ is translucent, but we can get a head start on coloring the new capital by mixing in our dye stains, which we used some "perfect brown" and "warm black ebony" (right).

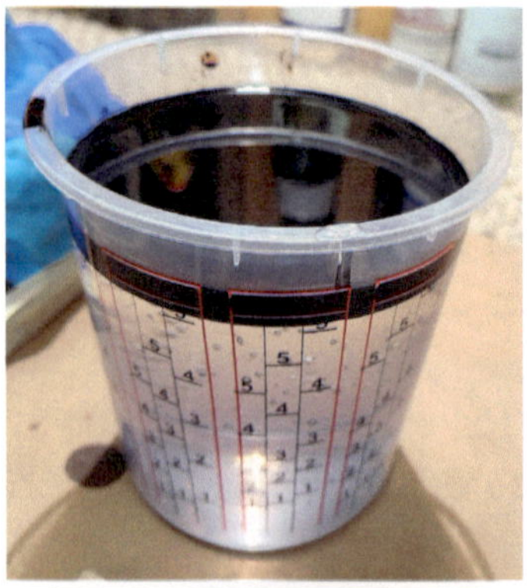

Once the casting material is mixed, pour it into your mold, shake it and tap the mold to attempt to remove any air bubbles, and let it sit undisturbed for realistically at least two days (48 hours) (second picture right).

The directions note that you have a 30-40 minute work time, but the material takes far longer to set up and will remain "soft" for at least 24-36 hours.

That could have been the case because of the large amount of material I was using, or because the additional dyes mixed in slowed the process. It's possible that a smaller amount may cure faster.

Once everything is completely cured, the product is very rigid, proceed to peel or rip the mold material off of the new capital.

The new capital will likely be a little rough, you can't always expect the item you make to be perfect and ready to go right out of the mold.

Often there will be areas where air bubbles may have been trapped (right) or other slight imperfections.

Any defects, you will have to fill or further address with Bondo®, and use some 400 grit sandpaper overall to smooth the surface to prepare it for painting.

Now that the new capital is prepped, we are tasked with matching the color to the original sample. Even though the sample is relatively dark, there is variation in the hues overall that we need to replicate.

I used a combination of various pigments including burnt umber, yellow oxide, black, and mars yellow, you'll see a fifth which didn't get used.

Along with the colored toners dark van dyke brown, light oak/natural, satin black, and a clear satin to seal in all our hard work.

I used a combination of brush application, application with a padding rag, and the spaying of the toners to apply color overall.

It's a tricky process sometimes to properly build up the finish. Some of the more advanced painting techniques will take time to learn and execute properly.

There will be moments where you pause the touch up and give the item another sanding with a finer sandpaper, like 600 grit, to further smooth out the surface, or possibly sanding to remove some applied color in an area where you need a different hue to show through from a previous application.

You will also be applying pigment with your padding rag, which assists in highlighting certain areas or edges, because the rag isn't going to get deep into the grooves or crevasses.

Patience is key most often. As you proceed through various repairs, you may think your project will never turn out well, but I think eventually your repairs will look great as long as you stick with it. Never give up!

Alumilite™ makes an array of cool products, feel free to check them out. Your imagination may be the only limitation for what you can create with their amazing line of materials.

We didn't have to alter or modify the original cabinet, and ultimately saved the insurance company thousands of dollars if this shrunk ended up not being restorable, and they had to pay the client's claim.

LEATHER

95% of the leather that I fix is not on furniture that you sit on, but hard surfaces, like leather tops of furniture such as desks, tables, or similar.

For the most part, I approach a leather repair the same way that I would approach any wood repair, but there are two very important warnings that you should be aware of.

First, keep any sanding to a minimum. Sanding will easily remove a large swath of color and depending on the leather surface, it may be near impossible to blend the area back flawlessly.

That may make it difficult to fill and repair deep gouges or scratches, because you will have to sand the filler. Just do your best to try and sand on the filler specifically, using a fine sandpaper, like 600 grit.

Try not to extend the sanding onto the leather surface, at least till you're sure the sanded filler is almost perfectly flat, then you may have to slightly sand the surrounding leather to complete the leveling of the filler.

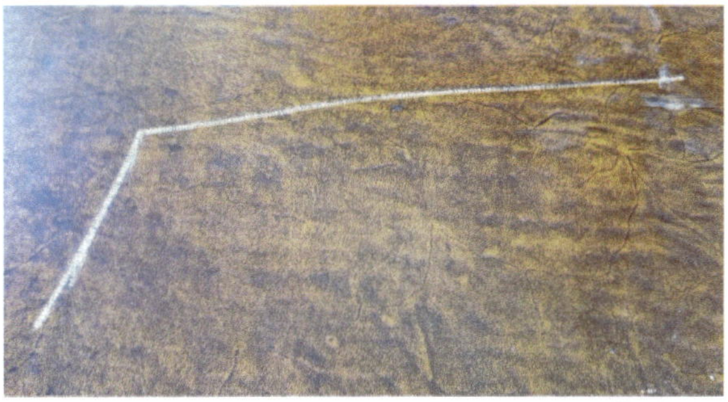

The second warning is to never clean the surface with any type of solvent, also along the same lines, never "scrub" an area of leather, both which could also lead to removal of a large area of color.

Once you've filled and sanded any damage, use My Repair Kit™, padding finish and pigments to perform the touch up, just as I recommend with a wood repair. You can seal the surface with a clear toner finish, or french polish the entire surface using padding finish to seal in your repair to make the surface beautiful again.

The only thing I did to the leather surface pictured, was clean it off with a water dampened rag, allowed it to dry, performed some small areas of touch up with a paintbrush, pigment, and padding finish, then I french polished the entire surface. I didn't use one iota of sandpaper.

If you don't want to be too aggressive, or your goal is just to clean a leather surface then I suggest you go to an automotive store and simply purchase a leather cleaner and conditioner. I prefer the brand, Lexol, and no they're not paying me to say that.

Cleaners and conditioners for the most part just clean off the surface and make the leather more supple. They should not have an adverse effect on any finished leather, as far as color removal, but they are not compatible with our touch up products, so you can't use both simultaneously during a restoration.

It's advised though in general, that you condition your leather furniture at least once or twice a year to stop it from drying out, which in turn elongates it's life span, that goes for hard surfaces as well as soft surfaces, like sofas and chairs.

Not all leather products are created equal. High quality (which usually means expensive) leather furniture will either be full grain leather, or top grain leather.

Full grain is leather that has not been mechanically altered, and left in its most natural state with minimal processing. Full grain leather is also very thick and may be difficult to work with due to its thickness, but it's considered the best!

Top grain leather is essentially full grain leather, but due to the thickness of the hide, it is split into two layers, creating the "top grain" (which is the thinner version of full grain) and a second piece which is referred to as "split grain".

Split grain is used to create suede, which has no apparent grain pattern and is "fuzzy" due to the fibrousness of the leather.

Bonded leather is not a new type of leather, it's often what lower tier "leather" furniture consists of.

Bonded leather is made by shredding leather scraps and leather fiber, mixing with natural rubber or polyurethane as a bonding agent, then extruding the mixture onto a cloth backing (cloth backing is used for furniture and clothes).

The material can then be embossed (stamped) with virtually any grain pattern, which can replicate the appearance of hides from any animal. Most animal species will have their own distinct grain pattern, similar to each wood type having its own special appearance.

Bonded leather is also essentially painted on the surface, unlike high end leather which is usually dyed thoroughly throughout.

The issue that arises is when people constantly sit on or move around, on a bonded leather sofa, the colored film may begin to delaminate from the cloth backing and could start to crack and peel. This type of damage to the right is often not repairable.

In my opinion, the only positive attributes to bonded leather is that manufacturers are able to use 100% of the leather from all hides, instead of simply throwing away the scraps, and the price is far cheaper for the consumer to have a product that could appear very similar to higher end furnishings.

The term bonded leather is considered controversial or at least debatable in the furniture industry, as some manufacturers may use the term to describe "non natural" upholstered items, which could be covered in a vinyl, a polyurethane laminate or some other composite material, that also appears similar to real leather.

The controversy lies with some manufacturers being deceptive about the product they are selling. The term "bonded leather" leads people to believe that they are purchasing a high quality leather item, mainly due to the fact the word "leather" is in the title.

There could be, for instance, a sofa sold with the description of "bonded leather". Often this sofa will have bonded leather only on the areas that your body "touches", essentially the seat cushion, back cushion, and top of the arm cushions.

The remainder of what you "don't touch" on that sofa, the back panel, side panels and front bottom panel will be made out of some other composite material, like vinyl.

In fact, it was such a problem that in 2011 the European Committee for Standardization published a key definition for the term which stated that any item listed as "bonded leather" must require a minimum amount of 50% in weight of dry leather.

Additionally the US Federal Trade Commission also states that an item that appears "leather-like", must be accompanied by a disclosure as to the percentage of leather or other fiber content.

So the lesson here is that you should be able to see exactly what you are purchasing, if you're interested in inquiring, as far as the quality and composition, when it comes to shopping for your new leather living room sofa set.

As I stated in the beginning, I don't often repair leather sofas and the like, but one repair I do perform often, is the repair of large depressions in leather panels.

The moving industry can keep us pretty occupied and often we see leather furniture with deep impressions, usually because something was packed up against it or on it.

Check out this rear panel to a loveseat, with a pretty significant dented area. There is only one tool needed for this restoration, a heat gun!

Basically holding the heat gun 8"-10" away from the surface and continually moving the gun in a circular motion, in and around the indented area, while also feathering out around the damage, will in essence shrink the leather panel, causing the indentation to work itself out until completely gone.

The golden rule is to never hold the heat gun too long in one area, or you may scorch or catch the leather panel on fire. Heat guns can become extremely hot.

This technique also works with vinyl, though vinyl is even more heat sensitive, and can easily be melted, so proceed cautiously when performing this type of restoration!

Just because I don't usually perform extensive leather restorations, doesn't mean I never perform a repair to scratched or torn leather.

Leather often has some type of finish, which lends itself well while performing repairs with My Repair Kit™. The repair to the side of this leather sofa was fairly easy, and a perfect example of the type of damage that can be easily repaired using techniques found in this book.

Basically, I only used epoxy to glue down the loose fibers (middle), then I only used red and black pigments along with some padding finish to touch up the damage which basically is now virtually invisible (right). This repair only took 15-20 minutes, and three quarters of that was waiting for the glue to dry.

Leather repairs can be simpler than you think. Just approach each task with patience and try to keep the affected area as minimal as possible and you'll be just fine!

ODDS & ENDS

GLASS & MIRROR

Glass and mirror replacement is usually a straightforward type of repair, the glass or mirror is broken and you need to replace it. Glass and mirror are essentially the same thing, only a mirror has a reflective material applied to one side of the glass.

Long ago, the reflective material used to create a mirror would have been mercury, spread thinly over a piece of tin, then a piece of glass applied over that.

A chemical reaction takes place between the mercury and tin, and the metal becomes adhered to the glass, but due to mercury's toxicity, nowadays, a mirror's reflective coating will either be just tin, chromium, aluminum, nickel or silver.

In fact, even though silver is not always used, the process to apply a reflective material to the rear of glass is called "silvering". Silvering is accomplished by one of three techniques, electroplating and chemical or vacuum deposition.

Often you can tell a mirror is old/antique because of tarnishing, oxidation and/or peeling of the reflective material which may cause a "sparkly" or crystalline appearance seen through to the rear of the glass. In addition, there may be defects/imperfections in the actual glass.

There's probably a glass shop within minutes of your home. Most glass shops should be able to fabricate standard shaped mirrors and glass panels in general, but not every shop will have some of the more advanced machines needed to fabricate specialized items, like custom contours, beveling, drilling, or CNC fabrication.

Replacement of broken glass or mirror also may occasionally take more than your local glass shop if you're dealing with antiques, as not all glass throughout history is created by the same processes used today.

Glass that is readily available at most shops is referred to as sheet glass. It's going to be perfectly smooth, without any imperfections, but "antique glass" could be "wavy" and include air bubbles or inclusions, often called "seeds".

This glass is referred to as "seeded glass or old float glass". There are also grades of waviness, seeding or other distressing that can vary from minimal to extreme.

It will be difficult to find an actual authentic piece of antique glass, but that doesn't mean it would be impossible, a lot may hinge on the size of glass needed. Try checking into architectural salvages for large pieces.

Most glass shops may not stock reproduction/antique glass, though some may be able to order the product. There are a few companies in the US, if you search hard enough, that can ship new or reproduction glass/mirrors anywhere in the world.

Another pain in the keister is bubbled, bent or curved glass. As far as bubbled glass (to the right), good luck, that will most likely need to be custom made by a professional glass blower.

Curved or bent glass is most common on china cabinets or display cases. The most difficult aspect of obtaining a piece of curved glass is measuring to ensure the new piece has the precise curvature as the original.

The proper way to measure would be to measure the girth, the chord, the depth and height, along with the thickness of the glass.

Measurements may get tricky if the glass has a bend in a particular area, like the one pictured right. That pattern is called a "J-bend".

Other good information to be knowledgeable about prior to going to a glass shop usually would include the type of edge needed on any particular piece of glass.

If the glass goes into some type of frame then usually the way the edge is cut doesn't matter, we just say "clean cut", which means the edges will not be polished and could be extremely sharp!

If your piece of glass does not sit in a frame and the edges are exposed, let's say for example, a dining room table top, the edges need to be "seemed" to remove the sharpness, and there are several different edge patterns you can request.

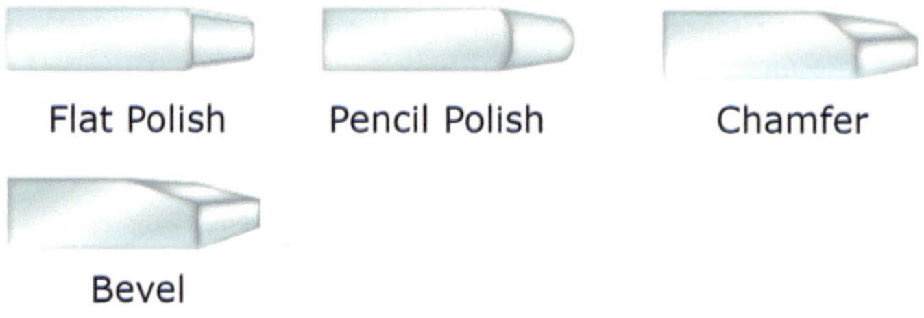

An example of the most common edges are to the right. There are several more edge variations, but not every company will have the ability to cut every type of edge, as it could require some pretty costly machinery.

Another important thing to know is glass that's 1/16" thick, common in picture frames and occasionally furniture, could be referred to as "Single Strength".

⅛" thick glass, commonly found in furniture, like the side panes to china cabinets, is often referred to as "Double Strength".

You (yes you) also have the ability to easily cut single or double strength glass yourself, with this medieval toothbrush, aka glass cutter, and a straight edge tool like a T-Square, which can be found at most local hardware stores.

Glass can now be obtained in different colors. The most common colored glass you may find on furniture is either bronze (a light or dark golden brown) or smoke (light or dark gray). Other special colors would likely need to be ordered as most glass companies do not carry stock of colored glass.

Probably the last, but not least, piece of information you may want to know is if you need "Plate" or "Tempered" glass.

Plate glass is cheaper than tempered glass in general but the big difference is what happens when these two different types of glass break.

Plate glass, otherwise known as annealed glass, is glass that is left to cool on its own during the manufacturing process. The problem that creates is when the glass breaks, it can shatter into large, sharp shards that can easily decapitate a fingertip or worse.

Tempered glass on the other hand, is cooled rapidly during manufacturing, which changes the chemical composition of the glass and gives it approximately four times the strength as compared to standard annealed glass.

The additional positive of tempered glass is it shatters essentially into blunt edged pellets that are significantly less dangerous than the large sharp shards created from untempered glass.

Jumping now to a completely different project with regard to glass, that once complete, creates something beautiful, truly unique, and is only limited by your imagination, that is the painting of glass!

This process has a few different names, some may call it reverse stenciling, back painting, gilding on glass or the French term is verre églomisé.

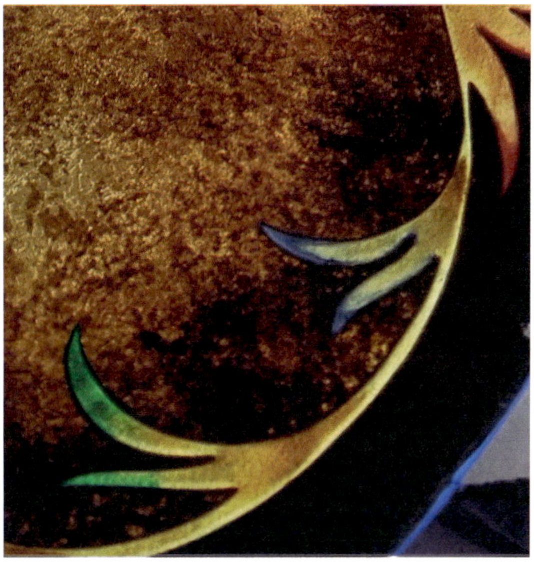

It's not called reverse stenciling because you're painting the backside of a piece of glass, the name is referring to the layering of the paint. All the various layers of paint are laid in reverse order, with the highlights applied first and the background applied last.

I reverse stenciled a large oval piece of glass, it was tedious, but it really wasn't as hard as it seems, and we'll go over the process!

It all starts with deciding which paints need to be applied in which order prior to start. Choose wisely as you only have one shot at it, unless you totally remove everything and start anew, so as my fiancé would say, "you need to have a plan of action".

Once paint is laid on the surface, that is what you will see from the opposite side, once you flip the glass over. If you mess up, it will be apparent. Also make sure prior to starting that the surface is completely clean and void of any dust.

So what is most prominent to me is the "vine", the pattern I painstakingly carved into some painters tape, around the circumference of the glass top.

What's the most distinct detail about the vine? Looking at the picture from the previous page, the "tips" of the vine are painted either green, blue or red.

Because I said that we apply the highlights first, as crazy as it sounds, that one little detail will be the first layer of paint that we will apply. To make it easier I chose to write on the tape, which color went where.

I'm still using the pigments from My Repair Kit™ for the colorwork, and my padding finish to paint the highlights onto the glass.

After the highlights, layer two, it's time to paint the remainder of the vine, which isn't a solid gold color, there are variations of darker and lighter areas of the gold, which I applied.

After we've applied the gold, we need to remove the tape from the outer edge of the vine because the next layer (layer 3) of paint we want to apply is black, which makes up the outer ring.

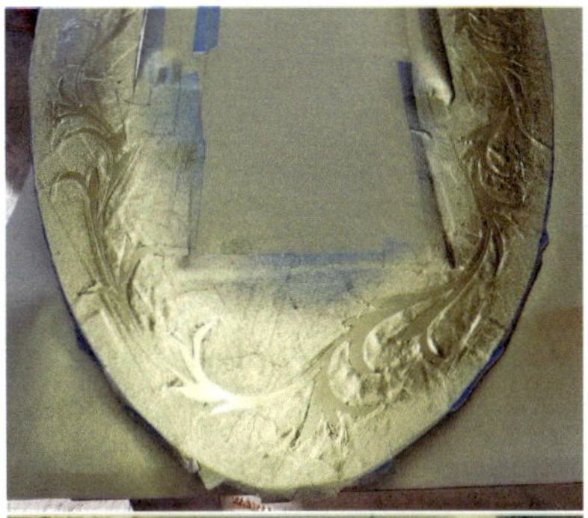

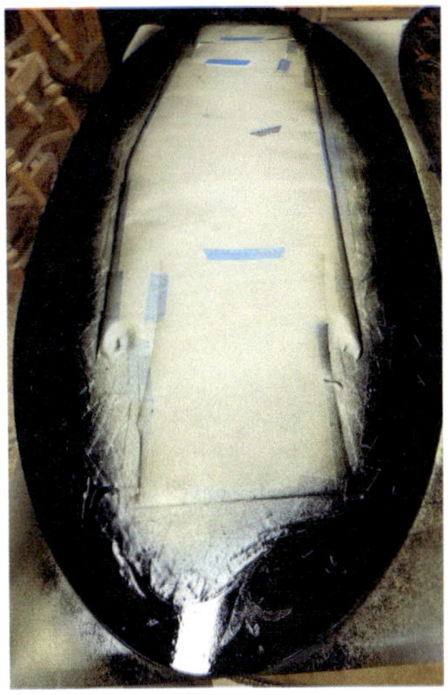

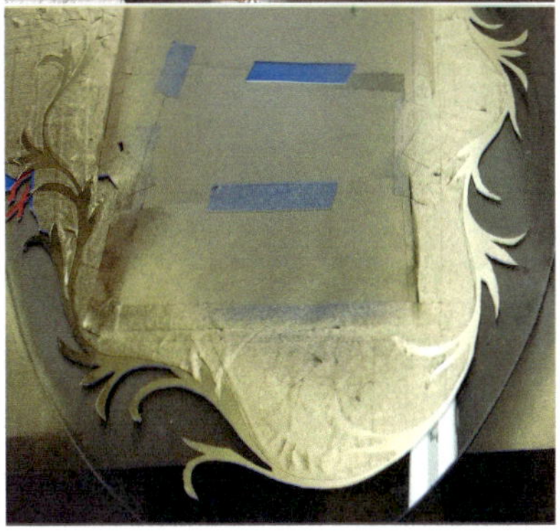

After painting the outer rim, I remove the remaining paper and tape from the center of the glass.

For the inside, I used a combination of black paint, actual gold leaf (see the squares in the bottom picture?) and various gold paints.

The order that I applied these is, spray adhesive on the glass so I could apply the gold leaf squares first.

After the gold leaf was installed, I used a natural sponge to apply additional gold paint (to give it a splotchy effect), then finished it off with the gloss black between the gold leaf and the inner vine.

Once completed, I put the piece of glass into a frame and secured it using liquid silicone between the rear of the glass and the wood frame. Custom coffee table done!

Furniture hardware can present itself in endless manifestations, knobs, pulls, screws, bolts, nuts, washers, shelf pins, escutcheons, hinges, lock and keys, t-nuts, plastic drawer guides or virtually anything that can be removed and/or installed onto a piece of furniture I would consider hardware.

Hardware could be made of wood, metal, plastic, ceramic, crystal/glass, and natural products like stone or seashells, if you're at a beach house.

One of the biggest issues we see in regard to a move (aside from physical damages) is that the crews love to disassemble things as much as possible, even some things that are not supposed to be disassembled.

What the crew is supposed to do is create a "parts box", in which every "part" that was taken off a piece of furniture is labeled and put into a singular box, to be one of the last boxes loaded and one of the first boxes off the truck at delivery so they are able to easily proceed with reassembling everything.

In theory that's a fantastic idea! In reality though, due to circumstances unknown, not every single piece of hardware makes it into that parts box in every situation.

In fact, more often than you may think, that entire parts box may end up missing and there may be numerous pieces of hardware to obtain for a variety of furniture pieces on a single job.

Looking for a particular type of hardware can often be very difficult to find and very time consuming. Let's say you have a 100 year old antique dresser with a missing handle.

It may be virtually impossible to locate and replace that one handle with an identical handle, so in some instances you may need to end up replacing all the handles so that everything matches.

You may, if you search hard enough online or at flea markets, be able to find a set of antique handles that are very similar and have a nice aged patina that you can purchase, install and use. If that's the case, consider yourself lucky.

If you do need to replace the hardware with new, then you'll have a plethora of options. You would need to decide what type of hardware you want: brass, pewter, bronze, wrought iron, a seashell, other metal type or something else unique?

Secondly, each type of metal will likely have different options with regard to the appearance, with brass (and other metals), there could be polished brass which is your standard super shiny brass you see all over the place.

Other options are satin brass, antique brass, tarnished brass, weathered brass, burnished brass, I'm confident there are more, each with their own unique appearance.

While on the topic of brass, if replacing hardware, the two main options to consider is whether to obtain solid brass or brass plated. There is a simple way to tell the difference, use a magnet.

Solid brass is non-magnetic, meaning that a magnet will not stick to it, but a magnet will stick to a piece of brass plated hardware. The other big difference is price, solid brass will be considerably more expensive than a plated piece of hardware, but solid brass is what may be needed when dealing with some fine, high end antiques.

One positive trade off is that solid brass, if tarnishing, can be polished to look new indefinitely, to which plated hardware can only be polished so many times before you start burning through the plating to expose the non brass structure.

If you do need to replace a handle, once you've figured out the finish style you are fond of, you'll need to measure to make sure that you are obtaining the correct size replacement.

You'll need to measure what is called the "bore". Bore is the distance between each hole on a drawer face or handle, from center to center. The bore on this handle is two and a half inches.

If there is only one hole on a drawer face, then that requires either a knob, drop/ring pull or something similar. You don't really need to measure anything because those would just require one screw or bolt coming from the rear of the drawer face to attach said knob.

Beds in my opinion, would be the furniture that we come across the most with missing hardware. Every bed in every move needs to be disassembled and often the hardware needed for assembly is unique to that bed.

There could be bolts, threaded rods, threaded insert nuts, half moon washers, screws, special brackets, the list could go on.

I'll use the example of bolts missing, there are several factors to be considered here also. One main factor is determining whether the threading on the bolt is "standard" (US measurement system), or "metric" (rest of world measurement system).

A very large percentage of furniture is manufactured outside of the United States, that means a good majority of the hardware that you will come across will be metric. Often you'll have to find metric hardware online, as most hardware stores in the US only carry a limited selection.

I would suggest buying a "nut and bolt gauge" (right) to carry around with you. They come in several different styles and they make identifying the bolt threading much easier.

Another thing to consider is the "head" (top) of the bolt. It may be possible to go to the hardware store to purchase a hex head bolt, or does the head need to be an allen head bolt or a different particular shape, size or finish?

The options are truly endless with regard to hardware replacement, and often finding an exact replacement is an exercise in futility.

There are numerous resources available that may assist you in your hardware exploration journey, most of these resources listed further, I have used, and ordered from quite a few times.

Van Dyke's Restorers® and Rockler®, each have a wide variety of reproduction and unique hardware, woodworking supplies and tools. Horton Brasses®, Whitechapel Ltd.®, Rejuvenation® and House of Antique Hardware®, each have a good selection of higher end hardware.

Of course there are random internet searches, if you want to browse through thousands of pages of mass produced hardware. Along with several other specialty stores online that you can browse through by simply searching "furniture hardware".

One last resource, if you want to find literally anything you can imagine with regard to furniture or your home for that matter, check out, The Complete Hafele. They have multiple different catalogs on several topics.

Good luck hardware hunting!

Be A Boss!

Remember in the beginning of this book I told you that you can turn My Repair Kit™ into a career? The opportunities are endless with practice, hard work, persistence and dedication.

When I started, and to this day, our clients include moving, insurance, warranty companies, furniture manufacturers, retailers, private individuals, military, commercial, antique dealers, interior designers, hotels, restaurants, the list could continue forever.

The point is, there is almost no place in this world that does not have a piece of furniture! The opportunities to perform repairs are endless, often with subpar competition.

If you excel with restorations similar to the examples in this book, you'll no doubt make a great living well into the six figures, but the most important thing is that you'll be your own boss! No one to answer to should be everyone's goal in life!

I would recommend preparing a letter introducing yourself and your business along with explaining what services you can provide. Look up the addresses of all the major national moving companies and local movers and send your introductory letter to their Customer Service and/or Claims Departments.

Include a few business cards, larger companies will have more than one adjuster.

It's almost mandatory these days to have a website that provides information on the services you offer, areas you cover, before and after pictures of completed repairs, among other information.

Feel free to check out our website that includes everything I just explained at www.jacobsonrestoration.com.

Moving/insurance companies always need reputable people to fix items they damaged. They also require companies like ours to inspect the damage, even if it's items not related to furniture like a microwave, lawnmower or anything else owned by a client.

Occasionally you are also inspecting property damage in which the movers may have damaged the walls of a staircase or put scratches on the hardwood floor.

If you are proficient at drywall repairs and painting, that's another way to create income, and since you're already inspecting everything, you should have first dibs at performing any and all restorations that you can quote. We patch and paint an abnormal amount of walls for a "furniture restoration" company.

Inspecting is going to the residence of a person or business the movers have just delivered to, look at all the damages, take photos, detailed notes and send an all encompassing report of the findings back to the entity that hired you.

These clients that received their goods are often referred to as "shippers". The shipper will file a claim form for the damage with the movers or insurance company

The movers, usually referred to as "carriers", then process and forward the claim forms to companies like ours with instructions on exactly what they require.

Some may only allow an inspection, but if you create a good rapport with these adjusters, some may give you pre-authorization to simply go out and fix whatever you can as long as repairs don't exceed the values claimed for whatever item is damaged.

During these inspections, you have to be able to determine whether the damage claimed is new and transit-related or pre-existing. There are a lot of unscrupulous people that may attempt to show you old damage and say it was caused by the movers.

It may be difficult initially to recognize the difference between old damage and new, but usually fresh damages appear to have no dirt/oils/soilage in the area and the wood should be clean and "bright".

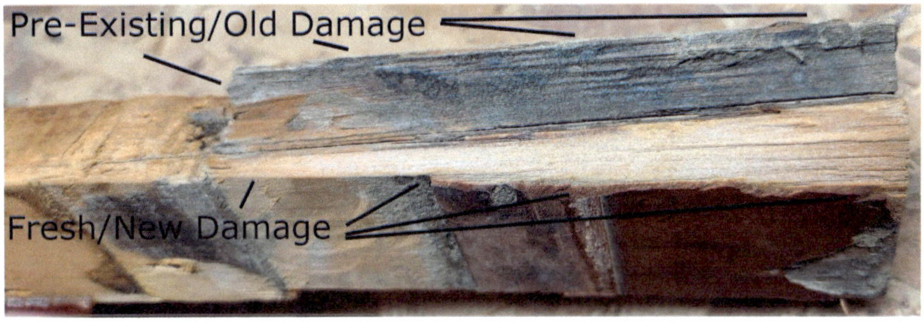

Older damage will often appear "darker/dirtier" from oxidation and/or soilage. Remember, just because there is damage, doesn't mean you'll always be able to figure out how, where, or when the damage occurred.

In some cases, we will state in a report that some particular damage may be questionable but we cannot verify whether it is transit-related. In most instances, the adjusters will compare claimed damages to their pre-move inventory sheets which should state any notable pre-existing damages.

As the shipper shows you the damaged items, you must document the location, size and any other pertinent information. Take photos, usually a picture of the entire item, along with close ups of the damage. There could be numerous photos for each item inspected.

Once the inspection is complete, type up the report on your company letterhead, explaining each individual item claimed, determining for each item whether the damage is repairable or not, while explaining what process you may need to perform the repair, and include a repair cost.

On occasion you will come across items that you will need to inspect that may not be in your expertise, like appliances, exercise equipment, the inner workings of a grandfather clock. In these instances, you still need to document the damage but you also would need to ask the adjuster for authorization to contract out a specialty company.

Some insurance adjusters may do that themselves but it's convenient if you have a circle of specialists that you can call on in your time of need to inspect and estimate repairs regarding their specialty.

You're the one with the local ties, adjusters can be anywhere in the world and you'd be saving them immense time and effort by handling as much of any particular job that you can.

Also remember, if you're the one contacting the specialty companies, usually you can add a little upcharge (aka convenience fee) to the bill, hence procuring additional money for your time and effort.

You may need to pay for their services upfront, but assuming it was authorized by the adjuster you will always be able to bill the authorized amount for reimbursement.

Repairs are your bread and butter, that's where you can begin to accumulate a good living. A proficient repair technician can usually charge anywhere from $100-$300 an hour based on what your repairing, skill level, severity of the damage, and how well the repair will turn out.

With experience comes speed, I would say that I can probably perform a particular repair now in a quarter of the time it may have taken me when I first started out.

To perform an inspection, most furniture restoration companies charge around $150-$200+. Our standard inspection includes up to twenty five items. For every additional 25 items, there are additional fees.

What you can charge some companies for inspections may vary. In some circumstances, you may not be able to charge a full inspection fee. One piece of advice is to take the work you can get, don't be pigeon-holed into thinking that you must always charge a set amount.

Some of those smaller jobs will help fill your day during some slower times, and once you've built a relationship with different adjusters or companies you may be able to negotiate higher fees at a later time.

It also depends on the type of work you are doing and who you are doing it for. If a private individual asks us to come out and look at some furniture, we likely would not be able to charge an inspection fee, but we are hoping to make up for any loss of income by performing repairs.

You may not always initially get the job or perform the repairs but if you always portray a positive image and you are respectful to your potential clients you are more likely to get their work in the future.

Adversely, if you are impatient or rude to a potential client, shipper or carrier, that's a good way to go out of business before you even get started. When in a job never act rushed, even if you may be, always take the time to answer any questions a client may have to the best of your ability in a respectful manner.

If you explain things well and are honest about the various steps and possible outcome of repairs, you will go a long way in this industry.

A secondary industry that we tap into is furniture manufacturer showrooms, like Ashley Furniture, Baker Furniture, Ethan Allen or even manufacturers similar to Bob's Furniture or Value City.

Lucky for us, furniture retailers always want the furniture that they are selling to look great, especially at higher end stores. In some cases we may go to a showroom and touch up all the furniture they have, or more often they may have sold a piece of furniture and before it goes out it may have sustained some type of damage.

You obviously can't send a new piece of furniture to a client damaged. In this case we may perform a repair, even to a new piece of furniture before it is delivered, without the customer's knowledge.

A client may not think that is ethical, but in reality we were hired by the furniture manufacturer, so regardless of the situation, we must perform the repairs we were hired for if we want to make money.

A good way to obtain this type of work is basically to go to the showroom or place of business and speak to a manager. It's almost guaranteed that they already have a repair technician, sometimes in-house, that performs repairs but there is always the opportunity to win their business.

On occasion, you can offer to do a small repair for free just to show them your skill level and proficiency. Leave a card, you never know when the manager may become unsatisfied with their current situation and look for a new restoration company.

Another good way to get your feet wet in the industry is to work for a warranty company. There may be several different companies but as an example, we have personally been contracted to work for companies like Furniture Solutions Network and Guardsman

Both companies and others similarly provide the servicing of warranties on new furniture that you purchase, when the furniture salesman also sells you on that furniture protection plan.

When contracting for warranty companies like those, It's also in your best interest to expand your repair abilities to more than just wood, like having the equipment and ability to clean, mend (sew) or replace upholstery, the ability to install electronic parts like switches and recliner mechanisms, the ability to refinish wood items, leather repairs and much more.

One downside to contracting with these various warranty companies is that your price structure is already set and you really can't deviate from it no matter how long the repair takes. You may only make $50-$100 if you successfully complete a repair.

Another downside is that you can spend that same amount of time on the repair and the customer is not happy with the end results. If that's the case, you would then have to consider it an unsuccessful repair and may only make the minimum allowed which could be as low as $15.

Even though you may not always make a lot of money performing warranty repairs, the work is usually constant and because so many people do purchase the warranties, they can normally fill your day with more than enough jobs.

Even if you don't work for a warranty company it's good to have some certifications, in fact, some insurance companies may not work with you unless you have some particular certifications.

Some of these warranty companies even offer free training in the different fields, discounted supplies and much more because they always are in need of competent technicians.

In some cases, companies may require that you obtain certain certifications in which you may have to pay for. But those certifications are linked to you or your company and stay with you forever, as long as you pay any recurring membership fee which is minimal.

The most recognized training and certification institute in the industry is named IICRC which is the Institute of Inspection, Cleaning and Restoration Certification.

You also can become a contractor for websites like Home Advisor™ or Angie™. Individuals use these or similar websites to find companies to perform specialized work in certain areas that you cover.

Individuals go to these websites, and submit a job request. From there, the lead generating companies send the leads to the various contractors registered in their system.

You as the contractor will receive an email or text from the company advising you that a client is looking for the services you provide, along with the client's information. It's entirely up to you to contact the client directly to introduce yourself and your company and to try to successfully obtain the job.

I say "try to successfully obtain the job" because your company likely isn't the only company to receive that job request. Job leads can and will be sent to numerous companies, in essence creating a race between contractors to contact the interested party. Hopefully you can sell your expertise and business to the client better than the other contractors that will be calling.

I've even been told by a few of the clients that they thought it was a mistake to use that type of service because they were inundated with phone calls for days or weeks from an "uncountable amount of different companies".

After you have talked to the prospective client, obtained the job and scheduled an appointment, you can theoretically charge anything you want. You're the contractor, there are no set fees for the work you perform (at least not in the furniture restoration business).

Keep in mind though, you can do everything right, call the customer, schedule the appointment, go to the client's home, look at the damage in question, quote the repair price and the client may still opt to not have the work done or go with a competing company, which means you technically lost money through this whole transaction.

The biggest downside of obtaining work in this manner is that as soon as you are sent the job request from the lead generating company, you are charged a lead generation fee, per job.

These lead generation fees can range anywhere from $15 - $50 or more depending on the company and what type of lead it is. There are usually options in the lead fees. For a higher fee, some lead generation services make you the only company that receives a particular lead.

If you opt for the lower fees, lead generating companies may send the same lead to up to ten or more competing companies at the same time you've received it. With each lead charging $20 bucks or so, this lead generating company may have made $200 just off distributing one email they received to ten different companies.

You have to pay that fee whether you are successful in obtaining or completing the job or not. It's highly competitive in markets like heating, plumbing or carpentry, and even though furniture restoration may be considered a "specialty service", you surely won't be the only company in your area that provides furniture repair services.

We have contracted with these companies in the past and pretty quickly we came to the realization that these companies are easily milking our credit cards to charge the lead fees, but we may only have successfully worked on 10% or less of the job leads given.

As an example, let's say in a one month timeframe you receive 20 job leads, which could be on the low side, and each job lead costs $20. To break even on the leads you purchased for the month, you need to generate at least $400 in completed work.

This doesn't include the countless hours involved in phone calls, gas, wear and tear on your vehicle driving to house calls, or the time involved at a clients home.

If you successfully obtain even 10% of the job leads, that's only 2 jobs during that month that you have the opportunity to perform repairs on.

Now if you are a skilled technician you may be able to recoup those lead generation fees in a couple hours of work, maybe even on one job, but there are no guarantees that you will obtain even one job, and who wants to lose money, break even, or spend countless hours chasing leads that often never pan out?

The lesson that I would like to give you when dealing with these types of companies, is that it's often financially a break even or losing proposition, but what may be valuable is the exposure you get on the internet.

These lead generation companies will spread your company name out to several different outlets online giving you a greater presence online than you may be able to create on your own.

We've found that oftentimes clients will search for services they need on these lead generation websites, find companies that interest them, do their own research, like going to your company website, and they may contact you directly, which saves any lead generation fees.

What these lead generation companies may also offer is a listing fee for a certain amount per month so your company can be listed in their directories, but you do not receive job leads. So there may be a trade off on what you feel is important to help grow your business in the restoration field.

Last but not least, a final way that you may be able to make money with MyRepairKit™ is to go around to local yard sales, craigslist, open markets or a multitude of other places and purchase older worn furniture, use your skills to rejuvenate, beautify that piece of furniture and sell it for a profit, otherwise known as "flipping".

In total, you may need to combine some or all of these methods to create a full time business in restoring furniture, but I find great joy in the satisfaction that I bring to clients when they see the end result of that damaged piece of furniture, which in some cases may have been a family heirloom and extremely important to them, even bringing some people to tears.

Not to mention you are always going to new and exciting places and working for different interesting people everyday. You'll hear the history and countless stories behind certain pieces of furniture or items that are intriguing.

I've made countless friendships and working relationships through this rewarding type of work, and I would recommend it to everyone!

In Closing..

As with everything there are limitations when performing repairs. Sometimes you could be doomed from the start because the finish on the piece of furniture in question may be too badly deteriorated, faded, cracked, or "alligatored". So it may be that your only option is to refinish the piece of furniture.

You may even come across a surface that has a 14" long by ½" wide by ¼" deep scratch perpendicular to the grain pattern, on a very light wood like maple. Even for the most seasoned professional furniture restoration technician, that repair is going to be an extreme challenge that may still end up needing to be refinished, because the initial damage is just way too severe to reasonably be filled and touched up.

Ultimately success may depend on how proficient you become at repairs and/or how particular a client may be. Not every client is worried about perfection as long as you forewarned them about some of the difficulties and challenges associated with their particular project.

So what needs to be determined prior to starting a repair is realizing limitations and also understanding what your expertise level is at performing repairs. A lot of damages are not capable of becoming perfectly invisible.

I can confidently say that in my early learning stages my repairs were far from perfect, but with less time and practice than you think, you undoubtedly will get to a level where you are able to perform repairs that are virtually undetectable.

Every technique that you have learned in this book would, could and should be employed in most refinishing projects. With older pieces of furniture there are usually veneer chips, missing moldings, discolorations, scratches too deep to be sanded out of veneer, the list goes on.

Hopefully you now have the knowledge to confidently perform satisfactory repairs or at least acquired some techniques or skills to make your projects turn out better than you've ever imagined.

With the knowledge I have given, you should eventually be able to create your own company, become your own boss, make your own schedule, and eventually have the expertise needed in the furniture repair industry to make six figures per year. It's easier than you think!

I believe in you, simply because you're taking steps to improve yourself by making an effort to learn to increase your knowledge and skills in the furniture restoration process. You've taken the first step, now have a nice finish!

Thank you!!

Eric Jacobson

PHOTO CREDITS:

All photos, unless noted below, have been taken by Eric Jacobson.

All photos notated in this book are used within a Creative Commons license and/or I have been given authorization from the author of the photos to publish.

Some photos may have been modified.

Attribution and links to the original photos are supplied below.

Due to circumstances out of my control, I can not guarantee that every link will work indefinitely.

Pg 10. Wood Heart https://pxhere.com/en/photo/639818
Cut Tree Author: XXL Ray https://commons.wikimedia.org/wiki/File:Common_juniper_cut.jpg
Pg 11. Cut Palm Tree Author: Tangopaso
https://commons.wikimedia.org/wiki/File:Cut_palm-tree.jpg
Pg 12. Janka test Author: Nasa-verve
https://commons.wikimedia.org/wiki/File:Janka_hardness_test.jpg
USS Nautilus Author: US Navy https://commons.wikimedia.org/wiki/File:USS_Nautilus_(SSN-571)_underway_at_sea_in_June_1965.jpg
Pg 13. Cuipo tree Author: The Field Museum Library
https://commons.wikimedia.org/wiki/File:Cuipo_Tree._Very,_very_tall_tree_with_two_people_standing_at_bottom_for_scale._1911._(3607563829).jpg
Pg 20. Pine Trees Author: Carl Schlabach
https://unsplash.com/photos/B1k44aPBybs
Pine Wood Author: Hobbit House Inc. http://hobbithouseinc.com/personal/woodpics/pine,%20misc/pine,%20misc%201%20s50%20plh.htm
Pine Bench Author: Metropolitan Museum of Art https://commons.wikimedia.org/wiki/File:Settee_MET_85D_ACF144R6.jpg
Pg 21. USS Delaware Author US Navy
https://www.navsea.navy.mil/Home/Shipyards/Norfolk/About-Us/History/
Pine Nightstand Author: Bonsoni.com https://www.flickr.com/photos/bonsoni_uk/12587317344/in/dateposted/
Pine corner cabinet Credit: Wmpearl
https://commons.wikimedia.org/wiki/File:Maryland_corner_cupboard,_c._1815-20,_pine,_Dayton_Art_Institute.JPG
Pg 22. English Walnut Seed Author: El Caro
https://commons.wikimedia.org/wiki/File:Walnut_close-up.jpg
Black Walnut Seed Author: Gero Brandenburg
https://commons.wikimedia.org/wiki/File:Schwarznuss_Frucht.jpg
Walnut Piece Author Bonsoni.com
https://www.flickr.com/photos/bonsoni_uk/11784958645/in/photostream/
Walnut Credenza Author: Bonsoni.com
https://www.flickr.com/photos/101899087@N06/41429934785/in/photostream/
Pg 24. Ohio slant lid desk Dayton Art Institute credit: Wmpearl https://commons.wikimedia.org/wiki/File:Ohio_slant_lid_desk,_1819,_black_walnut,_Dayton_Art_Institute.JPG
Pg 25. Poplar wood Author: Hobbit House Inc. http://hobbithouseinc.com/personal/woodpics/poplar/poplar%2039%20s50%20plh.htm
Pg 28. Black Cherry Wood Author: Hobbit House Inc.
http://hobbithouseinc.com/personal/woodpics/cherry,%20american%20black/cherry,%20american%20black%20just%20cut%201%20s50%20plh.htm
Cherry Highboy Author: Los Angeles County Museum of Art
https://commons.wikimedia.org/wiki/File:High_Chest_with_Scrolled_Pediment_and_Shell_Carving_LACMA_60.46.1a-b.jpg
Black Cherry Author: AnRo0002 https://commons.wikimedia.org/wiki/File:20140808Prunus_serotina2.jpg
Cyanide Sign Author: Midnight Believer
https://www.flickr.com/photos/144957155@N06/50154503398/in/photolist-2jpYWvd-NjbXkZ-TE8aCL-MrZLR-4qoLL4-Jx79fM-pBXWWM-MrS7o-MrS7m-pUk7mD-MrS7u-MrZLV-MrS7q-MrZLP-TE8fzj-9sNgoi-2m41p5z-2m8HTDA-su6BSY-sqXh3N-9EoJur-rLu1TY-sr5BHX-sHxPig-sqVjfj-2m8Uimq-rLu1a3-KGC6Lp-J1SRyo-MrS7j-P5AQaY-dcCqyK-Lmw6Co-MrZLF-5o2euo-MrZLK-5nWY7X-2Vzzof-jaHASR-5nWWZR-5nWZeM-5nWVta-5XVF3U-2epqj5Z-Koktuq-5nWYrz-64Rz4J-64MhoK-Tk64Q1-5o2b99
Pg 29. Cherry Lowboy https://www.flickr.com/photos/101899087@N06/25892417598/in/photostream/
Pitch Pockets on Cherry Author: Hobbit House Inc
http://hobbithouseinc.com/personal/woodpics/_g_GH.htm
Pg 30. Mahogany tree in mahogany title Author: YourWorldExplorer https://web.archive.org/web/20161102173518/http://www.panoramio.com/photo/91612222
Genuine Mahogany Wood Author: Hobbit House Inc
http://hobbithouseinc.com/personal/woodpics/mahogany,%20misc/mahogany,%20misc%20quartersawn%20figured%20veneer%204%20s50%20web.htm
Mahogany Secretary Author: Metropolitan Museum of Art
https://commons.wikimedia.org/wiki/File:Desk_and_bookcase_MET_Kem_23.jpg
Pg 31. Mahogany Boat Author: Jukka Mahogany Motoring
https://commons.wikimedia.org/wiki/File:Mahogany_motoring_(8457449565).jpg
The Tree Author: NooPun https://imgur.com/gallery/8Ek7dGe
Pg 32. Serpentine front sideboard Author: Los Angeles County Museum of Art
https://commons.wikimedia.org/wiki/File:Serpentine-Front_Sideboard_LACMA_M.90.211.jpg
The Tree Guitar Author: Fay Guitars http://www.fayguitars.com/Guitars/Gallery/tonewoods.html
Pg 33. Teak Tree Author: Sakthibalan
https://commons.wikimedia.org/wiki/File:Teak_tree.jpg
Teak Wood Author: Hobbit House Inc. http://hobbithouseinc.com/personal/woodpics/teak/teak%204%20s50%20plh.htm
Pg 34. Boat teak Interior Author: Bob Johnstone
https://upload.wikimedia.org/wikipedia/commons/7/73/J40interiorteak.jpg

Teak Chair Gray Author: Sherri Barras
https://www.flickr.com/photos/theadventurecontinues/2539695344/in/photolist-4SqAWL-9AMWWt-3eA7dF-bvFoMH-9YRk7A-3eAhcn-avRYG9-9C4fT7-bwLxGT-9vFpEw-hZ1h7d-3eEtN7-eG8Hg6-8tpDTC-rnx8U7-bDb48E-7PAfrk-ag6t6p-2RgteC-8HxVHZ-af7ot9-bAWHTU-6au8md-bvZu95-9MA9LJ-9AN2mB-xkoBFx-3eEmML-bvFqWi-9GtSa7-HTZVx-3eA1DD-avNAoM-8dfLqN-JTSNGC-fgKHUC-gPnBNK-bvFrfD-bvFgyi-3ezGZn-dTpDmK-aQsS3g-bkuVGe-vytcwn-9Qpc29-fhhuCS-9wWWaV-adwraj-92g6V9-aBKEKa/
Pg 35. Teak Carving Author: Daderot
https://commons.wikimedia.org/wiki/File:Jainist_family_shrine,_Gujarat,_West_India,_18th_century,_teak_wood,_view_1_-_Ethnological_Museum,_Berlin_-_DSC01573.JPG
Pg 36. Rosewood Tree Title Author: Dinesh Valke
https://www.flickr.com/photos/dinesh_valke/588615133/in/photolist-U1NLM-AciU4s-zx2Fvz-96953h-2433dXE-8625U1-bXWvLJ-bXWuKG-2awwFjN-ks3BRx-243MNxv-bXWwhm-23ffZZB-24NikRs-4ruZar-267KGfh-26cZNUb-ez3u3x-ks5WHq-ez3CgB-27k4nNx-27fQ6jL-FUR2Fb-26kX1ZG-nKGT25-zHiPBt-GXJdKK-GUMW4x-HWTXFK-U1NPD-7mFfrq-TdYfd3-286Hmih-24rpziw-27SRCnv-8bEg9E-2ad18Wi-24Su7px-83fm26-27DgjKx-27xmjUM-6tNgMR-AMmKcW-7NzFum-28WPAAs-24Z9woE-M29Rny-KkG2qA-25EZj4T-25dZpfX
Rosewood Piece of wood Author: Hobbit House Inc. http://hobbithouseinc.com/personal/woodpics/rosewood,%20camatillo.htm
Rosewood Carving Author: Grannies Kitchen
https://www.flickr.com/photos/granniеskitchen/4892590567/in/photolist-7wMGTR-212ZsME-o7zkTj-Dk39jj-9wnDCm-TDTF3v-vQ1cfQ-QqjsTG-9NNZWb-9NL9oc-5WbAxm-oE293-fBijfQ-2hKH8oH-Mht2Vj-8J4aph-5WbAwd-yUWzCF-AckgHR-Lpax2H-dNxBEW-oE2bd-aQ3dhZ-X56npu-6HGRHz-yCjwTL-VETmtx-8T1XFi-k54PiP-VBDENW-8J4aqh-9P3pqw-Lw5dQK-9P3Cio-8skNMt-dhaS7y-6ZnopP-TAYsZG-8soSkG-2icVBfy-H8zj6R-TAZQP1-8skNHM-5Q7ku4-95Xeii-9P3Jgo-5WunoZ-VQG8tw-4qmoxY-tQ4Dw7
Pg 37. Rosewood Guitar Author: Fay Guitars
http://www.fayguitars.com/Guitars/Gallery/tonewoods.html
Rosewood Sofa Author: Metropolitan Museum of Art
https://upload.wikimedia.org/wikipedia/commons/2/2c/T%C3%AAte-%C3%A0-t%C3%AAte_MET_DT177.jpg
Pg 38. Oak Tree Author: Peter O'Conner aka anemoneprojectors
https://www.flickr.com/photos/anemoneprojectors/14446575900/in/photolist-o1AtGQ-9dG9gg-6oJCzT-spFTkj-wqve7C-M4ETB-5u4TVK-w7Fd8X-BUPL49-ouQ571-wLWE7u-CUxLM8-vLmZKs-x5aSt6-wqwm8j-ChLkQD-CMnTdT-CSsXUk-5msSCJ-8BgibW-3hzec7-CPJprR-2ij1P4P-BPpWdf-w7CPMj-vLAjsF-aLEBYZ-CKasNs-x5cKxZ-pVeuns-wquCdG-3sefAW-wF9oyo-w7oewH-wLWXVy-wMaRBg-JbYrR-CM8q3H-5msRSJ-ouQ4VQ-5moC7e-wHCYLP-3gmKP6-w7CVss-w7xwrY-AMmm42-8SPVvn-CgjtPc-5moBeF-CqiD4o
White Oak Wood Author: Hobbit House Inc.
http://hobbithouseinc.com/personal/woodpics/oak,%20white.htm
Red Oak Wood Author: Hobbit House
http://hobbithouseinc.com/personal/woodpics/oak,%20red.htm
White Oak Cradle Author: Metropolitan Museum of Art
https://upload.wikimedia.org/wikipedia/commons/e/ec/Cradle_MET_HR10.125.672.X.jpg
Pg 39. Different Cuts of Oak Author: Madelynn Keller
https://pngset.com/download-free-png-nhzcm
Pg 40. Oak Barrel Author: Gerard Prins
https://commons.wikimedia.org/wiki/File:Oak-wine-barrel-at-toneleria-nacional-chile.jpg
Tyloses Author: Hobbit House Inc http://hobbithouseinc.com/personal/woodpics/_tyloses.htm
Pg 41. Oak Cupboard Author: Metropolitan Museum of Art
https://commons.wikimedia.org/wiki/File:Cupboard_MET_DP246922.jpg
Pg 42. Maple Leaves
https://www.piqsels.com/de/public-domain-photo-jvmgq
Quilted Maple Author: Hobbit House Inc.
http://hobbithouseinc.com/personal/woodpics/maple,%20hard.htm
Pg 43. Fiddleback Instrument Pssviolin https://commons.wikimedia.org/wiki/File:Italian_Violin_by_Ansaldo_Poggi,_Bologna,_Stradivari_Model,_Back.jpg
Chest of drawers Author: Daderot
https://commons.wikimedia.org/wiki/File:Chest_of_drawers,_Daniel_Lewis_(1798-1833),_Shaftsbury_VT,_1817,_maple,_white_pine,_cherry_-_Bennington_Museum_-_Bennington,_VT_-_DSC08852.JPG
Spalted Wood Author: Hobbit House Inc.
http://hobbithouseinc.com/personal/woodpics/_spalted.htm
Pg 44. Spalted Bowl Author: Hobbit House Inc.
http://hobbithouseinc.com/personal/woodpics/_spalted.htm
Birds Eye Maple Box Author: damianpenney
https://www.flickr.com/photos/84556056@N00/3154277751/in/photolist-5NJuTa-5jhFSY-5jduhH-6jLYVi-5NNMUj-6oiA9Q-cY9S8U-KrnUq-68Uchn-5jijAu-5jdJSx-5je5ev-8m76vA-5jhVhY-5PCPQi-83irNS-668BK6-Qokyq-83it5U-8cEnkw-KrkQ1-9WtQXd-5jef9F-5jhYiU-9WtPcy-8cAD4k-KriAN-PMpbn-5NK2K6-5jemTP-5jdPsK-5je75e-ae1AuV-5jiELA-KrtdK-SNdG7G-2dQq9eJ-2dQq835-88HyuK-8bAVyx-5NNMKm-5jebB4-KriAc-5ji5EN-5jisLq-2dxxSha-2dQqgDJ-2dxxzXM-2eWmCgg-SNdCfo/
Birds eye maple close up Author: Philipp Zinger
https://commons.wikimedia.org/wiki/File:Ahorn-Maser_Holz.JPG
Pg 45. Maple drop leaf Author: Metropolitan museum of art at the Bequest of Mrs. J. Insley Blair, 1951Tavle
https://upload.wikimedia.org/wikipedia/commons/c/c3/Drop-leaf_Table_MET_DT240720.jpg
Pg 46. Conference table Author: Fabrice Florin
https://www.flickr.com/photos/fabola/14704187900/in/photolist-opmNM3-kds1Lt-89fNAU-7VhPbk-84DjMo-nB29YL-r5ZC5G-6s76gS-hFv8gY-8gN8Un-ookHn1-dmXbv1-4mw9TR-5ZwdaE-dPkBhC-pu2jkM-cpHot7-7GKGNY-ojng4V-3hjRkg-agCBMb-ABEX31-cqDRZW-Avxbu-8NYapN-dMzS2L-5KH8KZ-qpfA6w-8Wv2V9-ERMQ4b-fyxWNY-5Wtdke-8CUVFW-NGRAa9-qJhxNq-kqkdrn-kRkT7-azih96-7Vm4w1-bdLp5g-8QXb1a-4jModJ-dz4TEi-7tviuV-86Y3pN-8bgNXK-9d2AJz-87jEuL-j6xbN-GxABmb
Office furniture laminate Author: Tom Ipri
https://www.flickr.com/photos/tomspix/4245540862/in/photolist-ajZpew-8ciHAm-eWojyc-mCCU8p-qpsSNV-oA2igm-pzzEnD-6bjBef-uAt-bSSVsT-q2Ybj9-bH1Uxt-7osZfd-fzuUwY-QqzZbz-7TYMgj-bAw85y-bWhoTd-7tavoo-7bXeCL-e7RcEk-bnqbHK-oceHpT-e99iQj-5awC8o-SZzbv-qPVpb7-8XThgS-m2Qu6m-paGFAB-8M7F8w-pWrqQG-bP3Cvx-8PExMn-dyzc35-6KYcso-dg9ESG-pJbq3H-9Z9hFj-ogdBkQ-aRYgj2-fyxmXL-7DudVC-okT2nP-9sRxn5-4hYQBG-2tGHqN-jcpxzS-bu77tw-Aqw5S2
Pg 48. Red blue green spotlight Author: Datumizer
https://commons.wikimedia.org/wiki/File:Rbg_spotlights.png
Pg 49. Cave painting Author : Warchavchik
https://commons.wikimedia.org/wiki/File:Pinturas_Rupestres_-_Serra_da_Capivara_IV.jpg
Prussian blue Author: Keministi
https://commons.wikimedia.org/wiki/File:Moist_prussian_blue_Fe(Fe(CN)6)3.jpg
Pg 50. Entombment of Christ Author: Museum Boijmans Van Beuningen
https://www.boijmans.nl/en/collection/artworks/3157/the-entombment-of-christ
Charcoal Author: JM http://www.logodesignweb.com/stockphoto
ttps://commons.wikimedia.org/wiki/File:Charcoal.jpg
Clay Author: Carla Antonini
https://commons.wikimedia.org/wiki/File:Soil_Auroville.JPG
Pg 51. Snail Author: H Krisp

https://commons.wikimedia.org/wiki/File:Brandhorn_Bolinus_brandaris.jpg
Crown Author: Cyril Davenport
https://commons.wikimedia.org/wiki/File:Corona_di_sant%27Edoardo.jpg
Jesus purple cloak Author: Claire and Richard Stracke
https://commons.wikimedia.org/wiki/File:AnaValleElSantoNazareno.jpg
Pg 52. Yellow tin glass User:MatthiasKabel, Own work, 15 February 2011
https://commons.wikimedia.org/wiki/File:Roman_diatretglas.jpg
Lead Tin Yellow Author: Douma, M., curator. (2008). What are paintings made out of? In Pigments through the Ages. Retrieved August 31, 2021, from http://www.webexhibits.org/pigments/paintings.html.
http://www.webexhibits.org/pigments/indiv/recipe/leadtinyellow.html
Pg 52. Jewish bride Reference should be made to this publication: Van Loon, A., Noble, P., Krekeler, A. et al. Artificial orpiment, a new pigment in Rembrandt's palette. Heritage Science 5, 26 (2017)
https://heritagesciencejournal.springeropen.com/articles/10.1186/s40494-017-0138-1
Pg 54. Rods and cones Author: Helga Kolb
https://commons.wikimedia.org/wiki/File:Rrods_and_cones_of_the_primate_retina.jpg
Pg 55. The sun Author: NASA/SDO (AIA)
https://commons.wikimedia.org/wiki/File:The_Sun_by_the_Atmospheric_Imaging_Assembly_of_NASA%27s_Solar_Dynamics_Observatory_-_20100819.jpg
Visible Light Spectrum Author: Maulucioni, basado en un trabajo de Megodenas
https://upload.wikimedia.org/wikipedia/commons/9/9f/Spectrehorizontal.png
Fake lightbulb Author: Ming888 at English Wikipedia
https://commons.wikimedia.org/wiki/File:Lightbulb.jpg
Pg 56. Light bulbs w kelvin Author: Yerocus
https://commons.wikimedia.org/wiki/File:Incand-3500-5500-color-temp-comparison.png
Color Temperature Author: Bhutajata
https://commons.wikimedia.org/wiki/File:Color_temperature_black_body_800-12200K.svg
Blue red yellow color wheel Author: Sakurambo at English Wikipedia
https://commons.wikimedia.org/wiki/File:BYR_color_wheel.svg
Prism illustration Author: Spigget
https://commons.wikimedia.org/wiki/File:Dispersive_Prism_Illustration.jpg
Light color temperature Author: Flexfire LEDs, inc., Brenton Patrick Mauriello
https://commons.wikimedia.org/wiki/File:LED_strip_lighting_Correlated_Color_Temperatures_CCTs.png
Pg 57. Red yellow blue Homoatrox
https://commons.wikimedia.org/wiki/File:Location_dot_red-blue-yellow.svg
Primary secondary tertiary wheel Author:none listed https://www.kissclipart.com/color-wheel-primary-secondary-clipart-color-wheel-uv12bh/
Pg 58. Look in the eyes! Author: Alex Proimos
https://commons.wikimedia.org/wiki/File:Look_in_the_Eyes!_(6619614763).jpg
Pg 59. Subtractive Author: Cantus
https://commons.wikimedia.org/wiki/File:SubtractiveColorMixing.png
Additive color Author: Wintermute
https://commons.wikimedia.org/wiki/File:AdditiveColorMixingII.png
Tartan ribbon James Clerk Maxwell (original photographic slides) Author: Janke
https://commons.wikimedia.org/wiki/File:Tartan_Ribbon.jpg
Pg 60. Photoreceptors Author: www.scientificanimations.com
https://commons.wikimedia.org/wiki/File:Photoreceptor_cell.jpg
Pg 61. All 16,777,216 colors of 24-bit RGB palette (truecolor) Author: Marc Mongenet
https://commons.wikimedia.org/wiki/File:16777216colors.png
Colorblind Author: Jordirooca
https://commons.wikimedia.org/wiki/File:Color_Blindness_Ca.png
Pg 62. Blue bottle butterfly Author: Rahans
https://commons.wikimedia.org/wiki/File:Blue_bottle_%E0%B4%A8%E0%B5%80%E0%B4%B2_%E0%B4%95%E0%B5%81%E0%B4%9F%E0%B5%81%E0%B4%95%E0%B5%8D%E0%B4%95.jpg
Mantis shrimp Author: Silke Baron
https://commons.wikimedia.org/w/index.php?sort=relevance&search=mantis+shrimp&title=Special:Search&profile=advanced&fulltext=1&advancedSearch-current=%7B%7D&ns0=1&ns6=1&ns12=1&ns14=1&ns100=1&ns106=1#/media/File:Odontodactylus_scyllarus_2.png
Pg 63. Hue saturation value Author: Datumizer
https://commons.wikimedia.org/wiki/File:Color_solid_comparison_hsl_hsv_cube_cylinder_cone.png
Pg 64. Blue red yellow color wheel Author: Sakurambo at English Wikipedia
https://commons.wikimedia.org/wiki/File:BYR_color_wheel.svg
Pg 66. Asia Map https://www.freeworldmaps.net/asia/
Pg 67. Lac Bug Author: Majoros Attila
https://www.freeimages.com/photo/red-bug-1375674
Indian insect life Author: Harold Maxwell-Lefroy
https://commons.wikimedia.org/wiki/File:02-Indian-Insect-Life_-_Harold_Maxwell-Lefroy_-_Kerria-Lacca.jpg
Lac residue on branch Author: Jeffrey W. Lotz
https://commons.wikimedia.org/wiki/File:Kerria-lacca.jpg
Pg 68. Sticklac in bowl Author: Sailesh Patnaik
https://commons.wikimedia.org/wiki/Category:Lac_dye#/media/File:Lac_as_a_natural_dye.jpg
Button lac Author: Gixie
https://commons.wikimedia.org/wiki/File:Gommalacca_bottone.jpg
Pg 69. Shellac flake blonde Author: Ivory
https://commons.wikimedia.org/wiki/File:Schellak_kleur-echt.jpg
Pg 70. Pills w shellac Author: NLM Pillbox https://commons.wikimedia.org/wiki/File:000726lg_24_HR_Verelan_300_MG_Extended_Release_Capsule.jpg
Shellac record Author: Grammohund
https://commons.wikimedia.org/wiki/File:Shellac_Die_Fahne_hoch_%E2%80%A6!.jpg
Pg 73. Shellac liquid Author: Simon A. Eugster
https://commons.wikimedia.org/wiki/File:Shellac_liquid.jpeg
Pg 74. Shellac Piles Author: Nuberger13 at en.wikipedia

https://zh.wikipedia.org/wiki/File:Shellac_varities.png
Denatured Alcohol Author: Dluuc
https://commons.wikimedia.org/wiki/File:Denatured_alcohol.jpg
Pg 77. Mortar and Pestle Author: Metropolitain Museum of art https://commons.wikimedia.org/wiki/File:Mortar_and_pestle_MET_DP-1372-047.jpg
Pg 81. Map of France https://mapswire.com/countries/france/
Mechanics Magazine https://www.historyofinformation.com/#entry_4505
Pg 85. Unfinished Dresser
https://www.flickr.com/photos/indonesia-furniture/9479511918/in/photolist-frEYCE-qJUmmP-25qQnLw-MW6nUe-MW6nEX-bR7qmz-7svWyM-9JQrUF-7172a2-4CnLnv-MW6nRZ-MW6nGk-7171Gt-MW6nDe-8yCiPK-togM9f-71aZgL-MW6o4c-DLBJw-4GdVph-wdHP1P-2bBLHpU-zsTFv-7Sq6aq-2ede7xC-252yAiz-53UkKi-3a4ius-fZ68Fo-8yFoQN-81pUz6-V7LWmn-4uvGM6-7171hK-zkw4DY-8LWkN-pg8n2f-zdMEZc-6mFpcR-66KCzA-pWcKzc-2e7JruR-6mKF41-QNA6Ea-btYhGX-UbzFhu-9yKFNR-pg8n49-8Xbc6r-4B54KK
Pg 103. Amphibious Plane Author: Boeing Aircraft, Library of Congress
https://commons.wikimedia.org/wiki/File:Boeing_314_Clipper-cropped.jpg
Pg 111. Olive Oil Author: Oregon State University
https://www.flickr.com/photos/oregonstateuniversity/21959161494/in/photolist-zssrEE-4H18YF-4gcPPd-4gcQkW-K7v5bB-241RftK-auWKDh-rbuU5P-4gcRoE-4g8NHg-4g8KLV-4gcNnJ-aaNwQL-7kM4vC-2eK8hSj-2kBz3c1-4gcPiJ-BG8gn-4gcNRm-Gcm84-AyEY5y-4gcVBj-6ggpT9-9R2zP-241y7xE-ainbZ-5Re9Mp-cM9YaN-2PycT-7nHbRP-4gcWws-9fWB4z-5TC7oe-7nHaU2-2hiEJ4S-7nHbJ4-6GURc6-4gcWZs-RUbB4L-2BiZR-ntLgB1-2gUK5hg-ntLG4h-ntL8rK-nJdJdQ-kfVmJ-ntLCRN-ntLyXy-ntLnR6-ntLE1E
Pg 113. Gloss Meter Author: GNMF
https://commons.wikimedia.org/wiki/File:Gloss_meter_in_action.jpg
Pg 128. Oak cabinet light Author: Bonsoni.com
https://www.flickr.com/photos/bonsoni_uk/12587992294/in/dateposted/
Oak cabinet dark Author: Bonsoni.com
https://www.flickr.com/photos/bonsoni_uk/12587825774/in/dateposted/
Pg 133. Italy Map Author Gigillo83
https://commons.wikimedia.org/wiki/File:Italian_regions_provinces.svg
Pg 154. Black and gold secretary Author: Daderot
https://commons.wikimedia.org/wiki/File:Secretary,_England,_probably_1725-1750,_oak,_black_lacquer,_polychrome_painting,_gold_leaf,_brass_-_Museu_Nacional_de_Soares_dos_Reis_-_Porto,_Portugal_-_DSC00604.jpg
Pg 156. Gold Leaf Whale Author: David Adam Kess
https://commons.wikimedia.org/wiki/File:(John_Pydynkowski)_made_this.._hand_carved._a_custom_made_to_order._estimated_to_have_%CC%A9175_u.s.d._cost_on_gold_leaf...._sold_for_%CC%A9350_u.s.d._Gold_Whale.jpg
Pg 208 Wood pores author Woodsurfsc
https://commons.wikimedia.org/wiki/File:Pore_distribution_in_beech.jpg
Pg 221. Container ship JoachimKohlerBremen
https://commons.wikimedia.org/wiki/File:Container_ship_%22Rio_Blackwater%22_in_Hamburg.jpg
Pg 233 Microfiber towels Author: Sue Thompson
https://www.flickr.com/photos/sue90ca/9492717819/in/photolist-dLG1Pk-fsQEhB-pdSwpE-2kN7q9i-7AqPWo-oh4LZN-oj4qDw-bNknmF-o2ARLo-o2Cbrz-okRzPt-dLG2Sk-4ZCdt6-ebwg6S-dLMyQy-J8EeoF-bFdfHp-azp3bQ-azmnCk-2mxMXEL-S46Taz-pv5AfD-BQpUPq-xAjRG2-xAjQF4-4X1E3X-e2xNU3-e2sbde-2kN7q1x-8tsUvi-8GnSJq-3oWmAL-dQQe6D-8tvXbC-6ctJZ5-2kSkhUL-8AD6cQ-xiHmE3-9Rx5xV-87gdYG-6zwEed-bUym1i-6ztvTD-dCnumc-8tsStg-7x9rWV-agjskn-rRhKk-715Jcp-7xcL3U/
Pg 247. Lladro Clown Author:Tangerineduel
https://commons.wikimedia.org/wiki/File:Lladro_Clown-1.jpg
Pg 269. Bonded samples Author: Serepsa https://commons.wikimedia.org/w/index.php?curid=11831454
Pg 275 Glass Cutter Author: Gift of Fred and Nancylee Dikeman, in memory of his father, John Dikeman, 1980
https://commons.wikimedia.org/wiki/File:Glass_Cutter_MET_DP241959.jpg

Other Sources:

https://encycolorpedia.com/
http://www.webexhibits.org/pigments/
https://en.wikisource.org/wiki/Cyclopedia_of_Painting/Color_Mixing
http://www.procato.com/rgbfind/
http://hobbithouseinc.com/personal/woodpics/index2.htm
http://www.theplantlist.org/
http://www.artiscreation.com/Color_index_names.html#key
https://www.historyofinformation.com/
https://www.w3schools.com/colors/default.asp
https://colourlex.com/
https://commons.wikimedia.org/wiki/Main_Page

Made in the USA
Columbia, SC
28 July 2024

39507616R00164